The Place Names of County Durham
and some pub names too

Paul Chrystal

© 2021 Paul Chrystal
First Published in the United Kingdom, 2021
Stenlake Publishing Limited
54-58 Mill Square, Catrine, KA5 6RD
01290 551122
www.stenlake.co.uk
ISBN 978 1 84033 871 3

Printed by
Claro Print, Office 26, 27, 1 Spiersbridge Way,
Thornliebank, Glasgow G46 8NG

Coble Landing or Old Ferry Landing in South Shields. A ferry has run across the Tyne from here since at least the 14th century. The name coble comes from a type of open fishing boat that was used in the estuary and coastal fisheries. Cobles were small enough to easily be drawn up a beach when not in use.

Cover illustration:
Joshua Archer's early 1840s map of County Durham. published in *Curiosities of Great Britain*. The historic boundaries of the county are shown, including the exclaves lost in 1844. The boundaries of the main part of the county remained in use for administrative purposes until local government reforms starting in the 1960s. There was some time between when Archer finished his map and when it was published; the railway lines, shown in blue, illustrate this, since he included projected lines. It was a period known as the Railway Mania which saw rapid development of the network. with roughly a third of the railways promoted never built. The map shows some of those lines, like the Hartlepool Railway running from Durham, by way of Ludworth, to Hartlepool.

Contents

Introduction 7

PART ONE
The Place Names of County Durham A-Z 19
The Rivers of County Durham 101
The Ten Highest Mountains in Durham 105

PART TWO
Some Interesting Durham Pubs A-Z 107

Further Reading 127

View of the North Road Shop of Darlington Railway Works, established by the Stockton and Darlington Railway in 1864. The works continued working until 1966, when they were closed by British Rail. The locomotive hanging from the travelling crane is former North Eastern Railway No. 2101 which was built in Gateshead in December 1900.

The location is believed to be in or near Jarrow.

Staff of the 21st VA Durham, and patients at Herrington Hall Hospital.

BY THE SAME AUTHOR

The Place Names of Yorkshire: Cities and Villages, Hills, Rivers and Dales… and Pubs
Old Hartlepool & West Hartlepool
Hartlepool Through the Ages with Stan Laundon
Hartlepool Through Time
Hartlepool The Postcard Collection with Stan Laundon
Hartlepool History Tour with Stan Laundon and Simon Crossley
Darlington Through Time
Barnard Castle & Teesdale Through Time
Co. Durham's Days of Steam with Stan Laundon
Barnard Castle Shops, Pubs & Trades Through Time with Carol Dougherty
The Romans in the North of England
Old Stockton
Old Yarm

For a full list please go to www.paulchrystal.com

FROM STENLAKE PUBLISHING

Old Barnard Castle
Carrying Coals to Dunston, Coal and the Railway
Northumberland & Durham's Last Days of Colliery Steam
The Lost Railways of County Durham
The South Shields, Marsden & Whitburn Colliery Railway
Sunderland's Railways
Old Tyneside from Throckley to Walker

Scouts of the 1st Bishop Auckland "Lady Eden" troop.

A 1948 view of Seaburn.

Crimdon Caravan Park, near Hartlepool, began as a collection of weekend beach huts and shacks built by local people in the early 30s. By 1936 complaints about the ad hoc collection of buildings and caravans, and lack of sanitation prompted Easington Council to buy the site. They cleared the old buildings and began developing a lido and camping ground. Butlins reputedly tried to buy it in the 1960s, but were refused because they intended to restrict access to the beach. By the 1970s and 80s the park was in decline, mainly due to the affordability of foreign holidays. It was sold in the early 2000s to Park Resorts.

Introduction

Place names are invaluable, and essential, signposts to our history. They provide enduring and reliable evidence about a specific place or region, reaching back well before the invasion and subsequent occupation of the British Isles by the Romans in the 1st century BCE and CE. For any settlement the name it bears can tell us who owned the land, that it was where a river was forded or bridged, that it was under or on top of a hill, the nature of the land, or the flora or fauna that flourished there. In the case of Durham, much of it, pre-Roman, was populated by a Celtic tribe known as the Brigantes who spoke a hybrid form of Celtic made up of what we might call British – roughly centred on England and Wales – and Gaelic from Ireland. The Celtic language is today confined to modern Wales, but around 400 CE variants of the language would have been spoken in Durham.

The Angles from southern Denmark and the Saxons from northern Germany introduced to Britain a language which was the precursor of modern English. Over time the old Anglo-Saxon language changed massively with the gradual assimilation of Latin, Norman-French and other foreign tongues.

Durham and the north east is unique in Britain, being the region where the original Anglo-Saxon language has survived to any great extent. Here the old language prevails in a number of varieties, the most notable of which are Northumbrian, Geordie, the Wearside dialect (Mak'em) of Sunderland and Pitmatic in those parts of Durham centred on coal mining. It is from the ancient Germanic and Scandinavian language of the Angles that the unique local dialects of Northumberland and Durham primarily owe their origins. Geordie and Northumbrian words are more than 80% Angle in origin, compared to standard English, where the figure is less than 30%. All of this had a marked influence on local place names.

The Romans were very influential during their occupation (from about 40 CE to 410 CE). 'Chester' and 'caster' as prefix or suffix or just on its own indicate a Roman fort or fortified town, as in Lanchester, Ebchester and Binchester; anything with 'street' in it probably signifies the existence of a Roman road nearby, as in Chester le Street. The word 'wic' has a Roman provenance – it means a settlement and originates in the Latin word *vicus*, which originally described a settlement which grew up around a military camp or fort but, in time, came to mean an ordinary village. Examples include Butterwick and Elwick.

After the Romans left in the early 5th century CE, much of Durham was then settled by the Angles who became Angel-cynn, the English people, and whose Germanic language was the *lingua franca* of the day. The Northumbrian dialect, for example, had a vocabulary of 30,000 words, 80% of which have survived into modern English. This linguistic shift was accompanied by a surge in the number of new place names.

Places were given names to differentiate them from all other places and to make them accessible and reachable as destinations. Some also were named to proclaim that this place or that was owned by a particular person: it was his land, his property, his territory. Billingham, Claxton, Eldon and Bedburn are good examples. The most ancient of names are usually those of hills and rivers because these geographical features were always of most significance to the local population as places to live, farm, fish, cultivate, hunt and shelter.

The impact of the Anglo-Saxons was to erase many of the Celtic and Roman names and replace them with their own. Old English gradually took over and most of the ancient Celtic words disappeared from our language. We have the Anglo-Saxons to thank for the development of hamlets and villages which typically grew from farmsteads: 'tun' or 'ton'; examples in Durham are legion and include Carlton, Stockton, Brierton and Brafferton. Homesteads were designated by the word 'ham' (Barningham, Billingham and Middleham) while a settlement in a clearing in the woods is indicated by 'leah' or 'ley' as in Birtley; 'stan' (stone) tells us that local stone was used as a building material – Stanley, Stainton and Staindrop are examples of this.

'Ing' often means either 'belonging to the people of' or 'belonging to' so frequently is found with a personal name, as in Billingham and Barningham. The Old English *walh* means a Welsh speaker and survives in Walworth. The Old Norse suffix – *by* indicates a town or village but more often a farmstead, for instance Aislaby. 'Thorpe' is the Old Norse word for village or farmstead, surviving in Thorpe Thewles.

The survival of old words in the north east can be accounted for to a large extent by the region's remoteness and isolation from southern England, its seats of power and influence. The troublesome border issues and conflicts here up north were also influential in discouraging outside influence although some Viking words have infiltrated the local dialect from the neighbouring Viking areas of Yorkshire, South Durham and Cumbria.

Some names come from historical events or the influence of history. After 1066 it was the Prince Bishops and abbeys which had the greatest influence, rather than the beneficiaries of the land-grab by supporters of William the Conqueror. Archdeacon Newton, Bishops Auckland and Middleham, Bishopton, Sacriston and the Mitre pub in Bishopgarth prove this.

The Norman Conquest does, however, give us a number of place names; among them Witton Gilbert, Barnard Castle, Bowes Castle, Dalton Piercy and Houghton le Spring while Beamish, Bear Park, Belmont and Coatham Mundeville are all examples of French being murdered by English name-place makers. We fight the battles of Stella Ford, Neville's Cross and the Crimean Balaclava and Inkerman. Memories of North America are celebrated in Toronto, Quebec, Nova Scotia, Washington and Philadelphia. California Street (and Australia Street) were in Seaham. Less expected is Nakhchivan, a farm near Crook and a province in Azerbaijan. Industry too plays a great part with 'colliery' suffixed in Blackhall, Trimdon and Shotton.

Places conjure up all sorts of events: the places listed enable us to go on the Jarrow March and play mob football in Sedgefield and Five Court at Sacriston; we attend the mop fairs in Stockton. Sombrely we remember the terrible lifeboat disaster at Seaham and the endless litany of mining disasters at Seaham, Felling, West Stanley, Blackhall, Haswell, Houghton, Toronto and Trimdon, and many more – vivid reminders of the inherent dangers and stoicism of the mining community. In 1913, for example, there was a miner killed or badly injured every five minutes on average; 1,000 miners died that year.

Sources for place names are many and various and, in terms of spelling, of varying reliability. Invaluable as it is, *The Domesday Book* was written in 1086 by Frenchmen with little or no knowledge of Anglo-Saxon or of the Viking dialect which influenced that language. Their English geography must have been minimal. *The Boldon Book* contains the results of a survey of the bishopric of Durham that was completed on the orders of Hugh du Puiset, Bishop of Durham, in 1183. The charters of the great abbeys dating from the 12th century and parish registers from the 16th century also add massively to our knowledge. Wills and deeds and other legal documents are crucial, as are old maps, census returns and gravestone inscriptions. However, all of these primary sources have one thing in common: they manifest with varying spellings as can clearly be seen in many of the entries that follow: it was only with the establishment of the Ordnance Survey and its mapping in 1791 – and the proliferation of road and street signs in the 20th century that anything like consistency began to emerge.

The history of County Durham is informed and shaped by many things; but there are three which stand out and which are responsible for a large number of the place, and pub names, in the county. They are the Prince Bishops, coal mining and shipbuilding.

THE PRINCE BISHOPS

> There are two kings in England, namely the Lord King of England, wearing a crown in sign of his regality and the Lord Bishop of Durham wearing a mitre in place of a crown, in sign of his regality in the diocese of Durham.
> the steward of Anthony Bek, Bishop of Durham (1284–1311)

County Durham is unique in English political and constitutional history, since for 800 years it was more or less an independent state ruled not by the English monarch, but by powerful 'Prince Bishops', who were to all intents and purposes the 'Kings of County Durham'.

Soon after William the Conqueror became king of England in 1066, he realised that his kingdom could not be safely protected from Scottish invasion until Northumbria – the most extensive and culturally advanced of all his new territories – was under his rule. He appreciated the political and military significance of this earldom's remoteness and independence, and saw that it would not be easily controlled by him from the south of England, his seat of power. Northumbria's own power had been gradually eroded by successive invasions of troublesome Vikings and Scots, with the result that by the time William arrived it was reduced to an earldom extending from the River Tweed to the Tees. Northumbria's two most powerful men at the time were its Earl, at Bamburgh and the Bishop of Durham. The Earls of Bamburgh inherited their Royal powers from the old kings of Northumbria and had operated virtually independent of the Kings of England. The Bishops of Durham were also of great influence and were the successors to the earlier Bishops of Lindisfarne, one of whom was St. Cuthbert. William's conundrum was to acknowledge the remote independence of Northumbria while at the same time ensure England was properly defended from the Scots. The king gained the allegiance of Northumbria's Bishop and Earl and confirmed their powers and privileges, but Northumbrian rebellions followed and he realised the province could not be fully trusted.

William's plan was to install Robert Comine, a Norman noble, as the Earl of Northumbria, but before Comine could take up office, he and his 700 men were massacred in the City of Durham by hostile Northumbrians. William responded with the bloody and devastating Harrying of the North. Aethelwine, the Anglo-Saxon Bishop of Durham fled Northumbria, helping himself to many a Northumbrian treasure. The bishop was later caught by the Normans and thrown into jail where he died in confinement.

A 'saint-like Norman ecclesiastic', William Walcher, a trusted cleric from Liege, was appointed as the new Bishop of Durham to govern the region alongside Waltheof, a Northumbrian earl. When Waltheof was executed for his involvement in a Norman plot against William, the earldom was sold to Walcher who became the first 'Prince Bishop' in 1071. Walcher, however, was less than competent and was murdered at Gateshead in 1080.

William's son and successor, King William Rufus persisted with his father's policy and Walcher's successor, Bishop William St. Carileph (1081-96), was also invested with the powers of Earl. Now however, the powers were confined to that part of Northumbria south of the Rivers Tyne and Derwent, an area which became known as the 'County Palatine of Durham'. Today we know this as County Durham – 'The Land of the Prince Bishops'. The rest of Northumbria, to the north of the Rivers Tyne and Derwent, became the county of Northumberland, where the political powers of the Bishops of Durham were limited. Nevertheless the Durham bishops remained the religious leaders for the whole of Northumbria until the creation of the diocese of Newcastle-upon-Tyne in the 19th century.

And so William St. Carileph became the first head of the County Palatine of Durham. His Palatine was a virtually independent state, a 'buffer zone' between civilised England and the hazardous and conflict ridden Northumbria-Scottish borderland. Carileph, and successive bishops, enjoyed virtually all the powers within their 'County Palatine' that the king had in the rest of England and it is for this reason that history has named the old bishops of Durham, 'the Prince Bishops'. Bishops of Durham were invested with powers to hold their own parliament, raise their own armies, appoint their own sheriffs and justices, administer their own laws, levy taxes and customs duties, create fairs and markets, issue charters, salvage shipwrecks, collect revenue from mines, administer the forests and mint their own coins. Indeed the Prince Bishops lived the lives of kings in their castles or 'palaces' at Durham City and Bishop Auckland. In return the Prince Bishop was obliged to raise and maintain armies to defend the country from Scottish insurgents and to accompany the monarch on campaign when necessary. Several, including Puiset, Hatfield and Fordham – but perhaps most notably Bek, the 'Patriarch of Jerusalem' – led forces raised under their banner.

The Bishops of Durham title and power survived the union of England and Scotland into the Kingdom of Great Britain in 1707 until 1836. Except for a brief period during the English Civil War, the bishopric retained this temporal power until it was abolished by the Durham (County Palatine) Act 1836 with the powers reverting to the Crown.

Owing to the divine providence evidenced in the city's legendary founding, the Bishop of Durham has always enjoyed the title "Bishop by Divine Providence" compared with other bishops, who are "Bishop by Divine Permission". The Prince Bishops had their own court system, including the Court of Chancery of the County Palatine of Durham and Sadberge. The county also had its own attorney general.

COAL MINING IN COUNTY DURHAM

The Durham Coalfield extends from Bishop Auckland in the south across to the east coast, just north of Hartlepool, to the boundary with the county of Northumberland along the River Tyne in the north.

Coal was being mined in significant quantities from medieval times. Accounts survive in the Durham Cathedral archives for coal mining as early as 1458, during the Wars of the Roses, and in 1509-10, soon after Henry VIII had acceeded to the throne. There was a particular demand for coal from London as its population grew – coal sent to London by sea from the Tyne became known as 'sea coal'. Such was the capital's voracious appetite for coal, that a tax on it, provided massive sums for the rebuilding of the City of London after the Great Fire in 1666. The Industrial Revolution boosted this hugely when colliery owners were able to dig deeper and mine more productive seams. Two early developments were pivotal for coal production: Abraham Darby's discovery of a method of smelting iron with coal rather than charcoal in 1713, and Thomas Savery's invention of the steam engine, which was to have a twin effect on coal mining. Not only did it hugely increase the demand for coal when steam engines were installed in countless mills and factories, and later on the railways, but steam-powered beam engines allowed deeper mining by allowing water to be pumped out from underground. From the 17th century the Durham landowners, including the Bishop of Durham, were amassing huge wealth from their colliery holdings.

By the later 19th century the growth of the mining industry had transformed the landscape and greatly increased the population of the county. Colliery villages sprang up everywhere and migrant workers from all parts of the UK were drawn to the area. Tens of thousands of people migrated to County Durham from Cornwall due in part to their previous experience of tin mining between 1815 and the outbreak of the First World War, so much so that the miners' cottages in east Durham called "Greenhill" were also known locally as "Cornwall", and Easington Colliery still has a Cornish Street.

Horden Colliery near Peterlee mainly produced coal from seams that ran under the North Sea. In 1930 it broke the European record for coal mined in a single day, with 6,758 tons mined, an achievement that stood for 30 years.

The twelve 'aged miners homes' at Crookhill near Ryton. At a ceremony on the 16th October, 1920 organised by the Durham Aged Mine Workers' Homes Association, 15 foundation stones were laid, one for each member of the committee. The local MP for Blaydon, Major Walter Waring, a Coalition Liberal, gave an address to the event. In which he said, 'we are all indebted to the old men who have worked down the mine, some for 40 years, others for 50 years, and others for even 60 years'. Almost a year later on the 8th October the homes were formally opened by the Prime Minister, David Lloyd George.

The industry had a major, lasting effect on working conditions, trade unionism, public health and housing, and on mines safety.

The peak of coal production in Britain was in 1913 when over 270 million tons were mined, 58,700,000 tons from County Durham (22%). In 1923 there were 170,000 miners working in County Durham. From then on production declined, despite increasing mechanisation, and stabilised at about 200 million tons per annum. 1947 saw nationalisation of the coal industry which ushered in more co-ordinated operations, with a trend towards more intensive working of fewer mines. The National Coal Board took over more than 100,000 men in County Durham, producing 24 million tons of coal a year from 127 collieries. From the 1950s alternate sources of fuel percolated into the railways, shipping and electricity generation, as well as domestic heating, and demand declined. By 1974 County Durham employed only 25,000 men at 22 collieries, annually producing about 8.2 million tons of coal, the only consolation being that the productivity rate per man/shift had increased from 17.4 to 33.4 cwts.

The irony is that the mid-20th century also saw an increasing number of pit closures, particularly in the west of County Durham, with production increasingly concentrated at the large coastal pits. Over 8,000 families moved to the Yorkshire coalfield under schemes grant-aided by the NCB. Many other miners began to commute long distances to the coastal belt.

Bitter strikes in 1972 and 1984 focused public attention on the problems caused by contraction of the industry, and caused deep feelings that still rankle today amongst County Durham communities. In the 1980s the closure of coastal mines began in earnest. In 1993 the last deep mines closed: Easington, Vane Tempest, Wearmouth and Westoe. Work to remove disused colliery structures, to landscape pit heaps, and to clean up the seashore, has virtually erased all evidence of this once-powerful industry and the miners' skills, culture, language, and folklore that went with it in the communities left high and dry; sadly these will diminish further with time.

SHIPBUILDING IN COUNTY DURHAM

Shipbuilding has long been one of the region's vital industries. In 1294 a galley for the King's fleet was built in Newcastle and ships were built at Sunderland from at least 1346, and at Stockton from 1470. The early ships were built of wood but in the 19th century iron ships took over.

TYNESIDE SHIPBUILDING
South Shields born Charles Mark Palmer established a yard at Jarrow in 1851 and built its first iron collier the *John Bowes* in the following year. It was the first ever sea-going screw collier and was built for John Bowes for shipping coal to London. Palmers were also famed for building the first rolled armour plates for warships in 1854.

SUNDERLAND SHIPBUILDING
Sunderland was once "the largest shipbuilding town in the world" – an industry which dates back to 1346 when Thomas Menville opened a shipbuilding yard in Hendon. Over time Sunderland has had over 400 registered shipyards.

By 1790 Sundertand was building around nineteen ships per year. It became the most important shipbuilding centre in the country in the 1830s and by 1840 there were 65 shipyards. Over 150 wooden vessels were built at Sunderland in 1850 when 2,025 shipwrights worked in the town. A further 2,000 were employed in ancillary industries. Sunderland's first iron ships were built from 1852 and wooden shipbuilding ceased here in 1876. Sunderland shipbuilders included Austin and Son (1826), William Pickersgill (1851) and William Doxford (1840).

The advent of iron and steel construction brought with it a new group of workers – the boilermakers or "the black squad" who were paid by piecework which meant that they could earn a lot more money than the shipwrights, who were only paid timework.

The Sunderland built screw steamer *Durango* in Palmer's dry dock in Jarrow. She was built by Bartram and Sons in 1895 for the Neptune Steam Navigation Co., and had a number of owners over her career. *Durango* was captured and sunk in August 1917, by *U53*, 50 miles north west of Barra Head in the Hebrides, on her way from Liverpool to St. John's, Newfoundland.

Workers clocked on at 6am; latecomers found the gates locked and their pay docked by a quarter of a day's pay. Working conditions were hideous with death and injury ever-present while compensation payments were not regulated until the late 19th century. This had a ruinous effect on affected families.

Only by the 20th century did things start to improve, but accidents were still a daily occurrence. Medical officers were appointed at yards and safety equipment came into use. By the end of the 1960s there were safety committees in most yards and, with the introduction of the Health and Safety at Work Act 1974, accident rates were greatly reduced. Strikes were a regular event in shipyards. As the workforce grew more trade unions and more disputes developed. The Sunderland Engineers strike of 1883-85 was one of the longest on the Wear.

The shipbuilding industry suffered regular fluctuations in demand for new ships or repair with three great depressions: the first was in 1884–87 bringing with it mass unemployment and, for the lucky ones who were still employed, wage reductions. The second occurred in 1908–10 after a national fall in ship production. The worst was in the 1930s when there was a huge fall in demand after the boom of the First World War.

After the Second World War Sunderland continued to lead the way, but although production increased globally it became increasingly difficult for British yards to compete. Throughout the 1950s and 1960s more yards closed or merged. In 1977 the shipbuilding industry was nationalised and job losses followed. In 1980 the last two remaining yards merged, then only eight years later on the 7th December 1988 this last remaining yard on the Wear closed, bringing shipbuilding in Sunderland to a sad conclusion.

S.P. Austin and Son Ltd

One of Sunderland's biggest yards founded in 1826 by Peter Austin, who started by building wooden collier brigs on the north bank of the River Wear. In 1846 the firm moved over the river to a site near Wearmouth Bridge, where it remained until it closed.

1869 saw the last wooden ship built in the yard and in the next decade repairs were being made on iron ships. By 1881 the yard employed 396 men and 54 boys.

Austin's was famous for its pontoon, which opened in 1904. The pontoon was a platform that could be sunk below a ship, then re-floated to raise the ship out of the water.

Output during the First World War was 13 colliers of 28,979 tons along with five small naval craft. One of these vessels, *Icemaid*, became the prototype for war standard colliers of that size during the Second World War. In 1914 they were classified as 'Shipbuilders, Ship Engine and Boiler Repairers. Specialities: building steamers for cargo carrying purposes, chiefly vessels adapted for the coal trade. In 1954 Austin's merged with W. Pickersgill and Sons to become Austin and Pickersgill but the yard closed in 1956.

J.L. Thompson and Sons

Estblished by Robert Thompson in 1846 this shipyard turned out ships until the 1980s. The world-famous Liberty Ship was among the designs to be created, produced and manufactured at the yard's base at North Sands.

Other yards included **Swan Hunter**, **Shorts** and **W. Gray**.

SOUTH SHIELDS SHIPBUILDING

A shipyard was established here around 1720 by Robert Wallis, although possibly only a ship-breaking or repairing yard. By the late 18th century, three further (ill-fated) shipbuilders are recorded: William Forster, John Wright and James Evans. Forster's yard operated between 1773 and 1791, when his widow was forced to put it up for sale. Wright sold his yard and became a shipowner. James Evan's yard thrived until the early 19th century, but went bankrupt in 1831. Other short-lived yards were Messrs Attley, Brown & Swan, shipbuilders at the "Low End" 1803-08, and John and Philip Laing of Sunderland who owned yards in Pilot Street and Thrift Street. Their partnership dissolved in 1822, with Laing retaining the yard at the eastern end of Pilot Street. Thomas Marshall built over 100 vessels, mostly steel, 1839-59. Following his retirement, his sons relocated the business to Willington Quay. Thomas Wawn, John Blumer and Luke Bushell are also recorded as shipbuilders in this area in the 1840s. Readhead and Softley and W.P. Greenwell had yards in Shadwell Street and Pilot Street in the mid 19th century.

Readhead moved to Tyne Dock in 1872. In 1865 Alderman John Readhead founded his shipyard John Readhead & Sons, which built small cargo ships and colliers for clients all over the world until the yard was closed in 1968.

HARTLEPOOL SHIPBUILDING

At the beginning of the 19th century Hartlepool had a modest population of 1,400 people, most of whom were engaged in the fishing industry. There were ten fishmongers and curers in the town but only two butchers. Eventually, after the founding of West Hartlepool in 1847, fishing gave way to shipbuilding and the shipping of coal. When the first dock opened in 1847 this led to a significant increase in the population by the time of the 1851 census to over 4,000 people. By 1861 this had increased again to over 29,000.

The development of the dockyards was swift and sure with the enclosed Victoria Dock opening in 1842. The eight acre West Hartlepool Harbour and Dock opened on 1st June 1847; its first vessel was *Prince*, commanded by Captain Black, from Jersey. Ralph Ward Jackson lost no time inviting shipbuilders, timber merchants and sawmill owners to establish businesses there. The Coal Dock pre-dated this but soon traffic outgrew it and two more docks were built. The fourteen acre Jackson Dock opened on 1st June 1852 on the same day a railway connecting West Hartlepool with Leeds, Manchester and Liverpool opened. One of its early prime functions was to transport fresh fish throughout the country.

Next was Swainson Dock, on the 3rd June 1856 named after Ralph Ward Jackson's father-in-law and opened with a breakfast ceremony for over 1,000 guests entertained by a convoy of ships entering the new dock. Food and champagne were served – the latter being a unique, if intoxicating, treat for many.

William Gray shipbuilders was established in 1862 and went on to win the Blue Riband prize for maximum output in 1878, 1882, 1888, 1895, 1898 and 1900. The first ships at Hartlepool were wooden, built by shipbuilders such as John Winspear, Luke Blumer and Joseph Parkin behind the High Street and then in Middleton in the 1830s and 1840s; Parkin's first ship was the 1837 built *Castle Eden*. The problem with the High Street yard was that ships had to be manouevered over the town walls in parts and assembled in Middleton for launching. John Punshon Denton had built 56 ships at Middleton from 1839 and was joined by William Gray in 1862 to form Denton Gray and Company; this became one of the biggest of the shipbuilding companies with seventeen acres of yards around Middleton from 1871 and eighteen launches in 1878. By 1913, 43 ship-owning companies were located in the town, building 236 ships. It all ended 125 years later in 1961 with the *Blanchland*, the last ship built by William Gray and Company Limited.

STOCKTON

In 1470 a wooden ship was commissioned for the Bishop of Durham, using 32 stones of iron fashioned into nails at six and a half pennies per stone. Shipbuilding took off in the mid 17th century with 60 ships built between 1780 and 1800; the yards were at Smithfield and near to Stockton Bridge. In 1718 75 corn ships entered the Port of London from Stockton, more than the combined total from Sunderland and Hartlepool. In 1678 Stockton was building ships of 200 tonnes but it was in the late 18th century that shipbuilding really took off in Stockton.

Between 1790 and 1805 Thomas Haw was building ships which saw action in the Napoleonic wars. Three shipping companies were formed between 1822 and 1835: by then 272 ships with a combined tonnage of 51,000 were registered at Stockton, exporting coal mainly; none survived the impending surging rise of Middlesbrough. The first iron ship turned out here was a screw steamer, the *Advance*, built at South Stockton, Thornaby, in 1854 by the Iron Shipbuilding Company, later the aptly-named Richardson, Duck and Co.; by 1865 they had launched 80 vessels, 50 of which were steamers. At the same time, Pearse, Lockwood & Co. in Ropner's Yard launched 64 including 34 steamers. The first steel ship was *Little Lucy* built in 1858. Pearse launched their largest steamer, the 377 feet *Talpore* in 1860 – a troop ship which was dismantled, shipped and reassembled in India where it saw action on the River Indus; it was the world's largest river steamer at the time. Ships' boilers were much in demand, leading local firm Fossick's to move into marine engineering from 1853.

CLOSURES 1909-1979
The sceptre of shipyard closures in the 20th century took place mainly between 1909 and 1933 and 1960 and 1993. Early closures included Smiths Dock at North Shields in 1909, which became a ship repair yard, Armstrongs of Elswick in 1921, Richardson Duck of Stockton (1925), Priestman's of Sunderland (1933) and Palmers of Jarrow and Hebburn (1933). There were 28 north east closures in this period of which fourteen were on the Tyne, seven on the Wear, six on the Tees and one at Hartlepool. Six shipyards closed in the 1960s including W.Gray of Hartlepool (1961) and Short Brothers of Sunderland (1964). There were five closures in the region in the 1970s including the Furness yard at Haverton Hill, near Stockton, in 1979.

Middleton Iron Works at Middleton St. George near Darlington. The first blast furnaces were set up in the area in the 1860s. The works stopped operating in the 1880s through a combination of increasing steel production, and better quality iron ore being shipped in from abroad which made inland sites more expensive to run. Around the turn of the 19th century the iron works were reopened by the Linthorpe Dinsdale Smelting Company. They continued to provide employment in the area until 1931 when they closed during the Great Depression and were demolished in 1947.

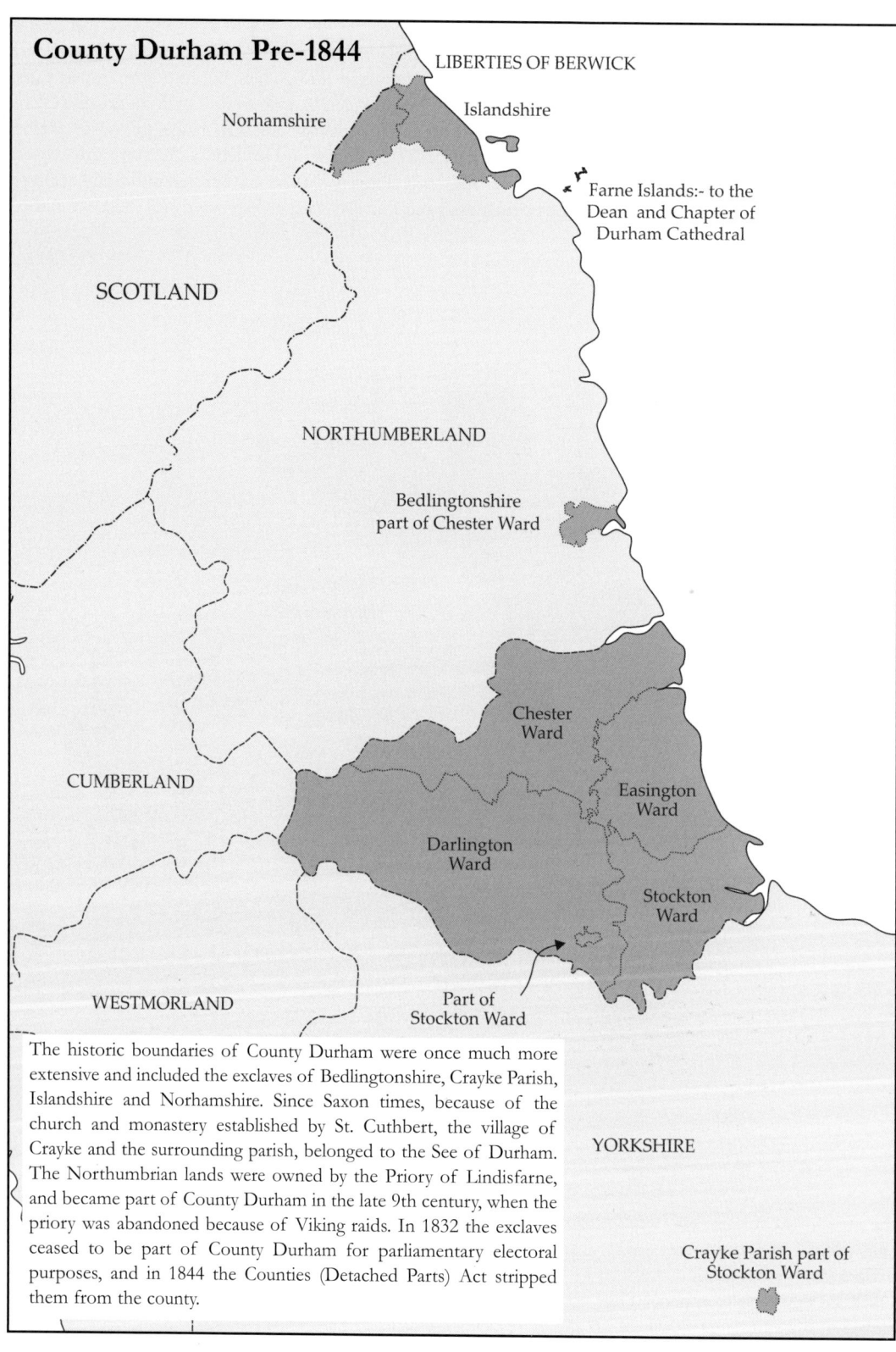

County Durham Pre-1844

LIBERTIES OF BERWICK
Islandshire
Norhamshire
Farne Islands:- to the Dean and Chapter of Durham Cathedral
SCOTLAND
NORTHUMBERLAND
Bedlingtonshire part of Chester Ward
Chester Ward
CUMBERLAND
Easington Ward
Darlington Ward
Stockton Ward
WESTMORLAND
Part of Stockton Ward
YORKSHIRE
Crayke Parish part of Stockton Ward

The historic boundaries of County Durham were once much more extensive and included the exclaves of Bedlingtonshire, Crayke Parish, Islandshire and Norhamshire. Since Saxon times, because of the church and monastery established by St. Cuthbert, the village of Crayke and the surrounding parish, belonged to the See of Durham. The Northumbrian lands were owned by the Priory of Lindisfarne, and became part of County Durham in the late 9th century, when the priory was abandoned because of Viking raids. In 1832 the exclaves ceased to be part of County Durham for parliamentary electoral purposes, and in 1844 the Counties (Detached Parts) Act stripped them from the county.

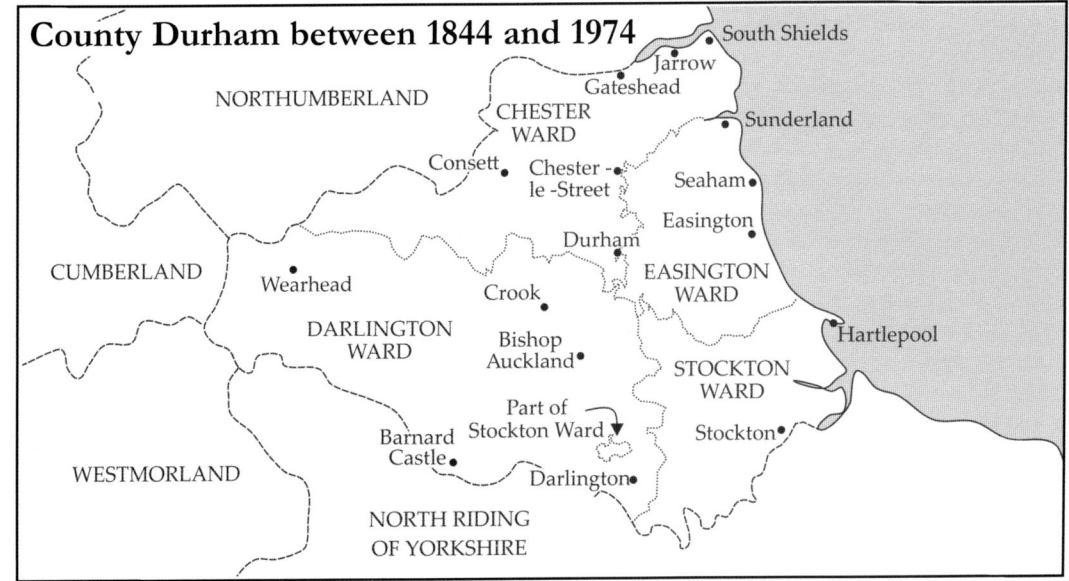

County Durham was sub-divided into six administrative units called wards which correspond to the hundreds or wapentakes in other counties. In 1844 this was reduced to four when Norhamshire and Islandshire became part of Northumberland. As the 19th century continued, the importance of the wards diminished, as their former powers were centralised in the city of Durham.

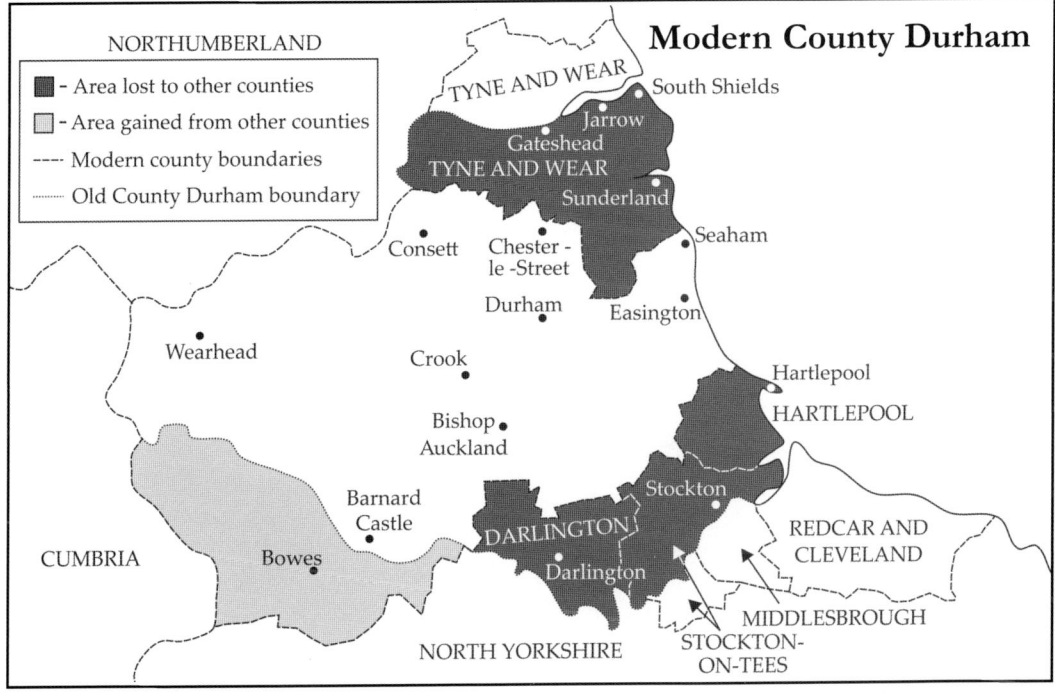

The boundary changed again in 1974 when the Local Government Act 1972 was enacted. Land was lost to the newly created counties of Cleveland, and Tyne and Wear, but was gained from the North Riding of Yorkshire. Cleveland lasted until 1996, when it was split into several borough councils. The last change was in 1997 when Darlington Borough Council was created.

A portrait of three County Durham ministers photographed in April, 1910. From right to left Rev. Croft, Rev. Francis Peacock and Rev. McKenzie. Rev Peacock was the curate of St. Stephen in South Sheilds, and later St. Ignanatius in Hendon, before he became vicar of Holy Trinity and Darlington in 1905. He became canon of Gloucester Cathedral in 1919 where he remained until his sudden death in April 1934.

The buildings that housed Castle Eden's cottage industries of bleaching cloth works and rope making.

The Place Names of County Durham A-Z

AISLABY
Historically and ceremonially Aislaby is located in County Durham, but for administrative purposes comes under the Borough of Stockton-on-Tees, which was made a unitary authority in 1996. Before then Aislaby was in the non-metropolitan county of Cleveland, set up on 1st April 1974 under the provisions of the Local Government Act 1972.

Aislaby is a small village and civil parish on the north bank of the River Tees to the west of Eaglescliffe and Yarm. The name first appears as Asulue(s)bi in 1086, is of Viking origin and means "Aslak's farm." There are other Aislabys in North Yorkshire near Sleights and near Pickering.

ALLENSFORD
Allensford is a hamlet just to the west of Consett, and to the east of Castleside on the River Derwent. Its first record is as Aleynforth, Alan's Ford, in Bishop Hatfield's survey of *c.*1382. The place name is sometimes listed as Allansford: "At Allansford...is a bridge over the Derwent into Northumberland, surrounded by some of the most beautiful scenery on that stream; there are a few cottages on each side of the river". There was a bridge there in the late 17th century when the structure was "very ruinous and in greate decay" according to the Northumberland Quarter Sessions for 1687-97.

Thomas Hatfield or Thomas de Hatfield (died 1381) was Bishop of Durham from 1345 to 1381 under King Edward III. He was one of the last warrior-bishops in England.

Denis Hayford, (*c.*1635–1733), a pioneer of the steel industry, acquired the lease of Allensford furnace and forge in 1692 which was upstream from his established business in Shotley Bridge.

The adjacent woodland forms the 43 acre Allensford Woods Local Nature Reserve.

ANNFIELD PLAIN
Annfield Plain village lies between Stanley, 2½ miles to the north east, and Consett, 5 miles to the west. Much of the surrounding landscape is rough moorland, dominated by the nearby Pontop Pike television mast.

"Anfield", the name, derives from "the fields of An", An being a man who lived hereabouts before the Norman Conquest. The "Plain" part was originally "Plane" and refers originally not to the plateau on which the village stands but to the inclined plane on the Stanhope and Tyne Railway of 1834. When this was linked to the Stockton and Darlington railway line in 1845 it became part of the national network by which time the Derwent Iron Company were also using it. The engine used by the plane was known as the Anfield Engine because of its proximity to Anfield House, built in the 18th century on nearby Loud Hill.

The spelling changed to "Annfield Plain" around 1856, when houses were built for miners on the nearby plateau.

In the 16th century, the main economic activity was sheep farming; mining started in the late 17th century. The Stanhope and Tyne Railway opened in 1834 for the transportation of coal. Several limekilns were built at this time and were fuelled by local coal, with limestone being brought in by rail. Deep coal pits were sunk during the 19th century allowing the village to grow with the construction of a brewery, mill, and candle factory, as well as a school, church, at least two nonconformist chapels, and shops.

The former Co-op supermarket was known as the Disco, an allusion to its previous name: the Annfield Plain Co-op and Discount Electricals. The store was dismantled and rebuilt at Beamish Open Air Museum in the late 1980s.

ARBEIA
See South Shields.

ARCHDEACON NEWTON
The hamlet's name derives from what is now an abandoned village, founded and built in the Middle Ages by the Archdeacon of Durham. An alternative derivation has it that the land was leased from the

BARRAS HILL
Near Sacriston, it features as Bararce in 1382 – bare arse, meaning exposed and unproductive land.

BEAMISH
The name derives from the 'beautiful mansion' here in the 13th century – Latin *bellus mansus* and Old French *beau mes*. In 1288 it appears as Bewmys; Bemyshe in 1505. Beamish was once called 'Pit Hill' and is situated to the north east of Stanley. The village is contained within Hell Hole Wood (completely at odds with 'beautiful mansion') and is home to the famous Beamish Museum. Its main public house is the Shepherd and Shepherdess. To the south is the village of No Place, also known as Co-operative Villas.

The local church is known as Tin Chapel – a nod to the amount of metal used in its contruction.

To the north of Beamish in Urpeth is Pockerley Manor – a rare example of a pele tower, probably dating from the 15th century with later alterations and additions. It is attached to a later farmhouse. The tower has living accommodation built over a stone basement, the first floor reached through a stair built into the thickness of the wall; the Welsh slate roof is largely original.

Peel or pele towers are small, free-standing fortified keeps or tower houses, built along the English and Scottish borders in the Scottish Marches and North of England, mainly between the mid-14th century and about 1600. They were built to defend against attack from the English, Scots and the Border Reivers of both nationalities.

By an Act of the Parliament of England in 1455, each of these towers was required to have an iron basket on its summit and a smoke or fire signal, for day or night use, ready at hand. Apart from their primary purpose as a warning system, the towers were also the homes of the lairds and landlords of the area, who dwelt in them with their families and retainers, while their followers lived in simple huts outside the walls. The towers also provided a refuge so that, when cross-border raiding parties arrived, the whole population of a village could take to the tower and wait for the marauders to depart.

Beamish Open Air Museum
Beamish was the first regional open-air museum in England opening in 1972; it pioneered the concept of a living museum. By displaying duplicates or replaceable items, it was also an early champion of the now commonplace practice of museums allowing visitors to actually touch objects and to literally feel history. Its guiding principle is to preserve an example of everyday life in urban and rural north east England at the climax of industrialisation in the early 20th century It is a significant educational resource locally. It can also demonstrate its benefit to the local economy while its unselective collecting policy has created a lasting bond between museum and community. And a lot of stuff…

BEARPARK
Bearpark is a village two and a half miles west of Durham. The name is a corruption of the French *Beau Repaire* – "beautiful retreat" and is recorded as Beaurepayre in 1267. Half a mile to the north of the present village lies the ruins of Beaurepaire Priory, built in 1258 by the Prior of Durham, Bertram de Middleton, as a retirement residence. The manor was largely destroyed by the Scots in 1640 and in 1644 during the British Civil War. In 1872 Theodore Fry helped found the Bearpark Coal and Coke Company, which established a coal mine in Bearpark until 1984, when the mine was closed.

BEDBURN
Bedburn is a village near Hamsterley, and Hamsterley Forest first recorded in 1291. It means the stream (Old English *burna*) of a man called Beda.

BELMONT
Old French *belle mont* – beautiful hill and Durham city suburb, originally a coal mining village. The house "Beechcroft" situated on Broomside Lane was used as a location in the 1971 film *Get Carter* as the home of character Cliff Brumby. It was here that Michael Caine as Jack Carter delivered the line "You're a big

man, but you're out of shape." Despite a vigorous campaign to preserve it, the house was demolished in December 2008. Belmont Stadium was used in the 1954 film *The Gay Dog* – a 1954 British comedy directed by Maurice Elvey and starring Wilfred Pickles, Petula Clark and Megs Jenkins.

BENFIELDSIDE
Also Benelands and Benefeldside in the 12th century meaning the cultivated land where beans are grown.

BILDERSHAW
Bildershaw is between Darlington and West Auckland. Bildershaw is primarily an agricultural village and is one of the only villages left in the world that still practices feudalism. The town is run by a group of local officials who meet every month to talk about legal matters such as farming boundaries and trades. It was established in 1169 under the rule of Henry II. Bildershaw mainly produced soy beans, squash, and peas.

BILLINGHAM
Billingham was founded around 650 CE by a group of Angles known as Billa's people which is where the name Billingham may have originated. Also Bellingaham in 1090 and Billingeham in 1291 – homestead of the followers of Billa. More likely is the hill village on the Billing – the ridge overlooking Billingham Beck on which the parish church still stands.

Today the town is famous for its Forum and for its chemical industry history. Aldous Huxley visited the newly opened and technologically advanced Brunner and Mond plant at ICI and gave a detailed account of the processes he saw. The introduction to the most recent edition of *Brave New World* states that Huxley was inspired to write the novel by this Billingham visit. Henry Thorold in the *Shell Guide to County Durham* states:

> This is one of the most extraordinary of experiences, a sight almost unique in England. On either side of the road are the works. Steaming, sizzling—tall steel towers, great cylinders, pipes everywhere... At night the whole industrial world along the banks of the Tees comes to life... brilliant with a thousand lights, the great girders of the Transporter Bridge dark in silhouette: a magic city.

Salt deposits were discovered at Port Clarence by Bell Brothers in 1874. In 1882 they set up a salt works at Haverton Hill bringing in experienced salt workers from Cheshire to exploit the resource. Bell Brothers were bought by Brunner Mond & Co. of Cheshire in 1890 thus effecting the foundation of Teesside's chemical industry and the demise of competition from Tyneside.

The chemical industry in Billingham was established in 1918 when the government initiated the production of synthetic ammonia, originally intended for the making of bombs for the war. The site chosen was the 700 acre Grange Farm. The war had ended before the plant opened and was taken over by Brunner Mond in 1920 for the manufacture of synthetic ammonia and fertilisers. In 1926 ICI was formed by the merger of Brunner Mond with three other chemical manufacturers including Nobel Explosives. From 1928 anhydrite or dry gypsum was mined 700 feet below Billingham for the making of fertilisers. Plastics and nylons came to Billingham in 1934 and a new plant was opened in 1935 to produce oil and petrol from creosote and coal through the process of hydrogenation. In 1946 ICI Wilton opened at nearby Redcar and in 1962 the site on Seal Sands was reclaimed from the sea.

Also in 1962 coke ovens originally used for chemicals production at Billingham, were replaced by new plants utilising the steam naphtha process – a much cheaper way of making ammonia. Between 1964 and 1969 four great oil refineries were built at the mouth of the Tees, two by Phillips Petroleum and one each by ICI and Shell, their function being to supply the Billingham chemical industry. The 138 mile pipeline linking chemical Teesside with chemical Runcorn for the transportation of ethylene was built in 1968.

Billingham Forum now offers a theatre, business standard conferencing facilities, a swimming pool, a large Ice Arena, a state-of-the-art Activ8 Gym with TechnoGym Digital exercising equipment, a sauna and steam room, fun indoor climbing (GoClimb), a sports injury centre, and dry sports and drama facilities.

BILLY HILL
Originally *billig* – a prominent hill.

BILLY ROW
Billy Row village is to the north of Crook. Legend has it that the name Billy Row was given by Sir William Row who owned the land on which the village was built; it was Billyraw in 1425 – the hill of Billing. Other variants include Burnigill (1313) and Burnyngill (1343) – followers of a man called Bruning. More popular etymology would have it that the name refers to Will o' the Raw – William de Rawe (d. 1350), a scoundrel who seized half of the manor of Cornsay.

BINCHESTER
The village is situated between Bishop Auckland and Spennymoor. Binchester takes the first part of its name from the first element of its Roman name *Vinovia*. This was Anglicised with the addition of the Old English word *caster* '(Roman) fortification' and perhaps through identification with the Old English word *binn* 'manger'.

Established around 80 CE to help defend the newly built Dere Street, four coins of Vespasian confirm that initial building of the Roman fort here coincided with Agricola's march northward into the territory of the Brigantes. The first fort was built in timber, most probably by troops of the IXth Legion. It was rebuilt in stone by the VIth Legion during the early 2nd century and was one of the largest forts in the area south of the wall. A large *vicus* (civilian settlement) soon sprang up. There is still a superbly preserved stretch of Roman road at the site, as well as remains of a bathhouse with underfloor heating. It can be found just over one mile to the north of Bishop Auckland on the banks of the River Wear, the crossing of which it defends. Binchester was the largest Roman fort in County Durham. The *via principalis* at Binchester is actually part of Dere Street, which runs through the centre of the fort.

The Binchester site has had more than its fair share of calamities: the bathhouse was found in 1815 when a farm cart accidentally fell into part of a hypocaust, and the ruins did not do very well under the early 19th century occupants of Binchester Hall – in 1828 'altars, urns, and other relics' were stolen and used as props for local coal pits. In 1891 the installation of water pipes caused destruction to the north east corner of the fort, particularly the rampart, Dere Street, and a few *vicus* houses, but did uncover a large Roman altar dedicated by Pomponius Donatus 'beneficiarius of the governor' to Jupiter and the Matres Ollototae – three Celtic mother goddesses originally from the continent.

BIRTLEY
Birtley crops up in numerous forms in the 13th century: Britlei, Brittele, Byrtelay and Bircteley, Brithley and Biretely in the 14th. It could mean the bright woodland clearing from Old English *beohrt leah* or else the first element may be a Saxon personal name. Birtley is north west of Washington; there is a Portobello nearby – lovely port, just like the one near Edinburgh.

BISHOP AUCKLAND
Bishop Auckland is about 12 miles north west of Darlington, 12 miles south west of Durham and 5 miles south east of Crook at the confluence of the River Wear and the River Gaunless.

Much of the town's early history revolves around the Bishops of Durham. Auckland Castle (known locally as The Bishop's Palace), has been the official residence of the Bishop of Durham since 1832 but it was established as a hunting lodge for the Prince Bishops of Durham. The castle is surrounded by 800 acres of parkland, which was originally used by the Bishops for hunting and is today open to the public. This link gives us the first part of the town's name. In 1083, when Bishop William de St-Calais expelled a number of canons from Durham some of them settled in the area and established a collegiate church. Around 1183 Bishop Pudsey established a manor house in the town, with a great hall being completed in 1195 on the site occupied by St. Peter's Chapel today. Bishop Bek, who preferred the town as his main residence over Durham Castle due to its proximity to hunting grounds, later converted the manor house into a castle. The grounds of the castle were large enough to accommodate 16,000 men before the Battle of Neville's Cross in 1346.

The town was first attested in 1040 under the name Alclit, or Alcluith or Alcleat but this is nothing to do with Auckland. Auckland is now accepted to be Old Norse in origin, meaning 'additional land'. This could refer to the extra land granted to the Bishop of Durham by King Canute in around 1020. Just as likely is the derivation from *Alclit* meaning the rock or hill on a river called Clyde (perhaps the original name of the Gaunless?) Another suggestion is that Auckland derives from "Oakland", referring to the local forests.

We also see Auckland in St. Helen Auckland, West Auckland and St. Andrew Auckland, an old name for South Church, all of which are along the **Gaunless**. The name Gaunless (from *gagnlauss*) itself is of later Norse origin, meaning useless. This derives from the river's inability to power a mill, sustain fish or create fertile floodplains.

At the end of the 18th century the main industry in the town was weaving. Coal mining had existed on a small scale as early as 1183 in Bishop Auckland when it is mentioned in the *Boldon Book*, but it was restricted by the lack of transport to move coal away from the area. All this changed with the railways in the early 19th century, which allowed large scale coal mining and coal to be transported to the coast. In the second half of the 19th century there were around 60 collieries in the area working at any one time. By the 20th century 16,000 people were employed in the mining industry in the area.

The *Boldon Book* (or the *Boldon Buke*) contains the results of a survey of the bishopric of Durham that was completed on the orders of Hugh du Puiset, Bishop of Durham, in 1183, designed to assist the administration of the vast diocesan estates. The survey was similar to that of the *Domesday Book* in the previous century.

Lancastrian Arthur Stanley Jefferson, better known as Stan Laurel, spent his early days in Bishop Auckland, as celebrated by the Comedian pub. In 1903 he attended Gainford Academy (or Bowman's Academy) for a few months.

Nearby **Eldon** was Heldun in 1204 from Old English the hill of a man called Ealla, while **Etherley** appears as Etherdacres in the 14th century – the open land of Aethred. **Coundon** comes from Old English *cuna dun* – the hill where cows are reared.

BISHOP MIDDLEHAM

Old English *Middlel ham* – middle homestead owned by the Bishop of Durham. Bishop Middleham is about 9 miles south east of Durham close to Sedgefield. The first recorded mention of the village was in 1146 when Osbert, the nephew of Bishop Flambard, gave the Church of Middleham to the Prior and Convent at Durham – hence the name. Bishop Middleham became one of the favourite residences of the Bishops of Durham, two of whom died here. By the 19th century the village supported four public houses, a brewery, and a few tradesmen's shops. The village economy was mainly agricultural though there was some coal mining. The 1883 *Boldon Book* says that there were 32 houses here.

BISHOPSGARTH

Bishopsgarth – literally the garth – quad or yard – of the bishops – is an estate on the western outskirts of Stockton-on-Tees. There are two pubs here: the Five Alls pub, and The Mitre pub on Harrowgate Lane.

BISHOPTON

An 1104 document has it as Biscoptun – Old English *biscop tun* – the bishop's farmstead. Bishopton lies to the north west of Stockton-on-Tees. Its history is bound up in farming with rows of cottages and several farms forming a long wide village street, with a village green. Bishopton is famous for its castle – a fortification was built by Roger de Conyers in 1143. Constructed in a motte-and-bailey design, the castle had two baileys, rather than the usual one, and originally had two large enclosures beyond the baileys. In the 12th century it was surrounded by a low artificial lake. A licence to crenellate was granted in 1143 during the time of The Anarchy.

The Anarchy was a civil war waged in England and Normandy between 1135 and 1153, which caused much loss of law and order. The conflict was a succession crisis precipitated by the accidental drowning of William Adelin, the only legitimate son of Henry I, when the *White Ship* sank in 1120. Henry failed in his attempts to install his daughter, the Empress Matilda, on the throne and on Henry's death in 1135, his nephew Stephen of Blois seized the throne with the help of Stephen's brother, Henry of Blois, the Bishop of Winchester. Stephen's early reign was marked by fierce fighting with English barons, rebellious Welsh leaders and Scottish invaders. Following a major rebellion in the south west of England, Matilda invaded in 1139 with the help of her half-brother Robert of Gloucester.

The war dragged on for many more years; in England neither side could achieve victory but rebel barons began to acquire ever greater power in the north of England.

De Conyers built the castle during a dispute with William Cumin, who claimed to be the Bishop of Durham; de Conyers supported Cumin's rival, William of St. Barbara. In later years the castle was owned by the Bishop of Durham, hence the name.

Nearby **Galloping Hills** is where the horses were exercised and **Woogra** comes from *wulf grava* which means the grove where the wolves are.

BLACKHALL COLLIERY

Blackhall Colliery is a village on the North Sea coast between Horden and Hartlepool. From its opening in 1909 until 1981 when the colliery closed Blackhall was all about coal mining; Daniel Hall was at the forefront of the founding and development of the colliery, investing heavily in the establishment of the local mining infrastructure in the area. It is thought that the name Black-Hall came about as a result of Daniel's nickname 'Black' – which he earned from his association with coal mining – and his surname Hall.

Over the years there were 69 fatalities at the colliery, each of which underlines the dangerous nature of coal mining and the tragedies it caused; here is a random selection as listed at http://www.dmm.org.uk/colliery/b006.htm:

> Allen, Walter George, 20 Jul 1916, aged 15, Pony Driver, He was driving a pony and three tubs in the pit. Another driver saw Allen's lamp go out, and heard his shout "Back" to the pony. He was found lying with his neck broken; he had been jammed against a prop.
>
> Taylor, R., 28 Jan 1948, (accident: 07 Oct 1944), aged 70, Stoneman, died from injuries received.
>
> Cartwright, Percy, 13 Jan 1927, aged 32, Cutter, on 14th October 1925 he sustained injuries to his spine when he was caught by a fall of stone during his bait time. He had left the face and gone back about 14 yards, the fall occurred five minutes later. He spent six months at Sunderland Royal Infirmary before being taken home where he died from his injuries on 13th January 1927.
>
> Neasham, George, 10 Mar 1933, aged 20, Buried: Blackhall Cemetery

Note the wide age range; boys could work underground from age 14; they could do surface work from age 12.

The revolutionary electric winding gear installed here (which could excavate 18,000 tons a week) meant there was no need for chimneys to spew out smoke and steam and no requirement for a slag heap because the waste was dumped into the sea by aerial ropeway; the pit was the most modern in Britain in 1916. Sadly, this industrial enlightenment was not reflected socially in the housing provision which was shocking: initially, many mining families lived in huts and tents, even in the caves on the beach.

Blackhall Beach is famous for its appearance in the 1971 film *Get Carter* where, at the end, Michael Caine is involved in a chase across a sea-coal covered beach.

BLACKHALL ROCKS

Blackhall Rocks village is just south of Blackhall Colliery which it adjoins. One of the earliest mentions of Blackhall Rocks is in the mid-19th century, when the beach was extensively photographed at a time when the beach was a minor holiday resort, thanks to the presence of a hotel above the cliffs. It was around this time a railway station was established here (closed in 1960). Next to the station a siding and coal depot supplied coal from Blackhall Colliery. The hotel survived until the late 1960s when it was demolished.

Despite the presence of the hotel, it was not until the 1920s and 1930s that Blackhall Rocks really developed as a community and village. The truly awesome railway viaducts at Crimdon and Dene Holme were built in 1905, Blackhall Rocks Station opened for passenger trains and eight houses for railway workers were built.

Blackhall Coastguard closed in 1975; their cottages were built in the 1850s near the Rocks Hotel and demolished in 1967. Their equipment comprised a cart, a small rescue boat, cliff rescue gear and a large pole for the breeches buoy. In the 1950s the lifeguards shared the beach block in Crimdon with tents, deck chairs, windbreaks, a tearoom and the St. John's Ambulance Brigade; an extension to house the RNLI Lifeboat was built later.

Since the mine closed in 1981, over £10 million has been spent removing the colliery conveyor and its concrete tower and cleaning tons of coal waste from the beach. The 11 mile Durham Coastal Footpath, runs through Blackhall. The Turning the Tide project – which has cleaned up the coastline – was in 2001 the joint winner (with the Eden Project) of the prize for Outstanding Achievement in Regeneration, in the annual Royal Institute of Chartered Surveyors awards. The *Guardian* takes up the story:

> To encourage people to come and see this rejuvenated landscape, the coastal path was created. The route runs between Crimdon up the coast to Seaham. From the end of the First World War to the beginning of the 1970s, Crimdon was popular with holiday-makers and day-trippers. Leaving the dunes behind, the route reaches brooding Blackhall rocks, a series of magnesian limestone cliffs and caves. The area is rich with tales of smuggling and Deadman's Bank was supposedly the place where the dead were pulled from wrecked ships.

BLACK BOY COLLIERY
See Coundon.

BLACKWELL
Blackwell is in the south of Darlington and derives from the Old English *blaec wella*, black or dark coloured stream. We have Blakewell in 964 and Blachewelle in 1086.

BLAYDON
Blackden in 1333, Blakedene in 1345 and Bladal in the early 16th century. The derivation is a Saxon personal name plus Old English *denu* – so the valley of a man called Blac. Alternatively, Bladon in 1340 could mean Bleak Hill. Farming was the main occupation of most people here until the late 18th century when the construction of a smelting works changed everything with something of a population explosion.

The Blaydon Burn Belts Corn Mill, one of five or six water corn mills stretching from Brockwell Wood to the River Tyne was thriving by the early 17th century, although some mining and quarrying had begun in the medieval and post-medieval periods.

Coal, was the stimulus for industrial expansion when the Hazard and Speculation pits were established at Low Shibdon linked to the Tyne. The 18th century Blaydon Main Colliery was reopened in the mid-19th century and worked until 1921. Other pits included Blaydon Burn Colliery, Freehold Pit and the Blaydonburn Wagonway. Industries supported by the coal trade included chemical works, bottle works, sanitary pipe works, lampblack works, an ironworks, a smithy and brickworks. Cowen's Upper and Lower Brickworks were established in 1730 with a clay drift mine and coal-clay drops. The 19th century Blaydon Burn Coke Ovens were replaced in the 1930s by Priestman Ottovale Coke and Tar Works which was the first in the world to produce petrol, from coal, known as Blaydon Benzole.

Apart from this intensive industry Blaydon is famous for the pioneering Blaydon School Press; in the 1930s, pupils at Blaydon Intermediate School, under the guidance of English teacher Mr Elliott and art teacher Mr Boyce, developed a way of economically producing good quality hardback books. Their productions were highly regarded and favourably compared to other successful private printing presses of the time. In one volume produced in 1935, entitled *Songs of Enchantment*, Walter de la Mare was invited to write a foreword in which he praised their ingenuity and efforts.

The post-war surge in demand for electricity had an impact on Blaydon when the South Stella Power Station opened. Stella South was built on the site of the Blaydon Races. Their name derived from the nearby Stella Hall, a manor house. In the 12th century a Bishop of Durham, William of St. Barbara, granted Stellinglei to the nuns of Newcastle, and it remained a nunnery until the Dissolution of the Monasteries. The present house was built by the Tempest family, Newcastle merchants. They occupied Stella Hall for 150 years and then in 1700 it passed into the ownership by marriage of Lord Widdrington, a noted Jacobite.

The battle of Stella Ford (also known as the Battle of Newburn or Newburn Ford), is a little known but important battle which was fought on 28th August 1640; 20,000 Scots defeated 5,500 English soldiers who were defending the ford over the Tyne four miles west of Newcastle. The Scots had been provoked by Charles I, who had imposed bishops and a foreign prayer book on their church. The Scots army, led by Alexander Leslie, fought its way to Newcastle and occupied the city for almost a year before Charles I paid £200,000 for the Scots to go away. The battle brought to an end the so-called 'Eleven Years of Tyranny' by forcing Charles to recall Parliament. This was the last battle in Britain to feature the use of archers.

BOGGLE HOLE
Near Brancepeth – means haunted hollow. Elsewhere Boggle Hole is a pretty inlet south of Robin Hood's Bay. A boggle is a local name for a hobgoblin, the 'little people' who lived in caves along this coast and in the more remote corners of the North York Moors. More prosaically Boggle Hole itself was where smugglers used to land their prodigious contraband.

BOLAM
Bolam is between Bishop Auckland and Darlington. A 1317 reference gives it as Bolom – the place of the tree trunks. This comes either from Old English *bola* or Old Scandinavian *bolr* – either way the meaning is the same.

THE BOLDONS
The Boldons are three small villages – East Boldon, West Boldon and Boldon Colliery – north of Sunderland, east of Newcastle and south of South Shields and Jarrow. The villages get their first mention in 1170. Their names evolved from the words "Bold" or "Botl", meaning a building, and "dun", meaning a hill.

The pit here began producing coal in 1869, and was then known as Boldon New Winning. The village that developed nearby in the 1870s became known as Boldon Colliery. The mine was deepened and extended in the 1910s, necessitating further housing to accommodate the workforce; and built to the south of the pit in an area known as Boldon New Town.

BOLDRON
In 1180 this is Bolrum, Old Scandinavian *boli rum* and so the clearing used by bulls.

BOLLIHOPE
Bothelinghoppe in 1294. Near Stanhope, meaning a valley with a bothy or sheiling.

BOURNMOOR or BURNMOOR
Bournmoor is near to Chester-le-Street. St. Barnabas' Church is there, which houses the Frostley Angel. Originally part of the Lambton Castle estate, the village developed from 1783 onwards when the first of seven local coal mines that were to make up Lambton Colliery were sunk.

Bournmoor Colliery (or Lambton Colliery) was a collective title for the pits named A to E, for the William Henry Pit and the Lady Ann Pit. The Lambton Pithead Baths (not to be confused with Lambton Baths) were opened in March 1940 and demolished in April 2018. A contemporary news report of this event tells of:

> Accommodation for 1,300 miners at Lambton. Provided by the Miners' Welfare Fund, at a cost of about £24,000.
> Pit head baths to accommodate nearly 1,300 miners were opened this afternoon at Lambton Colliery by Mr Austin Kirkup, Managing Director of Lambton, Hetton and Joicey Collieries Ltd...Designed by Mr F.G. Frizzell of London, architect to the Miners' Welfare Committee, the building has 1,296 clean clothes lockers and 1,296 pit clothes lockers, with sufficient accommodation to enable all the men on the largest shift to take their baths without delay. Among the adjuncts are boot-cleaning room, boot-greasing room and bottle-filling room, while in the clean entrance lobby there are drinking fountains and access to a canteen. Adjacent to the clean locker room there is a first aid room in which scratches, sores and other minor injuries can be dealt with promptly.

For most of the 20th century, "Bournmoor" was known as "Burnmoor", taking its name from the Moorsburn, an alternative name for Hutton Burn which runs through the village. A mid-19th century Ordnance Survey map shows the old village centre as "Wapping", with the open country to the south of the Sunderland road and north west of Herrington Burn shown as "Bourn Moor" and the colliery complex later known as Lambton shown as Bourn Moor Colliery. The corresponding end-19th century map shows the settlement as "Bournmoor". Maps produced after the development of the 'Flowers' estate, dated between 1920 and 1960 show both as "Burnmoor", reverted to "Bournmoor" in later maps.

BOWBURN

Bowburn derives from Bowburn beck which loops tightly here – so 'winding stream'. Bowburn village is about 3 miles to the south east of Durham. Like many of its neighbours its history is tied inextricably into coal mining although life started here as a small farming hamlet, named after that bow shape of the small burn that runs through it.

The first "Bowburn Colliery" was a shaft sunk in 1840 but failed to find workable coal; the second was sunk a few years later, near Park Hill, one of several sunk in the Quarrington and Coxhoe areas close to the terminus of the Durham branch of the Clarence Railway. The pit was a small concern, worked first by Robson and Jackson and then the West Hetton Coal Company closing in about 1870. The third and most productive, the Bowburn Colliery Tub, was sunk in 1906 by Bell Bros. Ltd, using the 1840 shaft as the ventilation upcast shaft (and, later, for manriding). Gertrude Bell, daughter of the chairman of Bell Brothers, cut the first turf on 23rd July 1906 to begin the sinking of the downcast shaft. Its first coal was drawn in 1908. It merged with Tursdale Colliery in 1931 and grew to be one of the largest in the Durham coalfield, working six seams and with over 2,500 employees in the 1950s. Nothing much now remains of the colliery complex which closed in July 1967.

Mines apart, Bowburn is famous for its eccentric parish church, Christ the King, built between 1963 and 1978. This had a detached spire described locally as 'The Rocket' standing alongside the main church building, which featured a spiked dome roof and was nicknamed 'The Pineapple Church'. The church soon became dilapidated and was made redundant and demolished in June 2007; the spire fell over in gales in 2009. A new church building was completed in autumn 2008.

BOWES

The place name 'Bowes' is first attested in a charter of 1148, in which it appears as Bogas – the plural of the Old English *boga* meaning 'bow', probably signifying an arched bridge locally or where the river bends.

Bowes, next to Barnard Castle, is built around the medieval Bowes Castle. Roman Bowes was Lavatrae ("summit") with its wooden ramparts fort built in the early 70s CE by the then governor

Petilius Cerealis; this in turn was re-used as the site for Bowes Castle. Lavatrae was strategically important to the Romans: being as it was on the northern leg of the Roman equivalent of Watling Street in the section connecting Luguvalium (Carlisle) to Eboracum (York) and all points south. It controlled the eastern entrance to the Stainmore Pass through the Pennines, overlooking the River Greta. There is a stone altar from the bathhouse, erected by the 1st Cohort of the Thracians, in Cambridge Museum of Archaeology.

Bowes Castle was built by Alan, Earl of Richmond (Alan de Bretagne, the Count of Brittany or Alan the Black) around 1087; this timber structure was replaced by a more substantial stone castle between 1170 and 1174 on the orders of Henry II. A mill was built by the River Greta to supply flour for the garrison. The village of Bowes post-dates the castle forming a planned site running up to the castle; it comprised a church and a market place; all very unusual in England.

It was besieged in 1173 by King William of Scotland during the Great Revolt of 1173 to 1174 and so badly damaged as to need rebuilding in 1187. Around 1216 enemies of King John again besieged the castle, and again in 1322 in a regional feud between Henry Fitzhugh and the then Earl of Richmond. James I sold the castle in the early 17th century and the remaining fortifications were dismantled after the English Civil War.

The only pub in the village is The Ancient Unicorn, a 17th century coaching inn, where Charles Dickens would stay when in the area. His Dotheby's Hall is based on the Bowes Boys Academy and immortalised in *Nicholas Nickleby*. The building can still be seen in Bowes as can the graves of two of the people who inspired characters portrayed by Dickens. William Shaw (1782–1850) was the headmaster of Bowes Academy, and was the model for Wackford Squeers in *Nicholas Nickleby* – they share the same initials. George Ashton Taylor, who died in 1822 aged 19, was the inspiration for Smike in the same novel.

Bowes Museum

The Josephine and John Bowes Museum was under construction in 1869 to a design by architect Jules Pellechet and intended as a house and a place to house the Bowes' numerous antiquities. After the deaths of Josephine (French actress and Countess of Montalbo) in 1874 and John in 1885, the property was left to the public as a museum and park and opened in 1892. There is also an unfinished Roman Catholic chapel. Montalbo is a town in Spain not far from Toledo. Designed to evoke French chateaux (the Bowes also had a chateau at Louveciennes, in the western suburbs of Paris, between Versailles and Saint-Germain-en-Laye) the museum cost over £100,000, is 300 feet long and 85 feet high, and the central dome rises to 150 feet. The late Queen Mother, Elizabeth Bowes-Lyon, was related to John Bowes. Every country in Europe in the late 19th century is represented in his extensive collection. The museum boasts an El Greco, paintings by Goya, Canaletto, Boucher, Fragonard and a collection of decorative art. A great attraction is the 18th century silver swan automaton, which periodically preens itself, looks round and appears to catch and swallow a fish.

BOWLEES
Near Wolsingham. Could mean pasture with a house – Old English *bu* + *leah/leas* or a clearing where wood for bows is cut if we take Old English *boga* + *leas*.

BRADBURY
Near Sedgefield and part of the civil parish of Bradbury and the Isle, along with the hamlets of Great Isle and Little Isle. In 1040 it was Brydbyrig, Bredberi in 1200 and Bradberia in 1220. The first element may be from the Old English for plank *briden* or just *brad* meaning broad. Planks or boards would have been necessary due to the marshy land around the village.

BRAFFERTON
In 1091 this was referred to by the pleasant sounding Bradfortuna – Old English *brad ford tun*, meaning homestead by the broad ford. It is situated between Darlington and Newton Aycliffe. The famous Durham Ox was bred at Ketton Hall in Brafferton. Ketton means the farmstead of Ceatta.

BRANCEPETH
This village is 5 miles from Durham. Its name reputedly derives from "Brawn's Path" from the legend that Brancepeth was once terrorized by a monstrous boar or brawn, which was eventually killed by a knight named Sir Roger de Ferie in 1208. A commemorative stone marks the traditional location of the brawn's death. A more plausible derivation is from the 1170 Brantespethe – "Brandr's Path", after St. Brandon, the Irish patron saint of the parish church and who legend would have it discovered America years before Columbus.

It all started in Saxon days with a big house and a church – the first Rector was a monk called Haeming in 1085. The Bulmer family owned the village until the sole heir, Emma, married the nephew of William the Conqueror and then married Geoffrey Neville Lord of Raby in 1174. The Nevilles built Brancepeth Castle in the 14th century, but in 1569 the family had the misfortune to be on the pro-Catholic side of the Rising of the North, so Elizabeth I seized Brancepeth. Most of the present castle was built by the first Earl of Westmorland who fought at Agincourt and was grandfather of Warwick the king maker. The castle was extensively rebuilt in the 19th century by Viscount Boyne (later Baron Brancepeth); Tennyson was a relative of the family and wrote part of his epic poem *Maude* in the gardens here. The Great Hall boasted a suit of armour inlaid with gold, taken from King David of Scotland at the Battle of Neville's Cross; and an artwork by Hogarth.

During the First World War, like many such establishments, the castle saw service as a military hospital. In 1914, the castle's owner, Gustavus William Hamilton Russell, the 9th Viscount Boyne and Baron Brancepeth, offered it to the Red Cross while he and his family moved out to Hardwick Hall, Sedgefield, another family seat. The family, though, stayed involved with the running of the 104 bed hospital – Viscountess Margaret Selina received a CBE in 1920 for her contribution, and one of Lord Boyne's sisters was a masseuse adept in the fashionable electrical treatments. More than 4,000 patients, from the UK and the empire, passed through the castle over the course of the war with an average stay of about three weeks.

Perhaps the most famous patient was war poet Ivor Gurney, a casualty here towards the end of the war. Gurney had joined up in the forlorn hope that army life would help him cope with his mental issues. But he took a shoulder wound in 1917 and although he recovered well enough to return to battle he was later mildly gassed in September 1917 and sent to a V.A.D. hospital in Edinburgh after which he ended up in Brancepeth following a nervous breakdown as a result of deferred shell shock.

Brancepeth was not a casualty centre but one of County Durham's 28 Voluntary Aid Detachment (V.A.D.) hospitals where survivors were sent to recuperate after receiving acute treatment at a more clinical hospital. Because many of the patients were on the road to recovery, they were able to integrate with the community.

The small village of Brancepeth had something of a population explosion between 1939 and 1962 thanks to the presence of a 100 hut army camp which was the regimental headquarters of the Durham Light Infantry. At the end of the Second World War, the camp hosted hundreds of Polish soldiers who had fought with the Allies and were stationed at Brancepeth. Many eventually returned home to Poland.

BRANDON
South west of Durham it is Bromedune in 1190 from Od English *brom dun* – the place where the broom grows. Byshottles is the village's reputed alternative name deriving from *shodel* and *scaden*, to divide so it means the dividing road. Less ordinary is the derivation from *scytels* which would make it 'the town's midden'.

BRANKSOME
In Darlington. Possibly Old Welsh Branoc's water meadow from Branoc + Middle English *holme*.

BRIERTON
There are two Briertons: one is part of Hartlepool; the other is a village to the south west of the town up a dead end. Variants include Breretone in 1243, Breerton in 1508 and Brearton 1517. Old English *braer tun*, the bramble farmstead.

BRIGNALL
Bringhenale in Domesday so the nook of land of the family of a man called Bryni.

BROWNEY
Named after the River Browney which is Aqua de Brun in 1125 and Brune Flumen in 1170; both add up to brown waters, *ea* being Old English water. Browney Colliery closed in 1938. Browney British School was built in 1881 by the colliery owners, and had schooling for 407. The Browney Colliery Reading Room and Library was also provided by the owners of the colliery. The library offered over 1000 books, and the reading room had all the usual newspapers. This emphasis on education coincided with the focus on the benefits of literacy when the Worker's Educational Movement was in its infancy. The Mechanics' Insitutes were another fine example of provision of education for the working class.

BURNHOPE
Brunhop in 1317 and Burnhop in 1382 describes the *hop* – small valley – with a *burna*, or stream. Burnhope is a village in the Craghead Valley opposite Stanley; it overlooks Lanchester in the Browney Valley. Burnhope has the honour of being the only place that the Durham Miners' Gala has been held apart from Durham. In 1926 during the General Strike it was banned at Durham and so moved to Burnhope. There was another Burnhope village, to the west in upper Weardale. The village was inundated in the 1930s when Burnhope Reservoir was filled.

BURNOPFIELD
Burnopfield is a village situated north of Stanley. The name Burnopfield is Old English – *burna hop feld* – and means quite simply the "field by the valley stream". There is a legend, however, which insists that the village got its name after an attempted Scottish invasion of England was foiled by locals literally burning up the fields to stop the advancing armies in what amounts to a firestorm. In the 19th century, Burnopfield was usually referred to as the Leap, or in local dialect, as the Loup, after the area of Burnopfield named Bryan's Leap.

Burnopfield had a leper hospital, High Friarside Hospice, founded in 1312, and demolished around 1450. The remains of the original chapel can still be seen today along with Burnopfield Hall, which was built in 1720 by the coal-rich Newton family, Leap Mill Farm is a classic example of an 18th century mill with a working water wheel. The Gibside estate is between Burnopfield and Rowlands Gill.

The Blakiston family acquired the estate by marriage in about 1540. Sir William Blakiston (1562–1641) replaced the old house with a spacious mansion between 1603 and 1620. The estate included some of the area's richest coal seams. in 1693 Sir William's great-granddaughter, Elizabeth Blakiston, was married off to Sir William Bowes (1657–1707) of Streatlam Castle so Gibside was owned by the Bowes-Lyon family from 1713. While Gibside Hall is but a shell, the property is still most famous for its chapel. The stables, walled garden, Column to Liberty and Banqueting House are also intact. Turner produced several landscapes of Gibside Hall, which hang in Tate Britain. Streatlam Castle was a Baroque pile near Barnard Castle that was demolished in 1959 and owned by the Bowes-Lyon family, Earls of Strathmore and Kinghorne.

Work on the "Column to Liberty", started in the 1750s by the obscenely wealthy Sir George Bowes. Set atop a steep hillock, the monument sports Doric columns and is higher than Nelson's Column, with a standing bronze female figure, originally gilded, carrying a liberty pole, or cap of liberty on a pole on the top.

In 1767 the granddaughter of Sir William Bowes – the "Bowes heiress" Mary Eleanor Bowes – married John Lyon, 9th Earl of Strathmore and Kinghorne and founder of the Bowes Museum, who changed his surname to Bowes due to a provision in her father's will that any suitor had to take the family name. This was a device to continue the Bowes lineage in the absence of a male heir. The estate remained in the Bowes and Bowes-Lyon family until the 20th century.

For the aristocratic families of Burnopfield and Gibside there is no escaping that scoundrel and charlatan Andrew Robinson Stoney. In the late 1760s, Hannah Newton, daughter and heiress to the Newton family fortune, married Stoney, an Irish lieutenant and adventurer stationed in Newcastle. They went to live together at Colepike Hall in Lanchester, where his abuse of her became a local scandal; so bad was it that within a few years she was dead. Pocketing her £20,000 fortune, he set off for London, where he met the widowed Countess of Strathmore, who owned the Gibside estate. Stoney inveigled her into marriage, and obliged to adopt her family name of Bowes, became the infamous Stoney Bowes. Her subsequent wretched life with him became one of the biggest scandals of the times . His story was fictionalised and immortalised by William Makepeace Thackeray in *The Luck of Barry Lyndon*, later adapted by Stanley Kubrick into the 1975 film *Barry Lyndon*.

Cricket has always been all the rage in Burnopfield – played at two small cricket grounds. One is in **Lintz**, near Burnopfield, since 1905, and the other in Burnopfield proper. Both grounds were built on land given to the clubs by the National Coal Board. The Burnopfield Club produced two Test cricketers for England: Jim McConnon, who played for Glamorgan, and Colin Milburn, the "Burnopfield Basher", who played for Northamptonshire. When Milburn died in 1990, his funeral was the largest ever seen in Burnopfield.

BUTTERKNOWLE
West of Bishop Auckland with the name meaning the small hill near the dairy farm – Old English *buttere knoll*; Boterknoll in 1313.

BUTTERWICK
Butterwick is a small village just to the south east of Fishburn. Butterwick records begin in 1131, when it is called "Boterwyck" meaning the butter or dairy farm. The West, South and East Butterwick Farms of today are testament to what was a small medieval village, the earthwork remains of which still survive in and around the modern farm buildings.

BYERS GREEN
Records here begin rather late: Byers Green, north of Bishop Auckland, was first recorded in 1345 as Bires – the equivalent of the modern word 'byres' or cowsheds. The village name, therefore, means 'the green by the cowsheds'.

Byers Green remained a farming area throughout the medieval period and into the 16th and 17th century in which most people would have worked on the land. However, apart from the Trotters of Byers Green Hall, Byers Green is notable for at least two of its sons.

Thomas Wright, (1711–86), the famous 18th century astronomer, architect and mathematician was born and died here. Wright, son of a carpenter, was at first home-educated as he suffered from a speech impediment and then at King James I Academy in Bishop Auckland before being apprenticed to a clockmaker in the town, Bryan Stobart. He also took part-time courses on mathematics and navigation at a free school in Gateshead founded by Dr. Theophilus Pickering. Then he went to London to study mathematical instrument-making with Heath and Sisson and made a trial sea voyage to Amsterdam. In 1730, he set up a school in Sunderland, where he taught mathematics and navigation then moved back to London to work on a number of projects.

That was before retiring to County Durham and building a small observatory at Westerton. By 1734 he had begun making a huge working model of the universe, an orrery which included Saturn for the first time, for a wealthy London patron This project set him on the path of a stellar career which included the first accurate description of the Milky Way and to postulate that faint nebulae were distant galaxies – published in his *An original theory or new hypothesis of the Universe* (1750).

An orrery is a mechanical model of the Solar System that illustrates or predicts the relative positions and motions of the planets and moons. The first modern orrery was made in 1704, and one was presented to Charles Boyle, 4th Earl of Orrery – hence the name. Usually, they are driven by clockwork with a globe representing the Sun at the centre, and with a planet at the end of each of the arms.

When not gazing at the stars Wright made a name for himself as a significant designer of gardens for the aristocracy, doing work for William Capel, 3rd Earl of Essex at Cassiobury Park in Watford and in the 1750s he laid out the grounds of Netheravon House, Wiltshire. In 1769 he also designed the folly known as Codger Fort at Rothley, Northumberland, on the Wallington Hall estate.

Sir Percy Cradock, GCMG, (1923–2010) was educated at Alderman Wraith Grammar School, Spennymoor and St. John's College, Cambridge where he read law. Cradock joined the Diplomatic Service and, among other posts, was Ambassador to China. He was dubbed by the media as the 'UK's most senior spy' when he chaired the Joint Intelligence Committee (UK) in Thatcher's government.

CARLBURY

'The peasants' fortified place' from Old English *ceorl* or Old Norse *karl*.

There is not much left of Carlbury today; it is a hamlet a few miles to the west of Darlington, on the north bank of the River Tees between Piercebridge to the west, and High Coniscliffe to the east. High and Low Carlbury once was a larger settlement, but most of the hamlet at Low Carlbury became derelict and was demolished by the late 1940s. Its eventful history started in 1320 when Carlbury was given by the widow of Sir John FitzMarmaduke, Sheriff of North Durham, to Sir Thomas Earl of Lancaster and Leicester. After Sir Thomas was executed for treason in 1322, Carlbury reverted to the widow's family and then to the House of Neville. According to a 1553 document High and Low Carlbury were included with Summerhouse and Ulnaby in the estate of the Nevilles in their capacity as Earls of Westmorland from 1354 to 1601. However Charles Neville had to surrender it in 1571 for his part in the Rising of the North. Elizabeth I granted it to Ralph Taylboys or Tailboys of Thornton Hall in 1573; it was then left to Thomas Jenison in 1580 and to William Jenison in 1588. Carlbury still belonged to the Jenisons in 1616.

By the 19th century it was a hamlet served by Piercebridge Station on the NER Darlington and Barnard Castle railway (1858–1964). The hamlet comprised the Railway Inn, and Carlbury's own bridge over Dyance Beck, which in turn powered Carlbury Mill. The mill burned down one night in 1889.

CARLTON

One of the most common place names in the north of England. Other forms are Careleton and Carleton up to the 13th century. It means farmstead of the peasant, from Old English *ceorl tun*.

Carlton is near to Stockton; its history is unmistakably medieval and remained so until the early 20th century. 1200 CE saw Bishop Pudsey of Durham commission a survey to be made of all his possessions, including Carlton, in which there were 23 farmers, a miller, and that William, son of Orm of Carlton, was required to come to the great chase of the Lord Bishop with one greyhound whenever required. By the end of the 14th century there were 124 residents who shared a common bakehouse, the lease being two shillings paid to the Bishop.

The only water supply was from the village pump in the centre of the village; piped water was installed in about 1895, although the village pump was still in regular use for many years after. Transport and travel was by foot or horsepower until the railway opened to the east of the village and Carlton Station was built in about 1850. This acted as a magnet, attracting goods trains, chemical works, a coal depot and passenger trains. Farmers used the railway to send their milk to the dairies in the town, cows were milked, milk cooled and measured into churns and transported by horsepower to catch a train due before 7.00 am so that it could be delivered at its destination fresh for breakfast.

Travelling men with their stallions visited the village to service the mares owned by local farmers; the men would stay overnight at a farm in the village before going on to the next client. Up until the advent of the 'combine', a steam thrashing machine travelled the area, spending a day at each farm thrashing the corn. Thrashing day was a big event on the farms; about 20 local men and women worked on the thrasher starting about 6.00 am until dusk. Fruit and fishmen and butchers came weekly by horse and cart.

The Smiths Arms (now the Smiths) was built in about 1900 by Irish labourers lodged in the village to replace an ancient inn nearby. The South Durham Hunt met here twice in the season for the Stirrup

Cup. Christmas Eve 1935 was a big day for Carlton. The electricity was switched on for the first time and candles and oil lamps were thrown away. Street lighting was installed in 1963.

George Orwell lived at Greystone, the home of his wife Eileen's sister-in-law about half a mile outside the village, from 1944–45. He moved there with Eileen and newly adopted son, Richard when bombed out of their London flat. It was here that Orwell finished *Animal Farm* before leaving for France as a war correspondent in 1945.

CASSOP

1183 sees it as Cazehope; the name derives from Old English *catt hop* and means the valley frequented by wild cats.

It is a former mining village five miles from Durham city. Cassop Primary School is the first school in the UK to generate some of its own electricity with its own wind turbine erected in February 1999 as a joint partnership between Durham County Council and Northern Electric. The church of St. Paul, Cassop cum Quarrington was built in 1868 using stones transported by William Smith, innkeeper of the Half Moon Inn, Quarrington Hill, as he was the only man in the village who owned a cart. It was closed in the 1980s and is now demolished.

The short-lived Cassop Colliery opened in 1840 and closed in 1868, shipping its coal through Hartlepool. Even in that brief time at least 23 mine workers lost their lives; here is a random selection from http://www.dmm.org.uk/colliery/c021.htm

> Bainbridge, Henry, 13 Jan 1854, aged 12, Pony Putter, he got on the limmers to ride outbye. As he was going along, his head was jammed between the tub and the roof. He died soon after being released.
> Barrass, William, 25 Aug 1848, aged 7, [Not Employed], he was crossing the railway with his grandfather's breakfast when he was knocked down and run over by a waggon full of props which was going between the raff-yard and the mouth of the shaft; he died shortly after being taken home.
> Cuthbertson, Andrew, 25 Dec 1855 [Christmas night], aged 70, he was taking down stones at work in the waste for the purpose of forming an air course, when a piece fell from the roof and struck him on the back of the head, he died the same night.
> Lamb, William, 14 Dec 1853, he was travelling behind a set of tubs when he was knocked down and suffocated by a mass of coal falling from the roof, the tubs had apparently knocked out a prop.
> Price, John, 30 Jul 1862, aged 2, [Not Employed], killed by a rope sheave on surface railway.
> Stabler, Eleanor, 21st May 1853, (accident: 20th May 1853), aged 2, [Not employed], knocked down and crushed by coal waggons on the colliery railway.

This demonstrates just how dangerous pits were to the public at large; you didn't have to be a miner to die at a mine.

CASTLE EDEN

Castle Eden lies south of Peterlee and takes its name from the Eden Burn (Old English *burna*) that runs through it. Eden is a Brittonic river name that derives from *ituna* 'to gush forth'. The name is first attested around 1050 as Geodene and Iodene. Apart from the glorious dene here Castle Eden is famous for its brewery, former provider of Castle Eden Ale now produced at Camerons Brewery in nearby Hartlepool.

Both the *Domesday Book* and the *King's Book* record Castle Eden as a small village, but make no mention of any castle. There is no trace of the medieval castle of Robert the Bruce.

In 1764 the estate of Castle Eden was purchased by Rowland Burdon III from William Turner; the following year Burdon, a merchant banker, with the assistance of architect William Newton, built the three storey house which came to be known as The Castle, complete with its castellated parapet.

The beer started flowing here in 1826, when John Nimmo (*c*.1801-67) began to brew at the Castle Eden Inn in Castle Eden, which had its own brewhouse. By 1910 Castle Eden could claim to be one of the most up-to-date breweries in the country and output doubled between 1906 and 1914. In 1912 the company acquired Thomas Chilton of Seaham, including twelve pubs. Between 1912 and 1920, production reached a record output of more than 42,000 barrels. Nearly a third of the output was in bottles by 1942, and an automatic bottling plant was installed in 1950. When William John Nimmo died in 1952 without any sons his daughter, Eileen Denton Trechman (1905–2004), became chair of the company, and at the time was the only female to hold such a position in the UK. Whitbread acquired J Nimmo & Son in 1963, along with its 125 public houses. Castle Eden Brewery, then owned by David Soley, took over Camerons in April 2002 for £35 million, moving all operations to Hartlepool and closing down the Castle Eden plant.

Apart from the brewery Castle Eden could boast a rope works and a bleachery for sail cloth manufacturing all owned by the Saville family.

CASTLESIDE
No castle here and there never has been. South west of Consett. The name refers to a defensive feature at the crossroads here, on the Darlington to Edinburgh A68 with roads also to Stanhope and Consett. The pub is the Smelters Arms, indicative of the old smelting industry in these parts.

CAUSEY
1328 Caldesete – cold fold.

Just north of Stanley, Causey is famous for its Arch, built to traverse one of those ice age denes which are so characteristic of the east Durham landscape and coast. The arch was intended to supercede a bridge of wood from 1725 which had collapsed. A new bridge was built in 1726 which took more than a year to erect; its purpose was to carry coal down to the Tyne at Dunston. The rails were made of wood, and the coal trucks were pulled by horses. The bridge had a span of over 100 ft and is 80ft above the stream about 23 ft wide. The Causey Arch is the oldest single span railway bridge in the world. Children who attended Causey School in the 20s and 30s were let out of school early in the dark nights as the bridge was unfenced.

CHESTER-LE-STREET
The history here goes back to the auxiliary Roman fort called Concangis. This is the "Chester" (from the Latin *castra*) of the town's name; the "Street" refers to the paved Roman road, Cade's Road that ran north–south through the town, today's Front Street. There is Cestra in 1160 and Cestria in Strata in 1400.

The fort covered roughly 6½ acres and was built first in turf and timber, probably in the 70s CE by the Legio VIIII *Hispana*. It was later reconstructed in stone by the Legio II *Augusta*, probably during the early 2nd century at the same time as the construction of Hadrian's Wall. Finds include the usual pottery, fine table ware, coins, animal bones, but also a cheese press and, most exciting of all, a tile with a dog's footprint on it. Altars found range from Mars and Apollo, to Celtic and German deities such as Digenis and Vitiris.

Concangis or Concagium, is a Latin form of the Celtic name for the area, which also gave name to the river which runs through the town, Cong Burn. This may mean "Place of the horse people". Old English forms of the name include Cuneceastra and Conceastre, which takes its first two syllables from the Roman name, with the addition of the Old English word *ceaster* 'Roman fortification'. This was shortened over time to Chester. *An Universal Etymological English Dictionary* of 1749 gives the town as "Chester upon Street"; at some point this was shortened to the modern form.

Chester-le-Street is seven miles south of Newcastle upon Tyne and eight miles west of Sunderland on the River Wear. Long after the Romans had left, in 883 a group of monks, driven out of Lindisfarne seven years earlier, stopped here to build a wooden shrine and church to St. Cuthbert, whose body they had carried with them. The parish church of St. Mary and St. Cuthbert is where the body of St. Cuthbert remained for 112 years before being transferred with the monks in 995 to Durham Cathedral. It is also where the first translation into English of the Gospels was made when Aldred wrote the Old English gloss between the lines of the Lindisfarne Gospels there. Aldred the Glossator was a 10th century priest who was a provost of the monastic community of St. Cuthbert at Chester-le-Street in 970 CE.

In 1080 most of the huts in the town were burned to the ground and many inhabitants slaughtered in reprisal for the death of William Walcher, the first prince-bishop, at the hands of an English mob.

Another black day for the town came with a miners' strike during the winter of 1811-12. Collieries owned by the Dean and Chapter of Durham Cathedral were brought to a standstill by the strike, causing much hardship amongst the people of the town. The strike was broken on New Year's Day, 1st January 1812, when the Bishop of Durham, Shute Barrington, sent a detachment of troops from Durham Castle to force a return to work.

The evening of 5th October 1936 saw the Jarrow Marchers stop at the town centre after their first day's walk. They were accommodated in the church hall before they continued the next day.

St. Mary and St. Cuthbert Church is famous for its superb anchorage; these were built for anchorites, a hermit and comprised a walled-up cell which had a mere slit through which to observe the altar, and an opening for food; outside there was, ominously, an open grave made ready for when the occupant died. The anchorage, and presumably the grave, were occupied by six anchorites from 1383 to c.1538, and is now a museum known as the Anker's House.

Chester Burn Viaduct was completed in 1868 for the North Eastern Railway. It is over 230m long with eleven splendid arches. Chester-le-Street's Art Deco post office in Front Street opened in 1936 and is unusual because it is one of the few post offices that display the Royal cypher from the brief reign of Edward VIII. The Riverside Ground is home to Durham County Cricket Club, a first class county team since 1992.

Medieval football was popular in the town and was played annually on Shrove Tuesday between the "Upstreeters" and "Downstreeters". Play started at 1 pm and finished at 6 pm. To start the game, the ball was thrown from a window in the centre of the town – in one game more than 400 players took part. The centre of the street was the dividing line and the winner was the side where the ball was (Up or Down) at 6 pm. It was played from the Middle Ages until 1932, when it was outlawed by the police; anyone trying to carry on the tradition was arrested.

Notable former residents include Bryan Robson, former England football captain; Colin Todd, football manager and former England international player, and Bruce Welch of The Shadows.

Local pubs include the Church Mouse, and the Cookson in Cookson Terrace, named after Catherine Cookson (closed), the Falcon and the diplomatic Rose and Shamrock. There is the Olde Miner's Lamp which is not as 'olde' as we are supposed to believe, and the Warriors Arms, Butchers Arms and Smiths Arms.

CHILTON

Chilton is to the east of Bishop Auckland and was once a mining town called Chilton Buildings. In 1092 Chilton was recorded as "Ciltona". Chilton is derived from the Anglo-Saxon words *cild* (Child) and *tun* (small town, or estate), with 'child being either a young monk or young nobleman. Hence Chilton was "an estate belonging to a young nobleman". Agriculture and farming were the major sources of employment until the mid-1800s, when people living in the village either had to work in the collieries or at the steel works at Spennymoor. St. Aiden's Church was an iron structure built in 1877; it was burned to the ground in 1928 and rebuilt in stone in 1930.

CLAXTON

As in Claxton Bank south of Greatham, near Hartlepool. Clacestona in the 12th century; Claxtun in 1153 – means Clack's estate – Old Danish personal name.

CLEADON

There has been a Cleadon for over a thousand years. It was Clyuedon in 1183, Cledone in 1242, Clifdon in 1312, Cleadon in 1339, Clewdon in 1536 – the hill of the steep slopes.

Cleadon has a traditional village pond which is the remnants of an ice age lake; an early history of South Shields suggests that there may have once been a Roman watchtower on Cleadon Hills. The name of the village is derived from 'Cliffa-dun' meaning a hill with a cliff, which over years became Clevendona, Clyvedon (1280), Clevedon, and in the 17th century Cleydon. The village was first mentioned in the *Boldon Book* of 1183.

The oldest houses in the village date to the 15th century; one contains a priest hole. Charles Dickens stayed in Cleadon House on Front Street. A story he was told by resident George Cooper Abbs inspired the character Miss Havisham in *Great Expectations*.

Cleadon Windmill was built in the 1820s on the Cleadon Hills. It was severely damaged in a storm during the 1870s, and then suffered the humiliation of being a target for gunnery practice during the First World War. Also up there is a former water pumping station, which once provided water to the South Shields area. The site is dominated by the Cleadon Water Tower, which is in fact a chimney for the former steam-powered pumps, visible as far south as the Headland in Hartlepool.

Also on the hills is a small painted hill figure in the form of a white horse, six feet tall and nine feet long.

CLEATLAM

Cletlinga in 1050 and Cletlum in 1270, Cleatlam 1616 and Cleatlamb in 1717. From Old English *claete leah* – the woodland clearing where burdock grows.

COATHAM MUNDEVILLE

Just north of Darlington the village was first recorded in the 12th century as Cotum and then in Cotum Maundevill in 1344. The first part of the name is a plural of the Old English word *cot*, which means 'at the cottage'. The Mundeville part is the name of the Norman knight, Thomas de Amundaville, who hailed from Emondeville in Normandy and owned the village until 1274. A variant is Cotum super Scyren about 1200 – Cotum on the Skerne.
The Foresters Arms remembers the Ancient Order of Foresters, a friendly society.

COCANGIS

See Chester le Street.

COCKERTON

Part of Darlington, this means settlement on the Cocker; the cocker element is a Cumbric river-name, *cucra*, the crooked one.

COCKFIELD

The name is derived from Old English *cocc feld* – the open land frequented with woodcocks. In 1223 it is Kokefeld. When the south west of the Durham Coalfield was opened in the 19th and 20th centuries the population of the village grew significantly. The last coal mine closed in 1962.

George Dixon (1731–85) owned coal mines here and was a keen inventor – probably the first to use coal gas for illumination. His brother Jeremiah Dixon (1733–79), an astronomer, went to America with Charles Mason in 1763 to survey the boundaries of Maryland and Pennsylvania. Immortalised by Mark Knopfler in his *Sailing to Philadelphia* album; the title track, in turn, comes from *Mason & Dixon* by Thomas Pynchon. The novel narrates the story of how the two English surveyors established the border separating Pennsylvania and Delaware from Maryland and Virginia in the 1760s. This border later became known as the Mason–Dixon line and has been used since the 1820s to denote the border between the Southern United States and the Northern United States.

Cockfield Fell is "one of the most important early industrial landscapes in Britain". As well as four Iron Age (or Romano-British) settlement enclosures, there is evidence within the landscape of early coal mines (the Bishop of Durham licenced mining here at least as early as 1303), medieval agricultural field patterns, centuries of quarrying activity, a railway line established in the 1830s and several earlier tramways. All in all, Cockfield Fell forms England's largest Scheduled Ancient Monument, described as 'an incomparable association of field monuments relating to the Iron Age settlement history and industrial evolution of a northern English County'. One reason for its preservation – unusual for a lowland fell – is that it was not subject to enclosure in the 18th or 19th centuries, perhaps due to its highly industrialised past.

COLD HESLEDON
'The valley growing with hazels' from Old English *haesel* + *denu*. Cold Hesleden was given to the community of St. Cutebert by King Athelstan in 934.

The village, near Murton, comprises a large Victorian, Gothic Revival former water pumping station, designed by Thomas Hawksley for the Sunderland and South Shields Water Company. The engine house contains a pair of 72" single-acting non-rotative Cornish beam engines by Davy Bros of Sheffield, dating from the 1870s when the complex was built. The site was prone to mine subsidence which eventually led to the demolition in the 1960s of the striking campanile-like top section of the central tower-chimney.

COLLIERLEY
Near Chester le Street – Colyrley in 1284, Collyerley in 1339 – means charcoal burning clearing from Old English *colere* or surname Collier + *leah*.

CONSETT
Consett is 900 feet above sea level, the third highest market town in England and one of the highest towns in the United Kingdom. South west of Newcastle, high up in the Pennines on the River Derwent in a region historically known as Allensford the 145 strong farming community of Consett knew nothing of what the village was sitting on in 1845: coking coal, blackband iron ore, and (nearby) limestone. These were the three ingredients blast furnaces were greedy for to produce iron and steel. Before that there was lead mining in the area and steel industry in the Derwent Valley, developed by immigrant German cutlers and sword-makers from Solingen (the Sheffield of Germany), who settled in the village of Shotley Bridge during the 17th century.

In 1183 Consett was Covekesheued and Conekesheued in 1228 – both a combination of the Celtic *cunaco* and Old English *heaford*, giving us the headland of a hill known as Conek. Also Konkeshed in 1385, Conset 1415 and Conside 1580.

The Consett Iron Company was established in 1864 as a successor to the original Derwent Iron Company of 1840, when the first blast furnaces came on stream. Over the next 100 years, Consett became one of the world's leading steel-making towns, making the steel for Blackpool Tower and some of the UK's nuclear submarines.

Steel dominated Consett for 140 years; clouds of red dust hung over the town, consisting of airborne iron oxide belching from the steel-making plant. At its peak in the 1960s, the Consett steel works employed 6,000 workers. It remained relatively successful producing high-quality boron steel, and was making a profit in the year it closed – 1980, with the loss of 3,700 direct jobs and many more ancillary jobs. The town became one of the jobless black spots in Britain. In 1981, it peaked at 36 per cent – one of the worst unemployment rates of any town in the United Kingdom and around three times the national average at the time. The last steel ingot from Consett was made into a cross and resides at St. Mary's Roman Catholic Church, Blackhill.

Consett was the first town in the world to have a Salvation Army Corps Band. It formed in December 1879 with only four players.

Famous people with a connection to Consett include actor Alun Armstrong born in Annfield Plain but attended Consett Grammar School; he had jobs as a bricklayer and as a gravedigger before acting; Rowan Atkinson, born to Eric Atkinson and Ella May, Anglican farmers in Consett; Susan Maughan, singer, who reached No. 3 in the UK singles chart in 1962 with *Bobby's Girl*.

CORNFORTH
Old English *corn* and *ford* to give us the ford where the cranes or herons are. Corneford, north east of Ferryhill, in 1116.

CORNSAY

In 1153 it was Cornesho; in 1183 it was Corneshow, Cornesowe in 1301 and Cornesye in 1549. From Old English *cirn hoh* – the hill frequented by cranes or herons.

Cornsay is six miles south east of Consett and consists of nineteen dwellings, including four farms, and is the home of Greenacres Nudist Club. All formerly belonged to Ushaw College for the training of Catholic priests.

Greenacres Sun Club (as it is now known) was founded in 1953 on the site of an old Alms Houses site. In July 2002 the *Northern Echo* reported:

> A naturist group is inviting curious members of the public to see for themselves what goes on behind closed doors. The Greenacres Naturist Club, near Durham, is holding open days this weekend… Margaret Denny, from the club, said: 'If the naturist way of life interests people, come and see what does actually go on behind our hedges and fences.'

On the village green you can see the enigmatic "draw well": which on first sight looks like a bus shelter but, on closer inspection, is a building with a 17th century dedication. It was once the main source of water for the village, and later a site for the sale of paraffin when the village was larger.

Cornsay Colliery

This is extracted from *History, Topography, and Directory of the County Palatine of Durham* published by Francis Whellan & Company in 1894; it illustrates well a typical Durham colliery community:

> The Cornsay Colliery, worked by Messrs. Ferens and Love, was first opened out in 1868… [it] gives employment to an average of 700 men and boys. The royalties worked… are leased from Ushaw College, the Ecclesiastical Commissioners, and Miss Taylor-Smith. Hamsteels Collieries and Coke Ovens were commenced in 1867 … There are four seams met and worked…giving a total yearly output of (when fully working) 280,000 tons. Three-fourths of this output is converted into coke on the spot…
>
> The Church is a small plain stone building in the Early English style, built in 1875. It was originally built as a school-chapel, but was at the formation of the parish converted into a church. It will seat about 300…
>
> The Wesleyan Methodist Chapel is a neat stone building of Gothic style, erected in 1873 at a cost of £750, to seat 400. The colliery proprietors gave £150 in addition to the site. The Primitive Chapel, also of stone, was built in 1875, and will accommodate 300. The cost was £600, in addition to site, which with £150 was given by colliery owners. The Methodist New Connexion have a chapel at Cornsay Colliery, which was originally built for the day school by the colliery owners, but becoming too small, it was given to this body, who fitted it internally to seat 400… St. Charles' Catholic School, at Cornsay Colliery, was built in 1874, and is a brick building with accommodation for about 220. Attached to this school is a house for the master. The British School, Cornsay Colliery, is a good building of brick, built in 1876 by the colliery proprietors. It is for mixed and infants, with accommodation for 400 in all, and is fully attended. The Temperance Hall is a building with a seating capacity of about 300, and is well adapted for public entertainments, having a stage and ante-room.

COTHERSTONE

In 1086 the Domesday Book named it as Codrestune –Old English *tun* + a Saxon personal name, Cuthere.

The swing bridge in Cotherstone was the scene of a tragic accident in 1929 when football supporters at a game between Mickleton and Cotherstone crowded onto it; 25 of them fell the 22 feet into the river, and one, Mrs Sally Nattrass, later died.

Cotherstone is famous for its cheese: its reputation goes back to 1858 and is based on a nonmonastic form of Wensleydale originally made from ewes' milk. Hannah Hauxwell farmed nearby at Low Birk Hatt Farm and moved in to the village itself in 1998. The spelling of the station on the now-closed Barnard Castle to Middleton-in-Teesdale line was changed to Cotherston in 1906, reverting back to Cotherstone 1914.

COUNDON

The Boldon Book of 1183 mentions a mine in Coundon in the 12th century. The Auckland rolls of 1350 record a mine of sea-coal (i.e. coal which was transported by sea) in the field of Coundon. The name

Coundon comes from its original name, "Cunadun", which translates in Old English as "cow's hill". An 1856 Ordnance Survey map shows to the south east, at Tottenham, five of the early colliery rows, also Isaac's Houses. A sandstone quarry and limestone quarries are marked, and a brick works. Just to the north is New Coundon with the Hermitage public house.

A trades directory of the same year reveals 23 commercial entries for Coundon, plus four farmers and eight taverns and a beerhouse; a number of shopkeepers, a coal inspector, a colliery cashier and a coal owner, as well as the manager of the brick and tile works at Coundongate and an earthenware manufacturer. There are ten entries under Coundon Grange three of which relate to coal mining and one victualler.

By the 1894 edition the number of commercial entries has grown to eighty. Eleven are victuallers and two beerhouse keepers, (including Black Boy). There are two agents for the Prudential; Coundon now has both Conservative and Liberal clubs. There is a surgeon and a patent medicine dealer. Eight entries relate to mining. Coundon Grange has 35 entries: eight relate to coal mining, two are victuallers, and there is a reading room and library.

Black Boy Colliery is listed under Coundon Grange, which in 1851 had a population of 585, with 102 inhabited houses, and two uninhabited. Blackboy was a colliery village said to have got its name from a roadside public house. The colliery company maintained a school for about 160 children. Black Boy produced 450 tons per day, giving work to 410 men and boys. By 1898 Jawblades Colliery has gone.

Coundon had a football team called Coundon TT which played in the FA Cup in 1984 losing 2-0 against Billingham Town. The club folded in 1991

COWPEN BEWLEY

Cowpen Bewley is to the east of Billingham, near Hartlepool. Unlike most villages there are no shops or businesses here, only a pub. In 1154 it was Cupum, Coupon 1339, Cowpon 1575. Coopon 1668 – from Old English *cupe*, *cupum* in the plural – the place of the coops, which were wicker baskets used in the trapping of fish in the streams around the Tees Estuary providing a lucrative income for the prior. The Bewley element is French *beau lieu* – beautiful place and describes the manor of Bewley belonging to the prior of Durham who had a grange here. Cowpan Bewley in 1678.

COXHOE

Cockishow in 1277 – Old English *hoh* – the hill of a man called Cocc. Between Sedgefield and Durham the modern village of Coxhoe developed during the 18th and 19th centuries, with the help of coal mining, first recorded in 1750. Coxhoe Colliery was sunk in 1827; from 1801 to 1841 the population rose from 117 to 3904.

Coxhoe had two railway stations, one at the south end and one at the north of the village. There was a pottery here from 1769; in 1851 it began to make clay tobacco pipes. Coxhoe also had its own gasworks, which produced gas from local coal; it was then sent around the village by a system of pipes. Most other coal was transported out of Coxhoe by the Clarence Railway.

Poet Elizabeth Barrett Browning (1806–61) was born in, and spent her early childhood at Coxhoe Hall, although born in Kelloe. Born the eldest of twelve children, she first put pen to paper at the age of four, writing poetry. She claimed that at the age of six she was reading novels, at eight entranced by Pope's translations of Homer, studying Greek at ten, and at eleven writing her own 'Homeric epic', *The Battle of Marathon: A Poem*. Her mother's collection of her poems forms one of the largest extant collections of juvenilia by any English writer. At 15 she became ill, suffering intense head and spinal pain for the rest of her life. Later she also developed lung problems, possibly tuberculosis. She took laudanum for the pain, followed by morphine, then commonly prescribed.

CRIMDON

Crumedon in 1270 – crooked valley – from Old English *crumb* + *denu*.

Crimdon is situated on the North Sea coast, between Blackhall Rocks and Hartlepool and was a holiday resort popular with miners and their families from nearby towns and pit villages, on account of its affordability for low-income workers. During the 1960s Butlins tried to buy the Crimdon Dene Holiday Park from Easington District Council, but the sale was declined as Butlins intended to charge people to use the beach.

CROFT-ON-TEES

Not actually in County Durham but the place has such an interesting history that we shouldn't allow 100 yards or so to get in the way of its inclusion here. Croft appears in the Domesday Book as the somewhat unpronounceable Crofst; the name of course means a small enclosed field. Croft once had quite a reputation as a fashionable spa (hence its other name, Croft Spa) first coming to light in 1668; in 1713 the sulphurous spring water was famous enough for it to be sold in London as a cure for ailments and diseases as described in Robert Willan's study of the sulphur water at Croft, published London 1782 [Robert Willan, MD, *Observations on the Sulphur-Water, at Croft, Near Darlington*]. Croft Spa Hotel, originally a posting house was built in 1808 to cater for visitors from as far afield as London A.B. Granville's 1841 description of the "Old Well" and the "New Well" described the Croft Spa for which the railway station was both opened and after which it was named.

According to the village website, *Story of our Village, 1960* by Edith Lumley

> it was discovered that horses suffering from swollen legs and other troubles were cured after drinking from the spring and paddling in the pond. Humans drank the water and found similar relief. On investigation it was found that waters of remarkable healing properties underlay the Spa woods. Sulphur, magnesia and iron water equal to those at Harrogate and the Continent were soon in constant demand. A pump room was built, baths were installed…

Lewis Carroll (Charles Lutwidge Dodgson 1832–98) lived in Croft from 1843 to 1850. When Charles was 11, his father was given the living of Croft-on-Tees and the whole family lived in the rectory for the next 25 years. Carroll's photo of the niece of Alfred Lord Tennyson's wife was taken at Croft. Some historians believe Lewis Carroll's Cheshire Cat in *Alice in Wonderland* was inspired by a carving in Croft Church.

Dodgson wrote and received as many as 98,721 letters, according to a special letter register which he devised. His advice about how to improve one's letter writing skills can be seen in his *Eight or Nine Wise Words About Letter-Writing*.

Croft Bridge is a sight to behold: built in 1356 it is one of the best in the north of England with its seven Gothic arches which gradually increase in height in the centre of the curve. The bridge not only unites the village but also unites the counties of Durham and Yorkshire.

Croft Circuit is a motor racing circuit at Dalton-on-Tees; it is just over two miles long and is on the lands of an airfield. With the start of the Second World War RAF Croft was built on the site now occupied by the circuit. Also known as Croft Aerodrome, RAF Croft was home to Wellington, Lancaster, Whitley, Stirling and Halifax bombers.

CROOK

Crook has some eccentric sounding earlier names: Cruketona in 1267 and Crok in 1304 – from the Old English *croc*, the secluded corner of land. Also le Croke next Brauncepath in 1378.

The historic market town of Crook is about nine miles south west of Durham City. Crook first comes to notice as an agricultural village around 1795 with an inn and a blacksmith's. In the 1830s it became a thriving mining village: very soon there were over 20 mines in the area, and by the end of the 19th century the town had developed rapidly in population and economy.

Crook Town FC, have reached the third round of the FA Cup and formed a key role in the development of FC Barcelona, playing a number of friendly matches in the 1910s and 1920s.

The town is also home to the oldest purpose built cinema in the north, the Electric Palace which opened on 21st November 1910.

About two miles to the west of Crook at Fir Tree is the Second World War Harperley POW Camp 93. Harperley was built to accommodate up to 1,400 inmates, a work camp for low risk PoWs. It was the main camp for a number of satellite camps, also numbered 93. Nearby Bishop Auckland used Harperley PoWs for labour; Oaklands Emergency Hospital was another installation numbered Camp 93. It was built in 1943 by Italian PoWs to the specifications of other existing Ministry of War Standard Camps. The camp was officially disbanded in 1948. All the buildings had two entry/exit points and were heated by one or two cast-iron pot-bellied stoves. Accommodation buildings were one room, approximately 60 ft long, housing about 48 men in double bunks. There were never any guard towers at Harperley, because of the low risk 'White' category PoWs. The Allied categorisation of PoWs resulted in White (Non Nazi/Low risk), Grey (Medium risk) and Black (Staunch Nazi/High risk) internees. Prisoners within wartime Britain who were fervent Nazis, such as members of the SS and U-Boat (Unterseeboot) crews would be sent to camps in particularly remote locations such as the Scottish Highlands.

Harperley held between 800 and 1,500 PoWs, all other Ranks and Senior NCOs; they were utilised extensively as manpower to work on agriculture, dam, forestry and many other local labour-intensive projects. Six days a week, Monday to Saturday from 0700 hrs to 1900 hrs.

CROXDALE

Crokesteil in 1190, Croxstalle 1259 and Croxdaill in 1570 – *dael* is Old English for valley. However, the earlier of the two may well be made up of Middle Scots dialect tail – 'the irregular boundary of land jutting from a larger area' with the personal name Krokr.

Croxdale is a village about three miles south of Durham City. At one time it had a station on the East Coast Main Line which passes over the impressive Croxdale Viaduct built in 1872 by the North Eastern Railway Company just to the north of the village. The village has two pubs: The Daleside and The Croxdale Inn.

Croxdale is a small settlement clustered around Croxdale Hall. The earliest mention in records is as Crokesteil in 1195. Ownership of Croxdale dates back to 1291 when it belonged to Roger Routhberi. By the early 15th century ownership was with the Salvin family who still own Croxdale Hall and the surrounding estate.

Burn Hall is just to the north of Croxdale, built in 1821 by Durham architect Ignatius Bonomi for the Salvin family. The cost of owning and maintaining two grand halls proved prohibitive and it was sold in 1926 to Roman Catholic missionaries who used it to train boys as missionary priests. In 1995 it was sold again and became luxury apartments.

The Croxdale we see today owes its existence to coal mining which came in 1845 with the opening of the Croxdale Pit, a short-lived venture by the Salvin family; the pit was closed by 1870. 1875 saw a return of coal mining as the Weardale Iron and Coal Company opened Croxdale Colliery just to the south of Sunderland Bridge. Housing was built to accommodate mine workers and their families, a Methodist Chapel completed in 1877 and a school built in 1878-79 as well as St. Bartholemew's being extended in 1878. The colliery closed in 1934. During the Second World War the village was home to a munitions factory. The Honest Lawyer is the jokey pub – often depicted on signs as a headless man in his silks.

DADDRY SHIELD

A village on the south side of the River Wear in Weardale. It was known as Datherie Shiel in 1685. Disappointingly the first element remains a mystery while the second is from Middle English shele, a shieling.

DALTON PIERCY

To the west of Hartlepool. Daltun in 1150, Dalton Percy in 1381. Originally part of the Bruce estate it passed through marriage to William de Percy in the 13th century.

DARLINGTON

Darlington lies in the Tees Valley – it is a sizeable market town on the River Skerne which is a tributary of the River Tees. The town's extensive history is notable for two reasons: it is steeped in Quakerism;

and it is famous for playing a significant part in the world's first passenger rail service – the Stockton and Darlington Railway. In the 18th century, Daniel Defoe did the town no favours when he wrote that while there was "good bleaching of linen, so that I have known cloth brought from Scotland to be bleached here" it had "nothing remarkable but dirt".

First records of Darlington are as an Anglo-Saxon settlement. It was then overrun by the Danes for which evidence survives in the many street names of Danish origin. From very early days Darlington's market has been the focus of the town and remains so today. The town first appeared in writing in 1040 when it was called Dearthingtun. Its name was probably originally Deornoth *ing tun*: Deaornoth was the name of a local man; the word 'ing' meant belonging to and tun meant farm or hamlet. So it was the place belonging to Deaornoth; for the Normans the name was Derlinton, while during the 17th and 18th centuries the town was known as Darnton. In time its name changed to Darlington.

In the Middle Ages Darlington belonged to the Bishop of Durham; in the 12th century the Bishop turned part of the settlement into a market town which attracted locals and inhabitants of outlying farms and villages. The Bishop made a lot of money by charging tolls.

Most inhabitants of Darlington at this time were farmers, but there was other industry, not least wool which was woven and dyed in Darlington as Defoe noted. There was also a leather industry centered on Skinnergate.

In the 18th century Darlington gained a reputation for the manufacture of linen, especially towels and tablecloths. The first newspaper in Darlington was published in 1772 and the town's first bank opened in 1774. In 1809 a dispensary was founded where the poor could obtain free medicines. The first hospital opened in 1864 and on 27th September 1825 the world famous Stockton and Darlington Railway opened. In 1823 an Act of Parliament formed a body of men to clean the streets of Darlington and light them with oil lamps. They could also appoint night watchmen. From 1830 Darlington enjoyed gas lighting. A water company was formed in 1846 to supply piped water. In the 1850s a network of sewers came on stream. In 1870 *The Northern Echo* was launched. Although a regional paper it includes national and international news; William Thomas Stead was a pre-eminent editor who died in 1912 in the *Titanic* disaster.

By the 19th century the influential Quaker Pease family started to have a beneficial influence on the town. In 1875 the statue of Joseph Pease (1799–1872) was erected. A railway pioneer, he was the first Quaker Member of Parliament, for South Durham; like most Quakers back then, he always refused to remove his hat, even when he entered the House of Commons. South Park was laid out in 1877 and from 1880 horse-drawn trams rattled down the streets. Darlington's first public library opened in 1885 and Central Station was built in 1887.

By 1900 Darlington had a population of 50,000. The linen industry declined but was replaced by engineering and bridge building; iron foundries were constructed. The curtains went back in Darlington's first cinema in 1911.

J.M. Dent (1849–1926), the famous (teetotal) publisher, was born in Darlington in what is now the Britannia public house in Archer Street. In 1888 he founded J. M. Dent and Company. (J.M. Dent & Sons from 1909). Between 1889 and 1894 Dent published Charles Lamb, Oliver Goldsmith, Jane Austen, Chaucer, Tennyson, and many other classic authors. The publication of books in the Everyman Library began in 1906 with 152 titles issued by the end of the first year. Dent died well before publication of his target of 1,000 volumes, which was eventually attained in 1956.

The Shuttle and Loom pub remembers the importance of flax weaving to the town. Another 'commercial' nod comes in the Boot and Shoe. The Glittering Star and the Hope are clearly religious while the Burns Tavern celebrates the Scottish poet. The Falchion is interesting: A falchion (Old French: *fauchon*; Latin: *falx*, "sickle") is a one-handed, single-edged sword of European origin, whose design is reminiscent of the Chinese dadao, and modern machete. It may have been used to kill a mythical beast here or to execute Peasant Revolter Wat Tyler in 1381. The Pennyweight indicates a jeweller or apothecary – users of weights and measures. A pennyweight was the weight of an old penny – 1/240th of a Troy pound.

DAWDON

Dawdon was once a pit village to the south of Seaham. The township of Dawdon (often spelled Dawden) lay between the Durham coast and the townships of Seaham, Dalton-le-Dale and Cold Hesledon. Seaham Harbour was built in the township. Other variants include Daldene (1040), Dalden (1240), Dauden (1253) and Dawdon (1580) denoting Dale Valley.

The port and town grew during the 19th century, and in 1894 the township was given urban district status, under the name Seaham Harbour. In 1937 the parishes of Dawdon and Seaham were merged into the new Seaham urban district. The population in 1801 was 22 and in 1891, 9044.

In the 1860s the part of Seaham Harbour which would become Dawdon consisted of three industrial communities. The first had grown up around the Seaham Bottle Works from 1855, the second was next to a chemical works, and the third was at Swinebank – housing the Marquess of Londonderry's engine and wagon works staff. Dawdon was home to the Seaham Harbour Blast Furnace, in Dawdon Field Dene. The original Seaham Bottle Works was situated here in 1855. The blast furnaces closed in 1865 but were soon replaced by the Chemical Works. The Marquess's decision to sink a new colliery at Dawdon in 1899 due to problems at his collieries in Seaham had great and long-lasting significance for the town. The colliery finally opened for production in October 1907 after major problems. Dawdon reached the zenith of its employment in 1925, when 3862 men and boys helped to produce over one million tonnes of coal annually. The colliery eventually closed in July 1991 but not before 95 men and boys had lost their lives here.

The church of St. Hild and St. Helen's – the Pitman's Cathedral – was built by donations from local pitmen and consecrated on 10th February 1912.

A beach near Dawdon, known locally as "the Blast", a former waste coal dumping site, was used in the opening scenes of the film *Alien 3*.

DEAF HILL

Deaf Hill rises to the east of Trimdon Colliery. The origin of the name is shrouded in mystery and folklore – the alternative name for the village is Trimdon Station. Locally Deaf Hill is thought to have been called Death Hill. People believed if children were passed through the fork of a sycamore tree they would be cured of diphtheria; usually they died and the spot was badged Death Hill. Others subscribe to a more agricultural derivation:

> No one seems to know how this pit got its name of Deaf Hill, but the nearest guess is that in days of long ago, if land was very poor, the old farmers would say it was 'deed' or 'dead' land, which perhaps has grown into the word deaf. The rising land behind the pit is called Sleepy Hill, which does not sound very productive.

DENTON

Records begin around 1200 as Old English *denu* + *tun* – another farmstead in the valley. It is to the north west of Darlington. The village has about 20 houses, new and old, all surrounding Denton Hall Farm and contained within the vast Raby Estate. Most are whitewashed. Why? The most common explanation is that Lord Barnard got lost in the mist one day and sought refuge in a farm house. Believing it to be one of his own he entered and demanded he be fed and put up for the night, only to discover that the house was privately owned. To prevent a recurrence of this embarrassment he ordered that all his buildings be painted white.

DERE STREET

Deorestrete in 1040 and Derestrete – Roman road of the stags, or the road to Deira, (Old English: *Derenrice* or *Dere*) was an Anglo-Saxon kingdom previously inhabited by Britons and first recorded when Anglian warriors invaded the Derwent Valley in the latter half of the 5th century. Deira extended from the Humber to the Tees, and from the North Sea to the western edge of the Vale of York. It later merged with the kingdom of Bernicia, its northern neighbour, to form the kingdom of Northumbria. York was its capital.

The name is of Brythonic origin from the Proto-Celtic *daru*, meaning "oak", (*derw* in modern Welsh) in which case it would mean "the people of the Derwent",
The road north from York and Aldborough forked into Dere Street, running twelve Roman miles north east to Vinovium (Binchester), and the Roman equivalent of Watling Street, running sixteen or so Roman miles north west to Lavatrae (Bowes). These roads were key to communications and logistics relating to the Hadrian and Antonine Walls.

DRYBURN

Dryburn was Durham city's place of execution until the construction of Durham Gaol. Saint John Boste was executed here in 1594 because he was a Roman Catholic priest. Legend has it that the name Dryburn derives from a stream that dried up following the execution of a Jesuit, or else it is a corruption of Tyburn, London's place of execution. The name, from the Middle English for 'dry stream', was being used by at least the 14th century. A mediaeval leper hospital, St. Leonard's, is believed to have been sited just south of Dryburn until its demolition in 1652/53.

DURHAM

"To see Durham is to see the English Sion and by doing so one may save oneself a trip to Jerusalem" Symeon of Durham, *Libellus de exordio atque procurso istius, hoc est Dunhelmensis* (Tract on the origins and progress of this the church of Durham)

The name Durham derives from the Celtic element *dun*, signifying a hill fort, and the Old Norse *holmr* which translates as island. The Lord Bishop of Durham takes a Latin variation of the city's name in his official signature, which is signed "N. Dunelm". Some attribute the city's name to the legend of the Dun Cow and the milkmaid who guided the monks of Lindisfarne who were carrying the body of St. Cuthbert in 995 from Lindisfarne via Chester le Street to the site of the present city in 995 CE. The legend is first documented in *The Rites of Durham*, an anonymous account about Durham Cathedral, published in 1593. Dun Cow Lane is one of the earliest streets in Durham, taking its name from a depiction of the city's founding etched in masonry on the south side of the cathedral. The city has been graced with a number of names: the original Nordic Dun Holm was changed to Duresme by the Normans and was known in Latin as Dunelm.

Until the martyrdom of St. Thomas Becket at Canterbury in 1170 the shrine of Saint Cuthbert, situated behind the High Altar of Durham Cathedral was the most important religious site in England having gained spiritual kudos as the final resting place of Saint Cuthbert and Saint Bede the Venerable. The Cathedral Church of Christ, Blessed Mary the Virgin and St. Cuthbert of Durham, Durham Cathedral, was founded in 1093 and is generally regarded as one of the finest Romanesque cathedrals in Europe; the rib vaulting in the nave marks the beginning of Gothic ecclesiastical architecture. The cathedral is also home to the head of St. Oswald of Northumbria.

The castle was originally built in the 11th century as an unmissable projection of Norman power in Northern England; it is a fine example of the early Norman motte and bailey castles. The holder of the office of Bishop of Durham was appointed by the king to exercise Royal authority on his behalf and the castle was his command headquarters. Durham has always had an important place in the defence of England against the Scots; Durham Castle is the only Norman castle keep never to have been breached. The Battle of Neville's Cross, which took place near the city on 17th October 1346 between the English and Scots, is one of England's most famous and decisive battles.

The prodigious power and independence enjoyed by the Prince Bishops in Durham and County Durham have had a huge influence. The 1832 Great Reform Act negated the Prince Bishop's powers, although he retained the right to a seat in the House of Lords and is regarded as the second most senior bishop and fourth most senior clergyman in the Church of England. The Court of Claims of 1953 granted the traditional right of the bishop to accompany the sovereign at the coronation, another indication of his seniority.

Durham remained loyal to King Charles I throughout the English Civil War; it suffered badly during the war and Commonwealth. This was not due to any direct action by Cromwell but because of the abolition of the Church of England and the closure of religious institutions and offices pertaining to it. The city has always relied economically on the Dean and Chapter and cathedral.

The benefits of being a port were never lost on Durham; in 1720 it was proposed that Durham become a sea port by digging a canal north to join the River Team, a tributary of the River Tyne near Gateshead. Nothing came of it, but the statue of Neptune in the Market Place remains a constant reminder of Durham's maritime aspirations.

The 19th century witnessed the founding of Durham University – England's third after Oxford and Cambridge (or fourth if we count Northampton University 1261-65) – thanks to the benevolence of Bishop William Van Mildert and the Chapter in 1832. Durham Castle became the first college (University College, Durham) and the bishop moved out to Auckland Castle. Bishop Hatfield's Hall (later Hatfield College, Durham) was added in 1846 specifically for the sons of poorer families, the principal there inaugurating a system new to English university life of fees payable in advance to cover accommodation and communal dining.

The first Durham Miners' Gala in 1871 was thronged by 5,000 miners in Wharton Park, and remains the largest socialist trade union event in the world.

EAGLESCLIFFE and EGGLESCLIFFE

Egglescliffe, as opposed to Eaglescliffe next door on the opposite side of the bridge to Yarm, got its name after a misspelling on the local railway station sign, in which the 'a' was accidentally substituted for the 'g'.

There is no history of eagles living in either. Other derivations cite Old English *clif*, 'steep slope' while the first element has been etymologised as Latin *ecclesia* 'church' but the absence of 'l' is problematic, However, the first element could also be from an Anglo-Saxon personal name like Ecgi or Ecgel, in which case the name means 'Ecgel's steep slope. We have Eggescliva in 1155, Egglescliue 1197 and Eggyscllf in 1291.

In the 1870s the station, Eaglescliffe Junction, was extended to include four platforms, extensive sidings, and refreshment rooms, which were *the* place to meet in Eaglescliffe. Amongst the celebrities changing trains at Eaglescliffe was the opera star, Beniamino Gigli – one of the finest tenors ever – on his way further north to a concert. The pub is the Pot and Glass.

As noted under Billingham, chemicals was and still is an industry crucial to the region's economy and dependent on the Tees for the import of raw materials and the export of finished products. Robert Wilson founded a chemical works at Urlay Nook near Egglescliffe in 1833 to produce sulphuric acid and fertilisers; this was the Eaglescliffe Chemical Company, later British Chrome and Chemicals Ltd.

EASINGTON and EASINGTON COLLIERY

Esingtun in 1040: farm or village named after Esa or Esi. It seems likely that Easington Village was an important pre-Norman Conquest site, with fragments dating from as early as the 8th century found within the fabric of St. Mary's Church. Its main claim to fame, however, was when two men were hanged on the village green for their involvement in the plot to replace Queen Elizabeth I with Mary, Queen of Scots on the throne. There is more Popery: Pope Adrian IV (*c.*1100–59), born Nicholas Breakspear, lived here for a time. Easington Colliery, sunk in 1899, was the last pit to close in the Durham Coalfield in 1993, with the loss of 1,400 jobs.

Seaton Holme is here: one of the few remaining 13th century domestic buildings left in the country, it was an open hall medieval home, became an archdeacon's residence and was a children's home for a time before falling into disrepair. In 1992 it was finally restored.

Easington is the town with the highest percentage of white residents in England – 99.2% white in 2001. Apart from Pope Adrian IV, Matt Baker, television presenter, was born here. The film *Billy Elliot*, set in the fictional County Durham town of Everington, was largely shot in Easington.

EASTGATE

In 1419 it appears as Estyatshele – the east gate of the bishops' of Durham deer park. Eastgate, near

Stanhope in Weardale, is famous for two things: it is at the eastern border of the private hunting park of the Prince Bishops of Durham – second in extent only to the royal hunting park of the New Forest in Hampshire; and for being the site of the geothermal power plant that never was. In 2004 this plant was at the centre of a plan to heat the UK's first geothermal energy model village – Eastgate Renewable Energy Village. But the plan fell through, and instead the village had to make do with being the set for the filming of the ITV series *Beowulf: Return to the Shieldlands*, broadcast in 2016.

The exploratory geothermal borehole drilled in 2004 was the first to be completed in the United Kingdom for more than 20 years. The water temperature at a depth of 3,264 ft was found to be 46.2 °C, and it was estimated that the water temperature of a production borehole with a depth of about 5,900 ft would be in the range of 75-80°C.

EBCHESTER

Ebchester is to the north of Consett. Chester, of course, comes from the Old English word for a Roman fortification while Eb comes from an Old English personal name Ebba, thus 'Ebba's fortification'.

The church of St. Ebba was originally a monastery founded by Æbbe of Coldingham, the daughter of Æthelfrith, the first king of Northumbria. Ebba became abbess of Coldingham, where she died in 683. The monastery was sacked by Danish invaders. The current parish church is dedicated to St. Ebba, being of partly Norman construction with a foundation described as being pre-Conquest. Much of the stone was quarried from the Roman fort of Vindomora, on which most of the village sits.

The isolated nature of the village has been a magnet for hermits and the area was once known as the 'place of the anchorites'. The River Derwent is crucial: several water mills are recorded in the 18th and 19th century. A corn mill stood at Mill Lane, and a fulling mill and a stick mill are also attested.

Vindomora was an auxiliary fort on Dere Street north of Consett, in between the forts of Corstopitum (Corbridge) and Bywell to the north north west, and Longovicium (Lanchester) to the south. It also protected the River Derwent. It is about 13 miles south of Hadrian's Wall. Excavations of the fort have revealed two phases of construction dating from 69 to 117 CE, and from circa 150 CE to the end of the 4th century. Vindomora means bright waters, i.e. of the Derwent.

The Derwent Walk Inn is here.

EGGLESTON

A village near Barnard Castle. The second element is Old English *tūn*, 'enclosure, estate, settlement'. The first element could be the Cumbric word represented today by Welsh *eglwys* 'church'. However, it could also be from the Old Norse personal name Egill or an Anglo-Saxon personal name like Ecgwulf or Ecgel, in which case the name means 'Ecgel's estate'.

The eagles are never far away: local legend points to a large stone near Eggleston Hall with iron eyelets attached. The story goes that eagles used in falconry were tied to the stone with long leads while in training. The stone was known as the Eagle Stone which evolved into current place name Eggleston. The village is first mentioned in tax records of 1196. Many of the cottages date from the 18th century and were built by the Quakers who owned lead mines in the area. Forty men were employed as miners until 1904 when the company closed the smelting mills.

Egglestone Abbey is a ruined Premonstratensian abbey on the southern Yorkshire bank of the Tees, south east of Barnard Castle. The Order of Canons Regular of Prémontré is also known as the Premonstratensians, the Norbertines and, in Britain and Ireland, as the White Canons – from the colour of their habit; they are a religious order of Canons regular of the Catholic Church founded in Prémontré near Laon in 1120 by Norbert of Xanten, who later became Archbishop of Magdeburg. The Abbey was founded between 1168 and 1198.

ELSTOB

Elstob is a hamlet, just north of Great Stainton. Other forms are El(l)estob, Ellstobe (1235) – means elder tree stump.

ELWICK
Elwick appears as Ailewick in 1150, Ellewick 1174, Elevet 1199, Ellewi 1211, Elwyk 1250 and probably means Ella's dairy farm. Elwick is a pleasant village close to Hartlepool and boasts two pubs: the Spotted Cow and the McOrville Inn. Made up of a number of 16th and 17th century buildings the village became a conservation area in 1975. St. Peter's Parish Church has a 12th century tower and chancel and number of outstanding stained glass windows, the latest of which depicts marriage, designed by Alan Davis. The McOrville is named after two famous local horses – Old and Young McOrville.

An event which gruesomely connects Elwick, Hart Greatham and Stranton is the 1569 Rising of the Earls – the unsuccessful attempt to put Mary, Queen of Scots on the throne. Hartlepool was heavily implicated and while the nobility escaped with their lives by forfeiting their lands (for example, Robert Lambton of Owton Manor), the less privileged duly lost their lives: one rebel was hanged on each of the greens at Elwick, Greatham and Stranton while four swung at Hart.

EMBLETON
Elmedene in 1190 giving us elm tree valley.

Embleton is a hamlet and former chapelry east of Sedgefield and west of Hartlepool. The township was historically named "Elmdene", supposedly derived from the site's proximity to a woodland of elm trees which flourished in the dene nearby. From the 13th to the mid 16th century the manor was the seat of the Elmeden family who assumed the local name.

ESCOMB
Ediscum in 1040 meaning 'at the enclosures' from Old English *edisc*. Escomb is a village on the River Wear just west of Bishop Auckland. Escomb Church was built in the 7th or 8th century CE when the area was part of the Anglian Kingdom of Northumbria, and has been called "England's earliest complete church". The building includes long-and-short quoins – masonry blocks at the corner of a wall – characteristic of Anglo-Saxon architecture, and re-used Roman masonry from Binchester Roman Fort.

The Anglo-Saxon church only seated 65 people so in 1863 a new parish church, St. John's, was erected next to the vicarage while the old church fell into ruin. It was restored in 1875–80, again in 1927, and again in 1965.

In the 20th century church attendance declined to such an extent that it became too small for St. John's. In 1969 the Anglo-Saxon church reverted to being the parish church, and in 1971 St. John's was demolished.

The George Pit was sunk in 1837, and an ironworks was opened at Witton Park in 1846. WC Stobart & Co's Etherley Colliery was Escomb's major employer from the middle of the 19th century until the seams were exhausted in the 1920s. The 1851 Census recorded 1,293 inhabitants of Escomb, most of whom worked at the pit. Escomb's pub is the Saxon Inn, built in the 17th century.

ESH
Es in 1195; Essche 1298, Assh 1382 – the ash tree. Esh is a village five miles north west of Durham; it features a stone cross known as St. Cuthbert's Cross and bears the inscription I. H. S., and the date 1687.

Coal has informed the history and development of both Esh and Esh Winning. Population growth through the 1800 was phenomenal with 276 persons in 1801 and 6,392 in 1891. The Esh Colliery specialised first in mining coal and then from 1896 the manufacture of coke as well. Employment in the collieries peaked in 1914, with around 870 men employed just before the First World War. In 1947 production of coal peaked at 70,000 tonnes largely in response to the demands of the Second World War.

There has been a church on the site of St. Michael and All Angels since at least 1283. The present building probably dates to the early 18th century and was heavily restored in 1850. King Edward I attended mass here on 10th September 1306, while en route from Durham to Hexham and left an offering of seven shillings. It was not just the church he called in on, though; he paid a visit to Esh's only pub, the Cross Keys, which has been in the village since the 14th century.

ESH WINNING

Nearby Esh Winning is in the Deerness Valley five miles to the west of Durham. The village was founded by the Quaker Pease family in the 1850s to service a new mine on the Esh Estate.

The name of the village comes from two elements, first the older village of Esh (as above), and Winning, which was a Victorian term used when coal was found.

The Grade II-listed Memorial Hall is one of the village's largest buildings; it was built in 1923 as a memorial to the miners killed in the First World War. Initially it was used as a meeting hall and community centre, before being converted in the 1920s to a cinema and ballroom and renamed The Majestic by the locals.

ETTERSGILL

A village at the top of Teesdale, on the north side of the Tees between Newbiggin and Forest-in-Teesdale. Known locally as "Dirt Pit". It was Ethresgilebec in 1175 meaming in Old Norse Eitrie or Edred's ravine.

EVENWOOD

Efenwuda 1040 – level woods. 1588: Even Wodd. Evenwood is south west of Bishop Auckland and a former coal mining village; the major pit, Randolph Colliery with its associated coke ovens, was worked between 1893 and 1962, and at its peak in 1914 employed over 1,000 men.

FATFIELD

Part of Washington. Fatfield won national fame in the 1990s when the village was challenged to lose weight on the Fatfield Diet as part of a BBC television programme. In 1814 the Hall Pit in Fatfield exploded with the loss of 32 lives. Apart from this, Fatfield is well known for the legend of the Lambton Worm which terrorised the village.

The worm apart, the hero of the story is John Lambton, a bit of a rebel and heir to the Lambton Estate who, one Sunday skipped church and decided to go fishing on the River Wear instead. While setting up his equipment, John is rebuked by a witch who says that no good can come from missing church.

John Lambton fails to catch anything, that is until the church service finishes, when he pulls in a lamprey-like creature with nine holes on each side of its salamander-like head. This worm, or dragon, is about 3 feet long with legs. The witch returns and is told by John that he has "catched [caught] the devil" and is intent on disposing of it down a nearby well. The witch is not impressed and warns John about the nature of the beast.

John forgets all about it. As a penance for his rebellious youth, he later joins the Crusades and fights in the Barbary Crusade. John is not the only one who grows up: the worm grows huge and the well becomes poisonous. The villagers start to notice livestock going missing and discover that the fully-grown worm has emerged from the well and entwined itself around a local hill seven times – Worm Hill in Fatfield, Penshaw Hill on which the Penshaw Monument now stands.

The worm terrorises the nearby villages, devouring sheep, rendering cows unable to produce milk and snatching away small children. It then makes for Lambton Castle, where the Lord (John Lambton's elderly father) sedates the creature in what becomes a daily ritual of offering the worm the milk of nine good cows – twenty gallons, or a filled stone trough.

A number of attempts are made by courageous villagers to kill the beast, but they are quickly slain. Any chunks cut off the worm are simply reattached. Visiting knights also try in vain to kill the beast. When it gets angry the worm uproots trees by coiling its tail around them, then creates havoc by waving around the uprooted trees like a club. After seven years, John Lambton returnes from the Crusades to find his father's estates in wreck and ruin, he decides to fight it, but first seeks the advice of a witch near Durham.

The witch tells him to cover his armour in spearheads and fight the worm in the River Wear, where it now spends its days wrapped around a great rock. The witch also tells John that after slaying the worm he must then kill the first living thing he sees, or else his family will be cursed for nine generations – they will not die in their beds.

John prepares his armour and arranges with his father that, when he has killed the worm, he will sound his hunting horn three times at which time his father is to release his favourite hound so that it will run to John, who can then kill the dog and thus avoid the curse. John Lambton does battle with the worm by the river. The worm tries to crush him, wrapping him in its coils, but it cuts itself on his armour's spikes; the pieces of the worm fall into the river, and are washed away before they can join up again. Eventually, the worm is dead and John sounds his hunting horn the requisite three times.

Tragically, John's father is so excited that the beast is dead that he omits to release the hound and rushes out to congratulate his son. John cannot bear to kill his father and so, after they meet, the hound is released and dutifully dispatched. But it is, of course, too late and nine generations of Lambtons are cursed and do not die peacefully in their beds.

At least three generations met with a sticky end: 1st generation: Robert Lambton, drowned at Newrig; 2nd: Sir William Lambton, a Colonel of Foot, killed at Marston Moor; 3rd: William Lambton, died in battle at Wakefield. The 9th: Henry Lambton, died in his carriage crossing Lambton Bridge on 26th June 1761. General Lambton, Henry Lambton's brother, is said to have kept a horse whip by his bedside to ward off violent attacks. He died in his bed at an advanced age.

The story was made into a song (Roud #2337), written in 1867 by C. M. Leumane, which passed into oral tradition with several different variants, most notably the use of "goggly" or "googly" eyes meaning bulging and searching, a term formerly widely used on Wearside. The dialect is most effective when sung in a regional Mackem accent.

This is how it starts; tune from Tyne Pantomime 1867

> One Sunda morn young Lambton went
> A-fishing in the Wear;
> An' catched a fish upon he's heuk
> He thowt leuk't vary queer.
> But whatt'n a kind ov fish it was
> Young Lambton cudden't tell-
> He waddn't fash te carry'd hyem,
> So he hoyed it doon a well

Bram Stoker's 1911 *The Lair of the White Worm*, and Ian Watson's 1988 novel *The Fire Worm*, owe much to the Lambton Worm legend. It is retold in the graphic novel *Alice in Sunderland* by Bryan Talbot. The legend, including the subsequent death of Henry Lambton, is referred to in Thomas Pynchon's novel *Mason and Dixon*.

(THE) FELLING

Now part of Gateshead but once very much in Durham. Fellyng in 1214, Le Felling in 1326 – Old English for clearing. The name Felling is recorded as early as 1217 and comes about because it lies on the eastern descent of a fell, which rises from Team Valley in the west to Low Fell before descending down to the Tyne through Felling.

In 1509 the entire manor of Felling was granted by Deed of Partition to Robert Brandling and his heirs "for life and to the total extinction" of any other claims. Felling struck copper around 1750 and a large copper works was opened on the banks of the Tyne. And then coal: Charles Brandling commissioned extensive mining of near-surface coal on his estate and then, encouraged by the discovery of several strata below his estate, began boring operations in 1758 for deeper coal extraction. The result was the opening of Felling Colliery in 1779. A brown paper mill was also opened in 1798.

The Felling Colliery (Brandling Main) endured four disasters in the 19th century: in 1812, 1813, 1821 and 1847. Much the worst of the four was the disaster which claimed 92 lives on 25th May 1812; this terrible tragedy was one of the triggers for the development of the miners' safety lamp. Before the invention of the safety lamp, the only way of shedding light was by candle. Where explosive gas was suspected, a Spedding mill was used, that is a steel cylinder which revolved at high speed against a flint with the resulting shower of sparks shedding some light. Although safer than candles, the Wallsend colliery explosion of 1785 had shown that these mills could cause explosions too. It is worth pointing out that smoking and smoking materials were allowed in many pits including Felling at this date. It was not commonly realised at the time that firedamp was essentially methane rather than hydrogen.

So 25th May 1812 was indeed a black day for Felling – that was the day when despite the colliery having state of the art cutting edge safety measures in place, methane gas ignited and at around 11.30 am, "one of the most tremendous explosions in the history of coal mining took place". For half a mile around the earth shook and the explosion could be heard up to four miles away when clouds of dust and coal debris were thrown up from both William Pit and John Pit. The dust fell like a shower for up to a mile and a half downwind. The pit-heads carrying the pulleys at both pits were blown off, set on fire and the pulleys broken. The pulleys for the horse-whim at John Pit were mounted in a crane kept away from the shaft. As a result they were undamaged and could be swung over the shaft. Men on the surface worked the whim in place of the horses and brought 33 survivors and two bodies out of the colliery. Three of the survivors subsequently died. 87 men and boys were left entombed below ground:

> Immense quantities of dust and coal rose high into the air in an inverted cone...In the village of Heworth, this cloud caused a darkness like that of early twilight and covered the roads so thickly that the footsteps of passengers were deeply imprinted in it. As soon as the explosion was heard, wives and children of the workmen ran to the pit. Wildness and terror were pictured in every countenance. The crowd soon collected to several hundreds, some crying out for a husband, others for a parent or a son, and all affected by a mixture of horror, anxiety and grief.
>
> Baldwin (1823). *The annual register or a view of the history, politics and literature for the year 1813.* Baldwin, Cradock, & Joy

At 12.15 a rescue team went down the shaft with Spedding mills to light their way. They were forced back with difficulties breathing and retreated to the pit bottom. The party ascended, but while two were still below and at 2 pm the second blast occurred. All in all some 29 men were saved, but the remaining 92 men and boys were killed.

The rescue team all agreed that there was no possibility of the men left below ground being alive. Two explosions, blackdamp, fire and the lethal afterdamp put paid to any rescue attempt. Two days later the decision was made to seal the colliery to starve the fire of oxygen. However, local recollections of three men who had survived for 40 days in a pit near Byker led to shouts of "murder" and physical obstruction.

The parish priest for Jarrow and Heworth was the Reverend John Hodgson (1779–1845). As well as giving comfort to the bereaved, he persuaded them to accept a common, speedy burial. The bodies had lain for seven weeks in the pit while the fires were extinguished and were badly decayed. Dr. Ramsay gave his opinion that if the bodies were returned to their homes for a normal wake and burial "putrid fever" might spread throughout the neighbourhood.

Identification was problematic. Mothers and widows could not identify most of the bodies as "they were too much mangled and scorched to retain any of their features". Most were identified by clothes, tobacco-boxes, shoes and other personal items.

On Sunday 20th September, 117 days after the explosion, the pit was inspected by candle light. The furnace below William Pit was relighted and the whole mine brought back into production.

Just one year later, on Christmas Eve 1813, a further catastrophe occurred:

> About half-past one o'clock on the morning, an explosion took place in Felling colliery, by which nine men and thirteen boys were hurried into eternity, several others severely burnt, and all the underground horses but

one destroyed. The accident occurred at the time of calling course, or when one set of men were relieving another. Several of the morning shift men were standing round the mouth of the pit, waiting to go down, when the blast occurred, and the part who had just descended met it soon after they had reached the bottom of the shaft; these were most miserably burnt and mangled.

> Richardson, Moses Aaron (1844). *Local Historian's Table Book of Remarkable Occurrences Connected with the Counties of Newcastle-Upon-Tyne, Northumberland and Durham*. J.R Smith, London

This time the explosion caused the loss of nine men and thirteen boys along with twelve horses.

On Tuesday 22nd June 1847, just after 21:00, yet another explosion led to the death of six miners: four outright by a fall of rock from the roof, the other two by afterdamp, and two died of their injuries over the following two days. Eighteen horses were also killed either by the explosion or by the afterdamp.

By the early 19th century there were three distinct Fellings: High Felling; Low Felling – a more heavily industrialised village, containing Felling Colliery, a large chemical works and other manufacturers; to the north on the banks of the Tyne, there was Felling Shore – a densely populated and industrial village spreading across three miles of the bank of the river with a quay, coal staithes and ship building works. The copper works still thrived, there was now an oil and a paper mill along with forging works for anchors and shovels. In 1827 the Friars Goose Chemical Works was opened and in 1834 a second large chemical works was established by Hugh Lee Pattinson, John Lee and George Burnett soon employing around 300 men. Grindstone quarries were turning out high quality stone and a brownware pottery. In 1842, Brandling Station was opened at Mullbery Street in Felling on the Brandling Junction railway linking Gateshead, South Shields and Sunderland. This is one of the oldest passenger stations in the world.

Industrial decline was starting to have an impact by the 1930s. In 1932 the chemical works at Felling Shore closed and was left derelict, leaving behind a two million tonne heap of spoil. Felling Colliery closed in 1931 with the loss of 581 jobs. Fairs Boat Yard at Felling Shore had been sold in 1919 and became Mitchison's Ship Yard, but this too closed in 1964.

Author David Almond spent his childhood in Felling. His 1998 *Skellig* won the Carnegie Medal and Whitbread Book of the Year.

FERRYHILL

Ferryhill lies between Spennymoor and Sedgefield. In the late 10th century it is Feregenne. Ferie in 1156 and Ferye on the Hill in 1316. Ferry being Old English *fergen* for hill, so a bit of tautology here. The town grew in the 1900s because of coal mining. The last mine closed in 1968.

Alan White, the drummer with the Plastic Ono Band and Yes, was born in nearby Pelton and moved here as a child.

FINCHALE PRIORY

Finchale Priory (pronounced 'finkle') or Finchale Abbey was a 13th century Benedictine priory, the remains of which are by the River Wear, four miles from Durham. Around 1100 it appears as Finch, and ffynkal in 1220, hence the pronunciation. It means place on the river bend where finches are, from Old English *finc* + *halh*. Reginald of Durham would have us believe that the place was named after a King Finc. In addition to the priory there are some remains of the early 12th century stone chapel of St. John the Baptist, the site of Godric of Finchale's burial. The priory was built in the latter half of the 13th century, with alterations and additions continuing for the next 300 years.

Godric (*c.*1065–1170) came here in the early 12th century, creating a hermitage dedicated to St. John the Baptist. He pursued a Spartan and ascetic life for 50 years, living and sleeping outside and spurning expensive cloth and wholesome food. Indeed Godric slept on the ground with only stones and branches as his furniture. Not surprisingly, Godric's latter years were afflicted by sickness, and for almost a decade before his death he was confined to his bed and cared for by the monks of Durham. He was initially buried in Durham, but his remains were eventually moved to Finchale.

The Hospitium and part of the prior's house date from the mid-15th century. Finchale remained a priory until the dissolution of the lesser monasteries in 1536. During this time Finchale, from 1196 when Thomas was prior, had 52 priors; William Bennett was the last prior in1536. Most of the time the priory served as a resting house for the monks at Durham when four Durham monks would travel to Finchale for a three-week period to join the four monks in residence.

FISHBURN
Fishburn is twelve miles west of Hartlepool. The earliest recorded owners of the village and manor were the family of "Fissebourne". Theories vary on how the village got its name: it could be from the Saxon words *fisc* meaning fish and *bourne* brook; or it may be from the monks who fished here: "fish stream", Fishburn. Or it could even be that the family of Fissebourne gave its name to the manor explaining Fisseburn in 1180. It may also be a Flemish name associated with the Norman conqueror, Ranulf de Fishbourne. Old maps suggest that the village was named "Fissebourne" at one time, and then some considerable years later, it became "Fishbourne", later adopting its present name "Fishburn".

Coal mining boomed here between 1910 and 1973 peaking at over 1500 workers in the 1950s. Fishburn coking plant was built in 1954 alongside the colliery to produce high grade coke for industry and a coke for the domestic market called 'Sunbrite', as well as other by-products such as town gas which was supplied directly to the nearby Winterton Hospital and to the National Grid. The plant was closed in 1986 with the loss of 250 jobs.

Niall Quinn, (honorary MBE born 6th October 1966) lived here. He is an Irish former professional footballer and businessman, and the ex-chairman of Sunderland. He played for Arsenal, Manchester City and Sunderland from the 1980s to the 2000s.

FOGGY FURZE, HARTLEPOOL
Furze is another word for gorse, denoting that the area had lots of gorse bushes; in Victorian times the area was called Foggy Furrows. Foggy is an old word to describe an area where coarse grass grows and derives from *fogg*, an Old Norse word for grass, the term Yorkshire Fog comes from this. Foggy Furze is therefore, an old name meaning the gorsey fields where coarse grass grows.

FOLLY
Near Hamsterley means dirty clearing pit – Fullaypitte in 1441: Old English/Middle English *ful* + *leah* + *pytt*.

FOUL SIKE
More mess: Fowlesik in 1382; it either means the stream where the birds are or dirty stream or ditch – Old English *fugol*, genitive plural of *fugle*. Middle English *foule* or *ful* +*sic*.

FOXTON
Foxton is to the north west of Stockton-on-Tees, near Stillington. The origin of the name is from the Old English words *fox* and *denu* giving valley frequented by foxes, and appeared as Foxedene in *c*.1170.

FRAMWELGATE
Framwelgate (or Framwellgate) is in Durham; the origin of the place name is from the Old English words *fram* and *wella* together with the Old Norse *gata* and means street by the strongly gushing spring. It appears as Framwelgat in 1352.

The 'Borough of Framwelgate' grew up after the building of Framwellgate Bridge over the River Wear by Bishop Flambard in 1121. The area was initially home to wealthy Durham merchants and artisans until the 17th century but by the 19th century was mainly slums with coal mining to the north of Framwelgate. Durham Main Colliery was opened in the 1880s by J. Lishman & Co. and ten years or so later it became Framwellgate Coal & Coke Co. Ltd. with work for 152 in 1902. It closed in 1924.

There is the usual tragic death toll; here are just a few of the many fatalities:

> Mason, Thomas, 24 Aug 1885, aged 58, Shifter, took a fit while going on the main road and died
>
> Purdham, Richard, 05 Nov 1907, aged 39, Stoneman, when making width for a waggonway, some top coal and stone fell away and buried him; the timber was swung out by the fall, Buried: St. Cuthbert's Churchyard, Durham
>
> Richardson, Samuel, 03 Aug 1886, (accident: 14th May 1886), aged 46, Shifter, injury to head by a tram; he worked a week after and died from an abscess in the brain

FROSTERLEY

Frosterley is in Weardale, on the River Wear close to its confluence with Bollihope Burn (Bollihope meaning the valley of the man called Bol), between Wolsingham and Stanhope. The remains of 10th century St. Botolph's Chapel are to the north of the village. St. Botolph lived in the 7th century; the village may originally have been named after him. The earliest reference to 'Frosterley' occurs in the Close Rolls of 1239, where it appears as Forsterlegh, meaning 'the forester's clearing' from Middle English *forester* and Old English *leah*, clearing.

Frosterley Marble is a black limestone containing fossil corals of the Carboniferous Period, some 325 million years ago. When cut and polished the result is a beautiful ornate stone, much in demand for church decoration, particularly during the Middle Ages. It has been quarried from the Rogerley Quarry for more than 700 years; the decorative columns found in Durham Cathedral date from about 1350. Examples of Frosterley Marble can also be seen in the village – in the church of St. Michael and All Saints, and in the railway station.

FULWELL

Today Fulwell is the affluent part of Sunderland – far from the days when its name – from Old English *fula* + *wella* – meant the dirty foul spring. Fulwell was a farming village until it was sucked in to the urban sprawl that was industrial Sunderland in the 19th century. The relics of three windmills attest to this agricultural past. They include the 19th century Fulwell Mill, the only working windmill in the UK featuring a stone reefing stage (a design-feature peculiar to mills in north east England, equivalent to the gallery found on other mills). The mill, built in 1808, was restored to working order between 1996 and 2001 after over half-a-century of dilapidation.

GAINFORD

Gainford-on-Tees is on the north bank of the River Tees half way between Barnard Castle and Darlington, near Winston.

Geagenforda, 1040; Geinforde, 1105. Legend has it that those who lived on the opposite sides of the river disputed ownership of an all-important ford across the Tees. In the ensuing battle, residents of the Durham side of the river gained the ford, and their village became known as Gainford as a consequence. Or it might just be the ford on a direct route, from Old English *gegn* ford. On the Yorkshire side of the river lies the site of the deserted village of Barforth or Barford, said to be named in memory of its residents' failed attempt to barricade the ford during the dispute.

In Anglo-Saxon times, Gainford was part of the Northumbrian Congregation of Cuthbert of Lindisfarne. Later, this area was occupied by Vikings as attested by Viking sculptures here which exhibit both Northumbrian and Viking influence. Despite the Viking settlement, Northumbrian Angles remained major landowners along the banks of the Tees in Viking times.

In the 19th century Gainford village enjoyed its own spa.

In 1904 the family of a deceased Joseph Edleston owned a plot of land next to the churchyard of St. Mary's. His children asked the church authorities to erect a monument in the churchyard in memory of Joseph's 41-year tenure at the church. The church refused permission, alleging that the churchyard was full, but that the family could donate their land to the church and then build a monument on part of it. Not to be outdone by this insult the family began building a house on their land with a 40-foot column erected next to the churchyard so it towered over the trees and pointed a huge V-sign in stone towards the church authorities. The Edleston Spite House is still standing but while the 40-foot column survives, the 'V' sign is (sadly) now gone.

The twelve-foot cross on the green commemorates Queen Victoria's Diamond Jubilee in 1897, unveiled at a ceremony in 1899 led by Lord Barnard; its base is formed of an ancient cross excavated here. The church, St. Mary the Virgin, was built on the site of the 9th century church established by Egred, Bishop of Lindisfarne, and gifted to the monks of St. Cuthbert.

Amongst the liberties enjoyed by the parish were right of execution, and confiscation of goods of felons. The church recently won fame when the vicar married a Pigg, christened a Lamb and buried a Hogg all in the same week.

GARMONDSWAY

Via Garmundi about 1080 – Garmund's Road. We have no idea who Garmund was but we do know that King Canute (r. 1017–35) walked five miles barefoot from Garmondsway to Durham Cathedral on pilgrimage, and gave the church a large estate around Staindrop and Gainford.

GATESHEAD

Gateshevet in 1150; Gatesheued in 1153, Gateshed in 1385; Gatehead in 1400; Gatesyd in 1433; Gatesyd 1448 – Goat's headland, from Old English *gat* + *heafod*. An alternative spelling may be "Gatishevede", as in a legal record, dated 1430. In 730 Bede described it in Latin as *monasterium quod vocatur Ad Caprae Caput* – the monastery called at the head of the goat. Gatehead is today in Tyne & Wear but historically it was a Durham town. JB Priestley, writing of Gateshead in his *English Journey* (1934) said that "no true civilisation could have produced such a town", adding that it appeared to have been designed "by an enemy of the human race". Despite this slur fine architecture abounds here today: Gateshead Millennium Bridge (2001); the Sage Gateshead (2004), the Angel of the North on the A1, and the Baltic Centre for Contemporary Art, a tastefully converted flour mill.

In the Middle Ages Gateshead was under the jurisdiction of the Bishop of Durham on land that was largely forest with some agricultural land. The forest was the subject of Gateshead's first charter, granted in the 12th century by Hugh du Puiset, the then Bishop of Durham.

William Hawks, a blacksmith, started business in Gateshead in 1747, working with the iron brought to the Tyne as ballast by the Tyne colliers. Hawks and Co. eventually became one of the biggest iron businesses in the north, producing anchors, chains and the like. Robert Stirling Newall took out a patent on the manufacture of wire ropes in 1840 and in partnership with Messrs. Liddell and Gordon, set up his headquarters at Gateshead to develop a global wire-drawing industry in which submarine telegraph cable received its definitive form through Newall's initiative, involving the use of gutta-percha surrounded by strong wires. The first successful Dover–Calais cable laid on 25th September 1851, was made in Newall's works. In 1853, he invented the brake-drum and cone for laying cable in deep seas. Half of the first Atlantic cable was manufactured in Gateshead. Newall was also interested in astronomy, and his giant 25-inch telescope was set up in the garden at Ferndene, his Gateshead home, in 1871.

Sir Joseph Swan lived at Underhill, Low Fell, Gateshead from 1869 to 1883, where his experiments led to the invention of the electric light bulb. Underhill was the first house in the world to be wired for domestic electric light.

Famous residents include: William Booth – founder of the Salvation Army; Steve Cram – athlete and TV presenter; Daniel Defoe – writer and government agent; Jonathan Edwards – athlete and television presenter; Howard Kendall – footballer and manager; Lawrie McMenemy – football manager; Sir Bobby Robson – footballer and manager; John Steel – drummer in The Animals.

GLOWER-O'ER-HIM

The name of a farm near Sedgefield; it means to watch over a neighbour.

GREAT LUMLEY

Great Lumley is south east of Chester-le-Street, near Lumley Castle. It takes its name from the influential Lumley family as formerly part of the Lumley family estate who presumably took their name from the place when it was Lummalea from *lumm leah*, woodland clearing by the pools. The Lumleys are descended from Ligulf of Lumley, an Anglo-Saxon noble who fled from the Normans and found refuge in the lands of St. Cuthbert. He married Algitha, granddaughter of Uhtred the Bold, Earl of Northumbria. Uhtred's wife was Ælfgifu, the youngest daughter of King Æthelred the Unready.

John Duck founded Lumley Hospital in 1686 for twelve people aged 60 and over. John Pots and eleven widows were incorporated as "The Brethren and Sisters of the Hospital".

Great Lumley is built upon the Durham Coalfield with several workable seams beneath. Stobbs Hill Pit was opened in 1704.

The pit was plagued by gas and in the days before safety lamps there were a number of fatal explosions. Sixty lives were lost in 1727, a further 31 lost in an explosion on 11th April 1797. On 11th October 1799 a "violent explosion took place in Lumley colliery ... by which ... thirty-nine human beings were launched into eternity". On 9th October 1819 there was an explosion in George Pit. It is thought that a fall of the roof released firedamp which was ignited by a candle: eleven men were killed instantly, two more died the following day. In 1824 another explosion killed fourteen people and on 20th July 1827 a man went into the wrong area with a candle and triggered an explosion. Nine men were burnt, one of whom subsequently died.

In the 19th century, with the nearby coal mines flourishing, the village grew from 696 people in 1801 to 2,301 people by 1831. There was a clay quarry between Great Lumley and Little Lumley just south of the site of Lumley Brickworks.

GREATHAM

Greatham village is approximately three miles south of Hartlepool town centre. Known as Gretham in 1196, Grytham, Gretham and Grethame it means homestead on the gravel, from Old English *Greot* + *ham*. Most of the parish is on gravel on a subsoil derived from the Mercia Mudstone Group. In the 15th century an unsuccessful attempt was made to turn Greatham into a market town when Henry VI granted a Wednesday market in 1444 to the Master and Brethren of Greatham Hospital, with fairs on the vigils and feasts of St. George and the Exaltation of the Holy Cross and the two days following (22nd to 25th April and 13th to 16th September).

The extraction and processing of salt has a long history around here: George Weddell, a pharmacist whose first plant was at Seaton, bought the 1894 Greatham Salt & Brine Company and founded Cerebos in 1903; here he drilled to a depth of 1,300 feet to extract the salt. Before free running salt was available, household salt was bought in slabs. Weddell, while looking for a cure for his daughter who was ill with a form of osteoporosis, extended research by George Duncan Bowie and serendipitously added magnesium carbonate and calcium phosphate which kept it dry and ensured it was free running: he then launched Saxa Salt in 1907; hence the famous slogan "See How It Runs". Weddell hit on the name Cerebos because it was a compound of the Latin name Ceres, the Roman goddess of the harvest, and *os*, Latin for bone. Bisto Gravy Salt followed – developed by employees Messrs Roberts and Patterson whose wives had complained about the difficulty they had in making gravy. In 1919 Cerebos Ltd acquired Middlewich Salt Co. Ltd., giving them a total workforce of 850 women and 150 men. The company was acquired by RHM Ltd in 1968, which in turn was acquired by Premier Foods in March 2007.

Sapper's Corner is in between Greatham village and Hartlepool's Fens estate. The 'sapper', (Royal Engineer) is Tommy Blumer, a veteran of the First World War who began running buses from Greatham to West Hartlepool in the early 1920s with a Model 'T' Ford Omnibus christened *Greenfly*. He then started a service to Stockton in 1925 using American Rio Speed Wagons. In 1930 Blumer built the Sapper's Corner bus garage on a rhubarb field. Four years later he sold the Blumer Bus Company to the United Bus Company and moved on to run Reliance carriers, haulage contactors.

Greatham Hospital of God was first established around 1264 by Bishop Stichell of Durham as a sanctuary for five priests and 40 poor laymen. It is dedicated to God, St. Mary and St. Cuthbert. The arched facade dates from 1804.

> The statutes or ordinances follow: Andrew de Stanley, Priest, shall be the first Master, and there shall be perpetually maintained five other priests and two clerks, of honest life and competent learning, to sing matins...and forty poor brethren to be chosen from the most indigent within the manors of the Bishop...the poor brethren shall have a competent house to eat and to sleep in; they shall be chosen of the most infirm and indigent, without other preference. The Master shall have the power of ejection... Those who are able shall attend mass-hours in the Chapel, and let the infirm lie in their beds and pray as they may.
>
> From Robert Surtees: *'Parish of Greatham', The History and Antiquities of the County Palatine of Durham: volume 3: Stockton and Darlington Wards* (1823), pp. 134-143.

In 1353 it was decreed that the Master would grant to each brethren seven white loaves and seven pitchers of ale weekly, for life. From 1761 women too were cared for. In the 16th century the hospital briefly lost its way and became more of a 'house of entertainment for gentlemen'.

Dormer Parkhurst's Hospital is a row of almshouses founded by Dormer Parkhurst, master of Greatham Hospital in 1761. Once there were six, now there are four. The plaque reads: "This Hospital for Six Widows or Unmarried Women Above Fifty Years of Age Was Founded by DORMER PARKHURST ESQ., Master of Greatham Hospital In the Year 1761."

The Smith's Arms in 1902 was run by Rachel Whitfield who died that year. Her widower, Robertson Whitfield sold it to a Mr J.W.Baird who then, astutely, sold it to Cameron's, brewers of (then) West Hartlepool. His profit was a considerable £1,230 which he used to pay for a new forge – the pub seems always to have had a connection with smithing.

RAF Greatham was situated close by; also known as RAF West Hartlepool, it was little more than a grass airstrip and a satellite station for RAF Thornaby. It was home to four of 403 Squadron's Spitfires from June 1942 to January 1943— operating forward from RAF Catterick. The airfield was also once home to 645 Volunteer Gliding School, who operate Grob Vigilant Motor Gliders for the Air Training Corps. They are now at RAF Topcliffe in Yorkshire. The site at Greatham was developed after the war by British Steel.

In October 2019 Northern Archaeological Associates Ltd of Barnard Castle published *Life of Brine? Bronze Age and Later Discoveries at Marsh House Farm, Greatham, Hartlepool* (David Fell and Gav Robinson) which described how in the winter of 2012/13, a team from NAA worked with the Environment Agency during groundworks associated with the Tees Tidal Flood Risk Management Strategy which included construction of a new flood embankment and the creation of salt flat, freshwater and grassland habitats to the south east of Greatham village. Key findings included evidence of human activity along the fringe of the prehistoric and Roman salt marshes close to Marsh House Farm. This included previously unknown funerary and settlement evidence spanning several thousand years of activity (approximately 4000 BCE to 410 CE). This took the form of flint tools and flakes of the Mesolithic and Early Neolithic representing the first direct evidence for a hunter-gatherer presence in the Tees Estuary outside Hartlepool Bay.

GRETA BRIDGE

Near to Barnard Castle, the bridge is over the River Greta just south of its confluence with the River Tees. Greta Bridge is named after the river and is Norse, from *grót* + *á* meaning "stony stream".

Greta Bridge is bypassed by the modern A66 which follows the line of the Roman road from Scotch Corner to Carlisle. Evidence from the fort here, including a dedication slab to Septimus Severus and his two sons Antoninius Pius and Geta found near the north gate in 1793, and now in the Bowes Museum, suggests it was occupied from the early 2nd to the late 4th century CE. In 1929 excavators found the foundations of roads and buildings of 2nd century or later occupation, opposite the Morritt Arms and in 1972 they exposed a road with side ditches, Samian, mortaria and Caistor sherds, and evidence of an 'ancient inefficient smelting process'. The north defences are now lost beneath the Morritt Arms. Epigraphically speaking, Greta Bridge fort and *vicus* have yielded rich pickings: four altarstones, two building stones and four tombstones. Furthermore, a Roman milestone or honorific pillar has been recovered from the roadside near the settlement.

Greta Bridge gets a mention in Dickens's *The Life and Adventures of Nicholas Nickleby* as the site of Dotheboys School. Dickens mentions the "George and New Inn, Greta Bridge". This is thought to be a conflation of two coaching inns in or near Greta Bridge.

According to Peter Gilbertson of The Coach House, Greta Bridge, the link here is the publican "George Martin", who first of all ran the inn called the "George and Dragon" to the west of the River Greta; he then moved to the original "Morritt's Arms" built on the east bank of the River Greta as a coaching inn by the Morritt family of Rokeby, in 1756. He renamed it "The George" as recorded by Dickens. Later, Martin moved to be landlord of The New Inn a mile to the east of Greta Bridge and renamed that "The George and New Inn".

The famous painting the *Rokeby Venus* by Velázquez was originally housed at Rokeby Park, near Greta Bridge. It now hangs in the National Gallery. John Sell Cotman's (1782–1842) celebrated *Greta Bridge with the Morritt Arms* (1807) hangs in the British Museum. The arch of the bridge was a great feat of engineering, which Cotman, a lover of architecture and of bridges in particular, admired. The bridge was designed by John Carr of York, and built in 1773 for Morritt's father, John Sawrey Morritt, a prolific collector of classical antiquities. The bridge replaced a Roman single-arched bridge of the same design.

HAMSTERLEY

There are two in County Durham – one near Bishop Auckland, the other near Consett. Both derive from Old English *hamstra* + *leah* – the clearing of the corn weevils. Hamsterley Hall near Consett Hamsterley Hall was the birthplace of the hunting novelist Robert Smith Surtees, author of *Jorrocks' Jaunts and Jollities*.

HART

Hart, a village to the north west of Hartlepool, is Hert in 1141; Harte in 1312, meaning stag from Old English *heor(o)t* – a symbol of royalty as in a hall in *Beowulf*. Things really took off here around 650 CE with the establishment of St. Hilda's Monastery in Hartlepool. The monastery was destroyed by Vikings in the 9th & 10th centuries. Robert de Brus I gained control of the area around 1119, with control passing to the Clifford family following Robert the Bruce's coronation in 1306. Some say that Robert the Bruce was born here.

In 1587 the parish was afflicted by the plague; the parish register notes that "89 corpses were buried, whereof tenne were strangers." In 1652 when John Pasmore was buried "On Black Monday 29th March. There was a star appeared in the South east, ye sun eclipsed."

In 1596 Ellen Thompson was condemned as a witch and buried under the stile of St. Mary Magdalene church at the east entrance to the churchyard. Another woman, known as Old Mother Midnight of Elwick may have been buried in the same place in 1641. Other Hart women convicted of witchcraft include Helen de Inferno (1454), and Alison Lawe (1582). The Jesuit Thomas Ellerker was born in Hart in 1738. Ellerker, who is described by George Oliver as "one of the ablest professors of theology that the English province ever produced" was the author of *Tractatus Theologicus de Jure et Justitiâ* (1767) and *Tractatus de Incarnatione*.

Nearby Bogle Beck means stream of the phantom or hobgoblin. Shortcake Hill may be thus named from its shape or else because of the crumbly nature of the soil. Pudding Street tells of a muddy street. Fittingly, the pub here is the White Hart.

HARTLEPOOL

A sizeable town to the north of the Tees estuary. It is Hiartar Poll and Hiarta Poll in 1155; Herterpol in 1160 and Hertepol in 1211; Hertilpol in 1230; Hertlepoul in 1344 and eventually Hartlepool in 1531. All Old Norse for stag's pool.

When dealing with Hartlepool we are really dealing with what has, over the years, been three towns. The first is Hartlepool, the ancient seaport which dates from 647 CE and which received a Royal Charter from King John in 1201. The second is West Hartlepool, founded in 1847 – Ralph Ward Jackson's vision of a Victorian new town which went on to become a major industrial city and the third largest seaport in England by the 1880s. The third is, again, Hartlepool – an amalgamation of the two towns which took place in April 1967.

Hugo de Hertepol is one of the first, if not the first, Hartlepool person to have left us a picture. He was from the Franciscan Friary where the Hartlepools Hospital once stood and later was proctor of Balliol College, Oxford. He died in Assisi in 1302 where his lectures are preserved and is buried close to St. Francis himself.

Around 1807, during the Napoleonic Wars, there was much fear in Britain of a French invasion, and even more paranoia about French spies infiltrating the country. The fishermen of Hartlepool were no exception and so, when they saw a *Chasse-Maree* type French lugger sinking in a storm just off their coast, they could scarcely believe their eyes when the ship's pet monkey, unfortunately decked out in a military uniform, struggled ashore. Their disbelief was largely due to the fact that none of the fishermen had ever seen a monkey before, never mind a Frenchman, and so, easy mistake to make in the circumstances, the monkey was deemed to be a French spy and its fate was sealed. Subjected to a kangaroo court, or should that be a monkey court, it was found guilty as charged and was duly hanged from the mast of a nearby coble. There may be some credence in the belief that this so-called monkey was in fact a French Navy powder monkey, but there is no more evidence for this than there is for it not being a monkey.

The origins of Hartlepool go back to 640 CE; in 731 Bede in his *Ecclesiastical History of the English People* refers to it as 'Heruteu', the Anglo-Saxon name defined by him as *insula cervi* – the place where harts drink, and tells us how Aidan, Bishop of Linfisfarne, gave permission for the building of a nunnery at Heortha in 640, the Isle of Harts, to be run by an Irish nun, Heiu, or St. Bega – the first woman in the north of England to take the 'habit and life of a nun'. She was succeeded by St. Hilda in 649, a daughter of King Oswy of Northumberland, until she left to run the monastery at Whitby in 657. The nunnery at Hartlepool was destroyed by the Danes in the 9th century; there are records of a later attack by Norwegian Vikings under King Eystein in 1153 when ships and goods were carried off as booty from the port. The *Domesday Book* passes Hartlepool by, possibly because there was nothing left to record. Heruteu becomes Heorternesse and Hartness and the area is devastated in the Harrying of the North by the forces of Odo of Bayeux. The next mention we have is in 1201 when King John confirmed a charter owned by Robert Bruce V (the grandfather of Robert the Bruce) – a name which still lives on in the town as Bruce or Brus. The charter was extended in 1593 by Queen Elizabeth I.

Work on the walls was begun by Robert Bruce I and completed in 1322 as a defence at various times against either the cruel sea or the even crueller marauding Scots. The Bruce family received Hartlepool from William I after the Conquest although their tenure was marred by disputes with the Bishops of Durham over who owned the town. Parts of the wall are eight feet three inches thick, notably around the Sandwell Gate. Hartlepool had cause to be well defended as it was the chief sea port of the Prince Bishops of Durham.

From the beginning of the 19th century it was becoming increasingly clear that, in order to attract trade to the town and to save it from oblivion, maximum advantage had to made of the benefits that the new railways offered. Christopher Tennant of Yarm gained permission for a new railway linking Hartlepool to the Durham coalfields; unfortunately, he died before the new 'Stockton and Hartlepool Railway' opened. In 1835, a railway line from Haswell and Thornley in County Durham carried the first coals to Hartlepool for shipment and in 1839 the railway was taken over by a Stockton solicitor, Ralph Ward Jackson. Jackson was, however, frustrated by commercial restrictions at Hartlepool's Victoria Dock and established the West Hartlepool Dock Company to the south west of the old town on land he bought around Mill House Farm Estate. This event marked the birth of West Hartlepool, a town which was soon to overshadow Old Hartlepool in terms of population and industry. Hartlepool was soon shipping more coal than anywhere else in the north and in the 1840s Hartlepool railways carried more coal than any with twenty-seven per cent of all coal shipped from the region passing through the town. By 1881 Old Hartlepool's population had increased from 993 to 12,361, but the emergent West Hartlepool now had a population of 28,000. By 1862 the two towns handled goods worth more than three times that of all north east ports combined, exceeding Newcastle, North and South Shields, Sunderland, Stockton and Middlesbrough. Hartlepool was the fourth busiest port in the country behind Liverpool, London and Hull and overtook Hull for a time in the 1890s. In 1900 West Hartlepool's population alone had more than doubled to 63,000.

On 16th December 1914 the German fleet shelled the towns with 1,150 shells killing 63 civilians and nine soldiers in Hartlepool and 56 civilians in West Hartlepool; 400 or so civilians were injured and much housing stock was damaged or destroyed.

Middleton was the shipbuilding centre of Hartlepool; it is named after John Middleton, a local Methodist and friend of John Wesley. Or alternatively, less interestingly, *ton* is Anglo-Saxon and in this case means hill, so it means "Middle Hill".

In the medieval era it has long been believed to have served as part of both the sea and military defence for the harbour. However, as Hartlepool declined and the town's fate was compared (implausibly!) with that of Ancient Tyre, Middleton gradually lost its significance; by the late 18th century the neighbouring Victoria and Commissioners Harbour was recorded as being half-filled in and used as a cornfield.

In the early 19th century things changed as the town began to industrialise, and the Greys, the Swainsons, and the Jacksons invested in new docks. Gradually Middleton re-emerged becoming more or less an island in the centre of the new dockyards. At its height in the late 19th century, the island had three shipyards and two engineering works. Middleton was a community in its own right, consisting of houses and a number of pubs. It was also home to a "Rocket House" which was used for signalling ships.

In the 1940s this area of Hartlepool was home to many decommissioned or mothballed Royal Navy ships, as well as ships of Axis Powers, waiting to be refitted or dismantled including one of Adolf Hitler's yachts.

William Gray shipbuilders was established in 1862 and went on to win the Blue Riband prize for maximum output in 1878, 1882, 1888, 1895, 1898 and 1900. The first ships were wooden built by shipbuilders such as John Winspear, Luke Blumer and Joseph Parkin behind the High Street and then in Middleton in the 1830s and 1840s; Parkin's first ship was the 1837 built *Castle Eden*. The problem with the High Street yard was that ships had to be manoeuvred over the town walls in parts and assembled in Middleton for launching. John Punshon Denton had built 56 ships at Middleton from 1839 and was joined by William Gray in 1862 to form Denton Gray and Company; this became one of the biggest of the shipbuilding companies with seventeen acres of yards around Middleton from 1871 and eighteen launches in 1878. By 1913, 43 ship-owning companies were located in the town responsible for 236 ships. It all ended 125 years later in 1961 with the *Blanchland*, the last ship built by William Gray and Company Limited.

Famous Hartlepool people include Jeff (Jaffa) Stelling, presenter of 'Gillette Soccer Saturday', one time Burnley supporter and old boy of Hartlepool Grammar School; Reg Smythe; Andy Capp; Wayne Sleep; Bill Sirs, British trade unionist, who served as general secretary of the Iron and Steel Trades Confederation (ISTC) from 1975 to 1985; singer Chick Henderson.

HASWELL

Haswell is a village six miles east of the city of Durham. It is Hessewella in 1131; Hessenwell and Heswell in 1153, Hasilwell in 1580 and Haswell in 1587 –the spring where the hazels grow, from Old English *haesel* + *wella*.

The sinking in 1833 of the first shaft at Haswell Colliery, between Haswell and Haswell Plough, acted as a magnet for hundreds of miners from around Britain. However, the miners' strike of 1844 tore the village apart when Haswell – a blackleg pit – hired non-union staff in place of union workers. "Things had never been worse," recalled historian Lewis Burt in *The Echo* in 1964. "Unrelenting poverty was everywhere. Barefoot children begged for bread" adding "But it wasn't only the poverty, though that was bad enough, it was the recrimination, the malice, the spite, the ill-will and the hatred."

It took the mining disaster that September to reunite the village. When an explosion tore through Haswell Colliery, 95 men and boys perished. Several 10 year-olds were among the victims, including John Barrass, who was on his first day at the pit. His father, William, also died.

> Those killed by the flame were blackened and scorched, some barely recognisable even by their nearest relations," said Burt. "Those killed by choke damp showed no expression of pain. Twenty putters were found lying clasped hand in hand, huddled together in that long last sleep of death.

In Haswell's Long Row, every house except one lost loved ones. In one house, indeed, two coffins stood on the bed, one on the dresser and one on the floor. "Haswell was no longer a village of malice; it was a village of mourning. It had taken the Angel of Death to draw them together in a bond of common sympathy," said Burt.

HAVERTON HILL

In 1580 it is Haverton Hill possibly from Old English *hofer* – a hump or swelling.

Haverton Hill is to the north of the River Tees, near Billingham. Along with Port Clarence next door, it flourished when the Clarence Railway opened in 1833. The railway, owned by Christopher Tennant, was a rival to the Stockton and Darlington Railway and transported coal from the Durham coalfields to colliers for shipment. In 1874 John Bell drilled north of the river where he discovered a vast salt bed at Saltholme Farm, near Haverton Hill. Improved techniques for salt extraction were developed in 1882 which led to salt exploitation by Bell Brothers and other companies. This new industry led to further growth of Haverton Hill and neighbouring settlements with the salt companies building housing for its workers.

Casebourne's established a cement works on the Tees bank in 1904 while more growth took place in 1917 when the Furness shipyard (Haverton Hill shipyard) was built in order to replace ships sunk by German U-boats in the First World War. The first ship was launched in 1919, named *War Energy*. A model village or garden city was built to accommodate 500 skilled workers for the shipyard.

In 1920 the Brunner Mond company had a salt extraction industry in the locality; they then diversified into fertiliser production by setting up the company, Synthetic Ammonia and Nitrates Ltd. Brunner Mond in 1926 amalgamated with three other companies to form Imperial Chemical Industries.

ICI rapidly expanded in the area over the next few decades, and in 1928 took over the Casebourne's cement works, which used by-products from the fertiliser plant as raw material. Atmospheric pollution, primarily from a boiler and sulphuric acid plant built by I.C.I. was a huge problem after the Second World War. This led to the total demolition of the residential houses in Haverton Hill during the 1960s and 1970s with most of the inhabitants moving to nearby Billingham.

HEBBURN

Hebburn on the south bank of the River Tyne between Jarrow and Gateshead and to the south of Walker. We see Heabyrm in 1104; Heberine in 1160 – all meaning the high tumulus from Old English heah byrgen. The first record mentions a settlement of fishermen's huts in the 8th century, which were burned by the Vikings. In the 14th century you would have seen a peel tower (see Beamish). There was also a 4' 6" wall, a portion of which still remains at St. John's Church.

Coal mining here reaches back to the 17th century. Hebburn Colliery opened in 1792 and eventually operated three pits. It closed in 1932. 200 miners were killed during the life of the colliery, the youngest were 10 years old.

Hebburn Colliery had an important role in the development of mine safety, following the mining disaster at Felling Colliery in 1812. Humphry Davy stayed with Cuthbert Ellison at Hebburn Hall in

1815 and took samples of the explosive methane 'fire damp' gas from the Hebburn mine; these were taken to London in wine bottles for experiments into the development of a miners' safety lamp. Davy's lamps were tested in the Hebburn mine.

Hebburn hosted its own annual Highland Games from 1883 for the next three decades attracting professional sportsmen from as far as Oban to compete.

In 1936 Monkton Coke Works was built by the Government, in response to the Jarrow Hunger March in 1932. The plant closed in 1990, and was demolished in 1992.

Hebburn was a prominent shipbuilding town with many Royal Navy battle ships built at A. Leslie and Company. The most famous was *HMS Kelly*, launched in 1938 the men who went down with her when she was sunk are remembered in memorials at Hebburn Cemetery, erected by surviving members of the crew and workers from Hawthorn Leslie. *HMS Kelly* (F01) was a Royal Navy K-class destroyer of 1,695 tons commanded by Captain Lord Louis Mountbatten; she was bombarding German positions on Crete along with the destroyer *Kashmir*, when at 5.30am on the 23rd they were attacked by German Stuka dive-bombers, each carrying a 500-kg bomb. The *Kashmir* was hit by one bomb dead amidships and sank almost immediately with the loss of 79 crewmembers. There were 159 survivors. The *Kelly* was hit soon after just behind the engine room killing all in the front boiler room. Within minutes she had rolled over and sank taking the lives of half of her crew, a total of 128 men.

HETT
Hett is south of Durham. It derives its name from the low rounded hill on which it sits – shaped like a hat – Old English *hætt*. In 1369 it was referred to as Hett in Spen – Spen being Spennymoor.

HETTON-LE-HOLE
Hetton-le-Hole is a village in the City of Sunderland although historically in County Durham; it is on the A182 between Houghton-le-Spring and Easington Lane. The name derives from two Anglo-Saxon words which were joined in 1180 as "Heppedun", meaning hill where the wild roses grow. It is also recorded as Hepton, Hettone, Hetton in the Hollow; and Hepton in Valle. The name was adopted by the le Hepdons, who owned part of the Manor – a manor which was divided into two parts known as Hetton-on-the-Hill and Hetton-in-the-Hole. The village grew out of the latter.

Twelve former mining cottages from Francis Street have been re-erected stone by stone at Beamish Open Air Museum.

Bob Paisley, Liverpool player and manager, came from here as did Trevor Horn, bassist, singer, songwriter, music producer, and recording studio and label owner.

HIGH CONISCLIFFE
High Coniscliffe is four miles west of Darlington. Its history goes back to Anglo-Saxon times, while the earliest part of St. Oswald's Church is Norman. The name, Coniscliffe, means king's cliff, first recorded in 1040 as Cingcesclife, from the Old English *cyning* and *clif* together with the Old Norse *konungr*. It is on a ridge or cliff of limestone.

Much blood has been spilled here down the years. Æthelwald Moll of Northumbria, who may have previously murdered Oswulf of Northumbria for the succession, killed Oswin, a Bernician nobleman here in 761. In the year 778 a high sheriff called Elduf was slain hereabouts. Later there was a coup in which Æthelred I of Northumbria, Moll's son, was ousted by Ælfwald I of Northumbria, and several royal nobles were killed in this same village. Richard Thirkeld, a Catholic missionary priest from the village, was executed at York on 29th May 1583 for high treason due to his Catholicism. On 4th March 1590 another local Catholic priest, Christopher Bayles, was similarly executed.

Local legend has it that a man called Dickenson returned to this village on 28th June 1848 to attempt a cure for paralysis. He asked to be buried up to his neck in the riverbank for four hours, and after much pain his health was improved.

HOPPYLAND
Near Hamsterley it was Hopilaund in 1300 from Old English *hopig* or *hoping* + Old French *launde*. More probably, though, Old English *hopping* – hop garden or place where hops grow wild (as at Witton le Wear nearby).

HORDEN
Horetun and Horeden in 1040; it either means dirty valley to go with the dirty farm that is also here or it is derived from the Danish *yoden* or Yew Dene. Things came to life when Horden Colliery opened in 1900. By 1920 pitmen's homes were built, initially in rows of houses named First to Thirteenth Streets. The village continued to grow, reaching a peak of 15,000 in 1951; by 1964 there were three cinemas, cricket, rugby and football pitches and also a bowling green. At one time there was a swimming pool which was filled with the water pumped out from the mine, and you could only use it if you were able to swim a certain length. Since closure of the mine in 1987 Horden's population has fallen to around 8,500. 'Marra' is a sculpture of a miner with his heart torn out, by Ray Lonsdale (2015), which symbolises the death of mining communities.

Horden Colliery was one of the UK's biggest mines. From 1900 to Nationalisation in 1947 it was owned and operated by Horden Collieries Ltd, who also operated mines at Blackhall, Castle Eden and Shotton.

HOUGHALL
Houghall is a hamlet approximately 1.5 miles to the south of Durham city centre. It was Hochale in 1115 and Howhale in 1292 from Old English *hoh* + *halh*, water meadow by the hill spur.

Coal was mined in Houghall from 1840 and a colliery village built during the 1860s although many miners lived in nearby Shincliffe.

HOUGHTON LE SPRING
Hoh tun Old English for the farmstead by the hill spur + le Spring after the family. Equidistant between Durham and Sunderland.

The earliest mention of the town's name is in the *Boldon Book* in 1183 as 'Hoctona':

> In Houghton are thirteen cottagers, whose tenures, works and payments are like those of Newbotill; and three other half cottagers, who also work like the three half cottagers of Newbotill. Henry the greeve, holds two oxgangs of 24 acres [10 hectares] for his service. The smith – 12 acres [5 ha] for his service. The carpenter holds a toft and 4 acres [2 ha] for his service. The punder (one who impounds straying animals) has 20 acres [8 ha] and the thraves of Houghton, Wardon and Morton; he renders 60 hens and 300 eggs. The mills of Newbotill and Bidic, with half of Raynton Mill, pay XV marks. The demesne, consisting of four carucates and the sheep pastures are in the hands of the lord.

An ancient document dated 1220 describes the town as 'Houghton Sprynges'. In 1311 the village was owned by Albreda, widow of Sir Henry Spring, hence the addition of 'le spring'. An alternative derivation supported by the "Regester Booke belonginge to the Paryshe of Houghton in the Springe" (1598) says it comes from the medicinal springs which flow from the surrounding limestone rocks. This is reinforced further by the area of the town formerly known as the Lake and the stream/spring that still runs through the town, long since culverted.

Houghton was a thriving coal-mining town. The local mine sank its first shaft in 1823 and was active until its closure in 1981. At its peak in the early 20th century, the pit employed over 2,000 workers. Seven miners lost their lives here in an explosion in 1828 (three men and four boys were burnt to death) while in 1850 a further 27 died in an explosion when firedamp and coal dust was ignited by a safety lamp. Here is a report:

> A dreadful explosion of gas occurred in Houghton Colliery, the property of the Earl of Durham. From the close contiguity of the colliery to the town from which it derives its name, the alarm spread in all directions, and the usual quietude gave place to the greatest consternation by the report that 150 lives were destroyed, that

number being down the pit at the time of the accident. A number of brave men volunteered, with the usual magnanimity displayed under such circumstances, to make an attempt to save their relatives and friends, and, after five hours arduous exertions, they succeeded in rescuing one hundred and twenty four men and boys, many of whom were in a state of insensibility, the remainder, twenty six on number, were found dead. The sufferings of the survivors, during the protracted period which elapsed before their deliverance, were of the most intense character, both bodily and mental, and the meeting between them and their disconsolate families, who had given them up as lost, will never be forgotten by those that witnessed it. The sufferers, with two exceptions, were unmarried, and the Earl of Durham ordered that every necessary relief should be afforded them.

Local Records or Historical Register of Remarkable Events
by T. Fordyce, published in 1867

HURWORTH-ON-TEES
South of Darlington on the River Tees. Hurdewurda in 1154; Hurthewrth in 1190. There has been a settlement at Hurworth since the 12th century.

In 1665 the Great Plague almost wiped out the village population of 750 leaving only around 75 survivors. Three dips in the village green mark the site where as many as 1,500 people were buried in massive lime pits. According to old records, bodies from other nearby villages were ferried across the River Tees for burial in Hurworth.

HUTTON HENRY
Huton Henrie in 1611 and Hutton Hendry in 1717. Hutton Henry is near Peterlee, to the west of Hartlepool. In ca. 1050 the village was known as Hoton. Henry de Essh held it in the 14th century, hence the second part of the name.

During the 19th century it became a mining village causing its population to increase from 156 in 1801 to 3,151 by 1891. Hutton Henry Colliery was operational between 1876 and 1897 and was owned by Hutton Henry Coal Co. Ltd. In 1894 its average output was about 190,000 tons per annum, and it was said to employ 1,000 men and boys.

INKERMAN
Inkerman was a village to the north west of Tow Law built to accommodate ironstone miners in 1854-55. Just like Balaclava it is named after a Crimean War battle – the decisive and victorious Battle of Inkerman (1854). In 1930s the mining failed, and the village was demolished in 1938.

IRESHOPEBURN
Ishoppburn in 1647 and Ireshopeburne in 1685. It means Iri's valley or, Old Norse Irishman's valley – a reference to the fact that many Scandinavian settlers came from settlements in Ireland.
Ireshopeburn is a village in Weardale beneath Burnhope Reservoir near Daddry Shield west of Stenhope; it is pronounced locally as "Eye-ssup-burn". Ireshopeburn is the site of the High House Chapel, the oldest purpose-built Methodist Chapel in the world to have held continuous weekly services since its foundation in 1760. John Wesley himself preached here often.

> This is country where the fires of Methodism took hold. ….there are many chapels in these parts…many are early and handsome and Ireshopeburn is the best.
> *England's Thousand Best Churches* by Simon Jenkins

The Weardale Museum is also here.

JARROW
Now in Tyne & Wear but historically in County Durham, Jarrow is on the River Tyne west of South Shields and north of Gateshead. In 716 we find it as Gyruum, Gyrwe in 1104 Jaruum in 1158, Iaro in 1180 and Iaru ca. 1300. Jaroo in 1553, Gerra 1587, Yarrow in 1728. It can mean in or at the settlement of the Gyrwe, the fen dwellers, or else mud, dirt from Old English *gyr* – mud, marsh. Jarrow has a significant place in English history: in the 8th century, the monastery of Saint Paul of Tarsus in Jarrow

(now Monkwearmouth–Jarrow Abbey) was the home of Bede, who was possibly born in nearby Monkwearmouth, and is regarded as the greatest Anglo-Saxon scholar and the father of English history. From the middle of the 19th century until 1935, Jarrow was a centre for shipbuilding; it was the starting point of the Jarrow March against unemployment in 1936.

Bede's most notable works include the *Ecclesiastical History of the English People* and the translation of the Gospel of John into Old English. Along with the abbey at Wearmouth, Jarrow became a centre of learning and had the largest library north of the Alps, mainly thanks to the wide ranging travels of Benedict Biscop. In 794 Jarrow was attacked by the Vikings, who had plundered Lindisfarne in 793. The ruins of the monastery are now associated with and partly built into the present-day church of St. Paul, which stands on the site. One wall of the church contains the oldest stained glass window in the world, dating from about 600 CE. The world's oldest complete Bible, written in Latin for Pope Gregory II (r. 715-731) was produced here – *the Codex Amiatinus* – which is currently in the Laurentian Library, Florence. The double monastery was given a grant of additional land to raise the 2,000 head of cattle needed to produce the vellum for the Bible's pages.

Palmer's Shipbuilding and Iron Company opened in 1852 to become the first armour-plate manufacturer in the world and builder of the first modern cargo ship, as well as a number of warships. In total around 1,000 ships were built at the yard which also produced small fishing boats to catch eel on the River Tyne, a delicacy at the time. Palmer's employed up to 80% of the town's working population until its closure in 1933. One consequence of Palmer's was a large influx of Irish immigrants: one out of every four people in Jarrow and Hebburn in 1872 was Irish. By comparison it was about one in five in Gateshead and one in ten in South Shields. When Palmer's closed Jarrow was described by *Life Magazine* (14th December 1936) as "cursed." and was the starting point in 1936 of the Jarrow March to London to protest against unemployment in Britain. Jarrow MP Ellen Wilkinson described this in her *The Town That Was Murdered* (1939). It was decided 200 men would take part, selected from 1,200 Jarrow volunteers. There were to be no women on the march, except for Wilkinson who joined the marchers for parts of the journey.

Day 1 was completed at Chester-le-Street followed by overnight stops at Ferryhill, Darlington and Northallerton. At Leeds a donation was made for the marchers' journey home from London, at Barnsley they were given the use of the municipal baths and at Leicester boot workers worked throughout the night to repair the marchers' shoes. There were 21 stops in all. The marchers carried an oak box with gold lettering inscribed 'Jarrow Petition'. There were 11,000 signatures inside, simply requesting that employment returned to Jarrow. The march ended on 31st October at Marble Arch; Wilkinson presented the Jarrow Petition to Parliament on 2nd November but it received short shrift and scant discussion. The marchers returned home by train, disconsolate.

1938 saw the establishment of a ship-breaking yard and engineering works in the town, followed by a steelworks in 1939. In the 1950s and 60s, the town centre had 54 pubs.

Jarrow, in 1912, was the setting for the first of Monty Python's 'Spanish Inquisition' sketches. Famous residents include Catherine Cookson, writer; Steve Cram, Olympic athlete; Alan Plater; Alan Price, musician, born in Washington and brought up in Jarrow; Sir Patrick Stewart, actor, spent most of his childhood in Jarrow, although he was born in Mirfield, West Riding of Yorkshire; Paul Thompson, drummer with Roxy Music and Lindisfarne; Jimmy Thorpe, Sunderland goalkeeper who died helping the club win the 1936 League title – on 1st February 1936 when he was kicked in the head and chest after he had picked up the ball following a backpass in a game against Chelsea at Roker Park. He played on until the match finished, but collapsed at home afterwards and died in hospital four days later from diabetes and heart failure 'accelerated by the rough usage of the opposing team'. This led to a change in the rules, where players were no longer allowed to raise their foot to a goalkeeper when he had control of the ball in his arms.

KELLOE

Cited as Kelflaw in 1140, Kellaw in 1230 meaning calf hill from Old English *celf* + *hlaw*.

Kelloe is to the south east of Durham. The Lordship of the Manor of Kelloe was bought by the

Tempests of Broughton Hall, North Yorkshire, and bequeathed by Sir Henry Vane-Tempest to his daughter, Lady Frances Vane, who married the third Marquess of Londonderry.

Nearby is East Hetton or Kelloe Colliery where six men were killed by gases from the Trimdon Grange Colliery disaster in 1882.

The 12th century St. Helena cross has been described as "one of the most important items of Romanesque sculpture in the country". It was discovered in St. Helen's church broken into several pieces and used as walling stone in the south wall of the chancel and has since been reassembled. The cross shows scenes from the legend of the Invention of the True Cross including Saints Helena and Constantine.

KEPIER

The name derives from 'Kipe weir', meaning a weir with fish trap baskets. 1230 Kipe weir from Old English *cype* + *gear*.

Kepier is in the city of Durham close to Gilesgate and the River Wear. The medieval Hospital of St. Giles at Kepier was here. Kepier was also the site of a medieval corn mill which continued in use until it burned down in 1870 caused by a spark from the grinding of the stone millwheels.

KIBBLESWORTH

Near Lamesley it went by the name of Clibersode in 1145 and Kibelswroe in 1175. The name means Cybell's enclosure. Other variants include Kibbeswurhya, Hybelsworth and Kibelswig. The square at Spout Burn was built to house the miners of Robert Pit. It was demolished by 1966.

1855 saw a short test tunnel for the London Underground built in Kibbleworth, owing to it having geological properties similar to London. This tunnel was used for two years in the development of the first underground train and filled in in 1861.

Si King, one of the Hairy Bikers was born here.

KNOTTY HILL

In 1032 it was hopilandknottes meaning Hoppyland hillocks.

LAMESLEY

A suburb of Gateshead, it is famous since 1998 for Anthony Gormley's 'The Angel of the North'. It was Lameslie in 1200 and means either Lambi's clearing, or the lamb's clearing from Old English lambi, a lamb.

The Angel is a steel sculpture (66 ft) tall, with wings measuring 177 ft across. The wings are angled 3.5 degrees forward to create, according to Gormley, "a sense of embrace". The angel, like some of Gormley's other work, is based on a cast of his own body. According to Gormley, the angel has a threefold significance: first, to signify that beneath the site coal miners toiled for two centuries; second, to encapsulate the transition from an industrial to an information age, and third, to serve as a focus for our evolving hopes and fears. the sculpture was built to withstand winds of over 100 mph, so foundations containing 600 tonnes of concrete anchor it to rock 70 feet below. The sculpture was built at Hartlepool Steel Fabrications Ltd using COR-TEN weather-resistant steel. The components were transported in convoy—the body on a 48-wheel trailer—from Hartlepool 28 miles away on a night time journey which took five hours.

LANCHESTER

The name means long camp and appears as Langescestre in 1150. Lanchester (Longovicium) is a Dere Street auxiliary fort, eight miles to the west of the city of Durham and five miles from Consett.

A construction slab tells that the Legio XX *Valeria Victrix* built the fort, but we do not know exactly when. It would have housed around 1,000 foot soldiers and cavalry. In 88 CE the legion was called back from Inchtuthil (near Blairgowrie, Perthshire), so it may have been around that time. There is evidence that it was rebuilt around 230-40 CE during the reign of Gordian (238-84 CE) and again in the early 4th century. Over the years the site has been quarried: a column, probably from the colonnade of the

Commandant's House, can be found in the nearby All Saints' Parish Church, as can an altar dedicated to the goddess Garmangabis.

Longovicium could boast two 'aqueducts', one of which harnessed the water of 21 springs and was 20ft high and 110 yards in length, stone faced and clay lined on the inside – a major feat of engineering, and one of the best-preserved aqueducts in Britain.

LANGLEY PARK

Four miles west of Durham, Langley means long clearing from the Old English. Langley Park is home to one of Diggerland's four theme parks where children and adults can run riot when they take control of machinery and enjoy rides over the former colliery ground on bulldozers and Landrovers. The cemetery of All Saints has Commonwealth War Graves and has the only grave of the unknown soldier outside London. The cemetery has an astonishing tale to tell:

> On the morning of 30th May 1941 Mrs N Bolton of Langley Park received notification of the death of her son, William. She was advised by the war office that Trooper William Bolton had died in a military hospital, a casualty of the war. The body was returned home in a sealed coffin to Langley Park and was buried with full military honours in All Saints Churchyard on 7th June 1941.
>
> Two weeks after the funeral had taken place a motor cyclist, one William Bolton arrived home to Langley Park. A shocked, delighted Mrs Bolton could not believe her eyes, her son was home safe and well. He declared he had never been injured, sick or ever in hospital. The mystery which remains to this day is of course....who lies in that grave in All Saints Churchyard? The War Office have never been able to offer a satisfactory answer. Mrs Bolton vowed to tend the grave until the soldier could be identified. Her family continue to do so along with other folk that honour the memory of this soldier "known only to God".
>
> www.langleyparkdurham.com/War_Graves_Langley_Park_Durham.html

LAVATRAE
See Bowes.

LEADGATE

Leadgate is to the north east of Consett. The Roman Dere Street runs straight through the middle of the village. 'Leadgate' is first recorded in 1590 and derives from the Old English '*hlidgeat*', which means 'swing-gate'. We also get Lydyate (1404); Lidgate (1590) and Leadgait (1617) – nothing to do with lead. The Eden Colliery was here from 1844.

LINTZ

Sounding more Austrian than Durham, Lintz is to the south west of Burnopfield. We get Lynce and Lince in 1155, Lynth in 1301 and Lyntz in 1619. It comes from Old English *hlync*, at the bank or ledge. Lintz is famous for Miller v Jackson [1977] QB 966 – a Court of Appeal of England and Wales case in negligence and nuisance. The court considered whether the defendant, the chairman of a local cricket club, on behalf of its members, was liable in nuisance or negligence when cricket balls were hit over the boundary and onto the property of their neighbours, Mr and Mrs Miller, the plaintifs.

Famous residents include Eddie Chapman (1914–97), criminal and double agent for Nazi Germany and the UK; Colin Milburn (1941–90), cricketer; John Snow (1813–58), physician and champion of anaesthesia and medical hygiene; Dare Wilson (1919–2014), SAS officer who introduced attack helicopters to the British military.

LONGOVICIUM
See Lanchester.

LUDWORTH

Ludewrth in 1160 – Luda's enclosure. Ludworth is a pit village between Durham and Peterlee. Ludworth Tower was originally a medieval manor house, founded by the de Ludworth family. In 1422,

Thomas Holden added a rectangular pele tower, when he was granted licence to crenellate his manorial complex, by Cardinal Langley.

In its heyday Ludworth Colliery produced 400 tons per day, and employed over 300 hand. Thirty four men died here.

MAIDEN LAW

The first part suggests the involvement of maidens somewhere down the line. The second from the Old English *hlaw* meaning hill.

MEDOMSLEY

Medomsley is about two miles north east of Consett. *The Boldon Book* of 1183 records Medomesley. The 1190 *Vita S Godrici* records it as Madmeslei. The name is Old English and means the "middlemost clearing" or "Maethhelm's clearing". Other variants include Medomsle and Madmesl.

Medomsley was blessed with two collieries near the village: Medomsley Colliery south west of the village and Derwent Colliery to the north opened in 1856. Medomsley Colliery was opened in 1839; it was also known as the Busty Pit, and is not to be confused with South Medomsley Colliery near Annfield Plain. Both pits were opened by Edward Richardson and Co. The Consett Iron Company took them over in the 1860s. There were several mining accidents at the pits. One in 1923 killed eight miners.

MIDDLETON-IN-TEESDALE

The middle town, of course, qualified by the 'surging one', the Tees. Middeltona in 1180.

The London Lead Company had started operating in Teesdale in 1753 when it leased a mine at Newbiggin in Teesdale and then a smelting mill at Eggleston. It moved its northern headquarters from Blanchland in Northumberland to Middleton in 1815 where it built Middleton House and bought a sizeable part of the town. The drinking fountain-cum-road sign here was put up by Robert Walton Bainbridge, superintendent of the London Lead Mining Company in 1877 to mark a testimonial he received from the London Lead Company. The company was incorporated by Royal Charter in 1692; its correct name was The Company for Smelting Down Lead with Pitcoal.

The importance of lead mining to Middleton is reflected in the parish registers: for example, in 1837, of the 113 baptisms, 83 (73 per cent) were of infants whose fathers were in the mining or smelting industries. In common with other Quaker companies they did much to try and improve the home and working life of its employees, for example, they built company houses in what became known as Newtown described in a contemporary report as follows:

> Masterman Place or as it is sometimes called, New-Middleton, was erected in 1833 by the London Lead Company from the chaste and appropriate design of Mr. Bonomi and...consists of several uniform rows of neat and convenient cottages, situated in a spacious garden, a portion of which was appropriated to each dwelling... as vacancies occur, they place their most deserving workmen, thus combining general utility with the reward of personal merit. The first occupiers took possession of their new abodes in May 1824, accompanied by bands of music, etc.

Temperance was imposed by the company as a precondition of occupation. By 1900, however, it was virtually all over. The price of lead had fallen like the proverbial lead balloon and there was intense competition from Spanish imports and from other materials. The company was wound up in 1905, selling the mines to the Vieille Montagne Company who mined them for zinc up until the Second World War.

Middleton also has links to the early Co-operative Society and may pre-date the Rochdale Pioneers.

Locally we have **Vallence Loo**, from the French local landowner Hamund de Valines and first seen as Valineslieu.

MIDDLETON ONE ROW

The One Row refers to the fact that there is only one row of houses here on the green instead of the much more typical two. Midleton one Rawe in 1620; also known as Ouermyddelton in 1620.

MIDDLETON ST. GEORGE

Also Middlinton in 1259 and Middelton Seint Goerge in 1382; 1473 has Medylton George. St. George refers to the name of the parish church here. The village, also once known as Nethermiddilton (1320) and Low Middelton alias Middleton St. George in 1717, is a mile or so from Durham Tees Valley Airport, formerly RAF Middleton St. George, a Royal Air Force Bomber Command station during the Second World War. The station's motto was 'Shield and Deter'. The airfield was originally Royal Air Force Goosepool after the nearby farm, but in 1941 became RAF Middleton St. George when the aerodrome opened under Bomber Command. In 1943 it was allocated to No. 6 Group, Royal Canadian Air Force. A sub-station was located at RAF Croft just over the border in Yorkshire. Squadrons based here include: 76 Squadron, which flew Handley Page Halifaxes, 78 Squadron, which flew Armstrong Whitworth Whitleys, 419 Squadron RCAF, which flew Vickers Wellingtons, Halifaxes, and Avro Lancasters, 420 Squadron RCAF, which flew Wellingtons, and 428 Squadron RCAF, which flew Wellingtons, Halifaxes, and Lancasters.

Post-war the aerodrome served various squadrons and units including No. 13 Operational Training Unit (OTU), No. 2 Air Navigation School, No. 4 Flying Training School, and squadrons which flew Gloster Meteors, Hawker Hunters, Gloster Javelins and English Electric Lightnings. In 1947 the airfield became a satellite station of RAF Leeming, North Yorkshire. In 1962 Flight Officer Jean Oakes became the first woman to fly at over 1,000 mph flying up and down the north east coast at about 1.6 mach. The RAF left the station in 1964, but the aerodrome was reopened in 1966 as a civil airport named Teesside International Airport, and was rebadged Durham Tees Valley Airport in 2004.

A local pub, the Fighting Cocks, is nothing to do with belligerent fowl but is less dramatically named after the Cocks family, 19th century landowners.

MONKWEARMOUTH

This is where in 674 Benedit Biscop founded a monastery *ad ostium fluminis Uiuri at Wiremuth* – 'at the mouth of the River Weir at Wiremuth', and so gave us the name of the place. We also get Uiuraemuda (730) and at Wiremuthan in the 9th century; *aquilonis* Wiramutha – north Wearmouth in 1123. Wermouth monachorum in 1080 and Monkwermouth in 1431 from Old English *mutha*, monk.

Monkwearmouth is that part of Sunderland on the north side of the mouth of the River Wear and one of the three original settlements on the banks of the Wear along with Bishopwearmouth and Sunderland, now known as the East End. It includes the area around St. Peter's Church, founded in 674 as part of Monkwearmouth-Jarrow Abbey, and was once the epicentre of Wearside shipbuilding and coal mining. It now is home to a campus of the University of Sunderland and to the National Glass Centre. The locals of the area were called "Barbary Coasters".

MUGGLESWICK

The delightfully named Muggleswick first appears as Muclingewic in 1189 and describes the farmstead or dairy farm of a man named Mucel. Muglyngwye and Muclyngeswyk in 1183. Some say that it is named after a giant, Mug, who along with two other neighbouring giants, spent their days throwing a hammer to one another. The surrounding valleys and hills around Consett are a result of that hammer being dropped on the ground.

MURTON

Murton is six miles east of Durham and seven miles south of Sunderland. As with many other places this agricultural hamlet of less than 100 people once called Morton was transformed completely by the discovery of coal. Morton became known as Murton Colliery or Murton-in-the-Whins following the sinking of the pit in 1838 by South Hetton Coal Company, and the village became a highly productive coal mining community for over a century. The pit employed over 1,000 men at its peak; the population grew to 1,387 by 1851. In 1848 five years after the colliery opened there was an explosion near the Polka East shaft, which killed fourteen miners.

The South East Durham Cooperative Bakery was here too, and from 1955 a by-product works for coal for the production mainly of coke. Despite high productivity the decision was taken to close the pit in 1991. The following timeline gives a good picture of how communities developed in the East Durham coalfield:

1830	Population 69
1838	Work on pit starts
1843	First coals drawn
1851	Population 1,395
1889	Electricity first used in pit
1892	Murton toll gates removed
1902	Three putters killed in pit, two aged 14, one aged 18
1906	Colliery draws 4,131 tons of coal in one day
1910	Miners strike over Eight Hours Bill
1913	Foundation stone laid for first council house
1914	First public telephone for Murton, based in post office
1922	Cenotaph unveiled
1923	Coal drawn from West Pit for first time
1927	Bus service to Sunderland introduced by Northern buses
1930	First "talking pictures" at Murton Empire
1931	Flush toilets put in colliery houses
1935	Miners started carrying electric lamps
1939	Pit head baths opened
1950	X-ray van visited Murton for the first time
1953	The first paid annual holiday leave of two weeks was introduced
1957	A new library was opened in Barnes Road
1958	Murton Brickworks closed
1961	Murton's swimming pool was opened
1982	First memorial service held to commemorate fatalities at Murton pit
1990	Miners fought to keep the pit open
1991	Murton Colliery was closed
1994	Pit winding tower demolished, despite being listed

The Colliery Inn has obvious resonance, more so than the anodyne Village Inn.

NAKSHIVAN, near CROOK

Nakshivan is the bizarre name of a farm to the north west of Willington. It is famous for its name and for the 3,000-year-old Bronze Age axe found there.

Emeritus Professor Alan Townsend of Durham university tells us that Nakhchivan is also a town and province in Azerbaijan.

> "the province today is one of the detached pieces of Azerbaijan wedged between parts of Armenia and Iran. Nakhchivan is on the disputed border between Armenia and Azerbaijan – tensions between the two countries are such that in 2019 Arsenal's Armenian footballer Henrikh Mkhitaryan pulled out of the Europa League final which his club played in the Azerbaijan capital of Baku over fears for his safety".

The town in Azerbaijan was, according to local legend, founded by Noah after the flood and is where he died and is buried.

It appears on an 1890s Ordnance Survey map as "Nackshavan".

NEASHAM
Near Hurworth it means settlement at the nose = the nose-shaped bend on the Tees; Old English *nosu* + *ham*. Nesham in 1158; Nysom alias Neasom in 1765.

NETTLESWORTH
Near Chester-le-Street. From Old English *netele* + *worth* – nettle enclosure.

NEVILLE'S CROSS
Nevil Croyes in 1346. Neville's Cross is in the west of Durham. Who was this Neville and what was his cross? The mediaeval cross in question was erected by, or named after a member of the powerful local Neville family, owners of the Honour of Brancepeth. Neville's Cross would have marked the precise spot where pilgrims heading for Durham from the west, along the old Roman road from Willington and Brancepeth, would have first caught sight of Durham Cathedral which, of course, housed the shrine of St. Cuthbert – a truly astounding moment. Similar crosses stood by the main roads into Durham for the same reason from the north (Aykley Heads), east (Sherburn Road Ends), south east (Philipson's Cross near Mount Joy) and south west (Charlie's Cross near the New Inn).

Neville's Cross was also the site of the Battle of Neville's Cross at Redhills where in 1346 the English beat off a Scottish invasion force. Knowing that the English army was occupied in France, David II of Scotland slyly invaded England. After pillaging much of the north the Scots were confronted at Neville's Cross by an army of Lancastrians, Yorkshiremen and Cumbrians led by the Archbishop of York. The Scots were defeated by the smaller English army and David II was taken prisoner. To commemorate the event a further monument was jubilantly erected to the south of the battlefield by Lord Ralph Neville, 2nd Baron Neville de Raby.

NEWBIGGIN
There are two in Durham; one near Lanchester and this one in Teesdale; Neubinghinge in 1333. It is named from Biggin in Derbyshire – which comes from the old North England word for a building or house. Biggin, was originally known as Newbiggin; in the 18th century it was a centre of lead mining. When the lead started to be worked out, there was a migration of lead miners to Upper Teesdale, taking their name with them.

NEWTON AYCLIFFE
Newton Aycliffe was established in 1947 under the New Towns Act of 1946, which explains the first element of the name. The town is about five miles to the north of Darlington and is the oldest new town in the north of England, bordering on Aycliffe Village and the north part of School Aycliffe. For the second element Aycliffe (originally 'Acley') was the site of a Saxon settlement. The name Acley came from the Saxon words: 'Ac', meaning oak, and 'ley', meaning 'a clearing'. Aycliffe was the location of church synods in 782 and 789 CE. Another name was 'Yacley'. The town's motto is Latin for "Not the Least, but the Greatest we seek".

The town was bordered by the Bishop Auckland to Darlington railway branch line which is part of the 1825 Stockton and Darlington Railway. George Stephenson's steam locomotive *Locomotion No 1* was placed on the rails close to Newton Aycliffe near to Heighington Station.

Aycliffe was a potent and productive force in the Second World War munitions manufacturing. ROF 59 Aycliffe, was a Royal Ordnance Factory built on an 867-acre site off Heighington Lane, during the early 1940s. Around 17,000 women from the surrounding towns and villages worked tirelessly filling countless shells, mines and bullets (for example by the end of 1945 they had produced some 700 million bullets) and assembling detonators and fuses. They came in three shifts in their droves by bike, bus and train – resulting in the construction and opening of two new stations on the former Clarence Railway at Simpasture and, ironically, Demons Bridge.

The marshy land was an ideal location as it was often shrouded in fog, thus confounding the Luftwaffe. Huge grass-covered munitions factories were built and serviced by the nearby railway lines.

The women were dubbed the "Aycliffe Angels" and braved incredible dangers on a daily basis. They got their name after a Nazi propaganda broadcast from Lord Haw-Haw threatened that "The little angels of Aycliffe won't get away with it" and promised that the Luftwaffe would bomb them into destruction – they never did of course. Apparently, though, the site was infiltrated by several German spies during the war. The many injuries and fatalities went unreported due to reporting restrictions and the secrecy surrounding the factory and its workers, as were the occupational illnesses they endured, to say nothing of their inestimable achievements in the war effort.

The fatalities we do know of include:

> The four women who were killed in the incident on the night shift of 20th-21st February 1942: Edna Thompson, aged 30, single; Irene Irvin, aged 24, married; Alice Dixon, aged 22, married; Phoebe Morland, aged 24, married with two young children. Miss Rosie Robb was killed in an explosion at Aycliffe on Group 1 in 1944. Eight workers were killed at Aycliffe in an explosion on 2nd May 1945 (days before D Day) as reported in *The Northern Echo* on 3rd May 1945: Isabella Bailey, married; Elsie Barrett, widow; James Bunton, married; William Clark Hobson, married; William Mitchell, single; Christopher Seagrave, married; Edmund Smith, married; Alice Wilson, single.

In 2000 *The Northern Echo* launched a campaign to have their work officially recognised; this led to a memorial service which was attended by Prime Minister and local MP Tony Blair and Her Majesty the Queen. A permanent memorial was also placed in Newton Aycliffe town centre commemorating their efforts.

Newton Aycliffe was also hugely instrumental in the shaping of the Welfare State. In response to the government's request for a report on what he envisaged Britain to be like after the war, in 1942 William Henry Beveridge (1879–1963), with others, produced his pivotal report which still has major ramifications. Five giants, he said, were the blight of mankind – Poverty, Disease, Homelessness, Ignorance and Unemployment. To end this once and for all Beveridge proposed a state system of Social Security benefits, a National Health Service, council housing, free education and full employment which he termed the Welfare State. The Welfare State was introduced in 1948, but Beveridge chose one place which he wanted to be the shining example of how his brave new world would work. The moors between Aycliffe and Middridge were perfect – there was a huge ordnance factory that was now surplus to requirements and there was lots of poor farmland to build on. This is where Beveridge chose his flagship new town to be – Newton Aycliffe no less. Beveridge – one of the great shapers of modern Britain – came to live here in a house at the top of Pease Way.

The site of the ordnance factory became a very productive industrial estate, home to many key industries over the years, including Great Lakes Chemicals, which retained the munitions factories until 2004; Eaton Axles, and BIP (later Hydro Polymers) who were to become two of the largest employers of the town until the early 1980s. Union Carbide was taken over by Standard Telephone & Cables before being taken over by Sanyo. Businesses currently located in the town include Flymo, 3M, Ebac and Ineos. One of the largest factories in the district is Gestamp Tallent (formerly Thyssenkrupp), which now holds over six plants around the industrial estate. In 2015 Hitachi commenced production at their £82 million railway rolling stock factory at Newton Aycliffe, called Hitachi Newton Aycliffe. It employs 720 people.

Newton Aycliffe is the town with no streets. There are no places of residence with the suffix 'street' in Newton Aycliffe. The older 'streets' are named after Bishops of Durham and saints: Van Mildert (Road); St. Aidan's (Walk); Aldwyn (Walk); Biscop (Crescent); Bede (Crescent); Heild (Close) – she became Abbess of Hartlepool in 649 and then of Whitby in 657. Some are named after prominent local families such as Shafto (Way), Eden (Road), and Bowes (Road). Some are named after New Town Movement pioneers such as Lord Lewis Silkin (Silkin Way) and Lord Beveridge (Beveridge Way). Elizabeth Barrett Walk speaks for itself; Bell Walk recalls the inspirational Gertrude Bell CBE (1868–1926) – writer, traveller, Arabist, administrator, and archaeologist who explored, mapped, and became highly influential to British imperial policy-making due to her knowledge and contacts, built up through extensive travels in Greater Syria, Mesopotamia, Asia Minor, and Arabia. Along with T. E. Lawrence,

Bell helped support the Hashemite dynasties in what is today Jordan and Iraq. She lived in Redcar and was daughter and granddaughter to the Bell steel dynasts.

James (Jim) Moir better known as Vic Reeves did a five-year engineering apprenticeship at a factory in Newton Aycliffe with the intention of pursuing a career in their technical drawings department.

NEWTON BEWLEY

In the early days this was simply le Neuton (1305) but when the prior of Durham built a manor house here between 1258 and 1273 the suffix was added – presumably it was a nice looking house so it was called beaulieu. Neuton de Beaulu in 1358; Neuton Beule in 1364; Neutonbeaulieu in 1387.

NO PLACE

Despite its name No Place does exist and is near Stanley. It is fortunate enough to be home to an award-winning real ale pub, the Beamish Mary Inn dating from 1897 and originally known as the Red Robin; No Place is near the Beamish Mary coal pit. As noted under **Beamish** the local church is known as the "Tin Chapel".

As might be expected, the origins of this distinctly unusual name have forever been mired in mystery and controversy; theories include a truncation of "North Place", "Near Place" or "Nigh Place", or that the original four house village which 259 inhabitants later called their home in 1954 bestrode a boundary between two parishes, neither of which would accept the village. It could also be a play on the word "Utopia", which comes from the Greek: οὐ ("not") and τόπος ("place") – "no-place". But that is no more likely than it being inspired by Odysseus's encounter with the cyclops, Polyphemus, in Homer's *Odyssey* Book 9 where he dupes the monster when he asks Odysseus his name. Odysseus tells him "Οὖτις", which means "nobody" and Polyphemus promises to devour this "Nobody" last of all. With that, he falls into a drunken sleep. Odysseus had meanwhile heated a wooden stake in the fire and drove it into Polyphemus' eye. When Polyphemus shouts for help from his fellow giants, saying that "Nobody" has hurt him, they think Polyphemus is being afflicted by divine power and recommend prayer as the best solution.

In 1937 the residents of the terrace of houses to the north, now known as Co-operative Villas, demolished these houses, but adopted the name for their own village. Derwentside Council tried to change the name of the village to Co-operative Villas in 1983; however, they met with strong objections from local residents at the removal of all signs pointing to No Place. Today the signs say both No Place and (at the request of some residents) Co-operative Villas.

NORTON-ON-TEES

The village is of Anglo-Saxon origin, developing into a market town, and for centuries Norton parish included Stockton; but this status was reversed in 1913 when Norton became a part of the borough of Stockton-on-Tees. Northtun in the 10th century; Nortuna in 1108 – north town In relation to Stockton – Old English *north* + *tun*.

The market was at a place called Cross Dike, near the pond. It was established in Norman times by Henry II and Bishop Flambard of Durham but ceased trading around the time of the Civil War in the 1640s. A rural myth has it that the market only opened on the sabbath and this offended God so much that he caused the market to be swallowed up by the sudden appearance of a chasm caused by an earthquake; this then formed the village pond.

Despite its decidedly leafy character, Norton had its fair share of industry: there was a brick works, the Clarence Pottery and the Clarence Windmill.

A farm called Holm House was near the old Portrack meander of the River Tees; it was in the 18th century the home of Thomas Baker, farmer Quaker and preacher who became known as 'Potato Tom' for introducing the potato to County Durham at Norton in about 1736 – Norton's own Sir Walter Raleigh. Holm House is long gone but its site since 1992 is in part occupied by the Holme House Prison built in 1992.

In 1982 human bones were discovered by schoolchildren near the Mill Lane area of the village; an Anglo-Saxon pagan cemetery was subsequently unearthed. Excavations in 1984 revealed 120 burials

(117 inhumations and three cremations) in graves that contained personal items such as spears, belt buckles, tweezers and brooches dating to around 540–610 CE.

The fourteen cottage style Fox almshouses are off the High Street, founded in 1897 at the behest of local brewer John Henry Fox whose will directed that the business be discontinued and the brewery razed to the ground. Nine pubs were sold by the trustees in 1894.

Westminster's Big Ben's first bell was cast by John Warner & Sons in Norton in 1856; sadly it was tested and found to be perfect but there was a delay of 16 months in having it fitted and it was then found to be fractured.

NOVA SCOTIAS

Nova Scotia Pit is part of the Harraton Colliery complex, on the banks of the Wear close to Chester-le- Street and Sunderland. Its history is steeped in tragedy. The villages of Chaters-Hough, Fatfield, and Picktree are nearby.

Row Pit, Harraton Colliery was the scene of a fatal explosion on 30th June 1817 when miners were sent to work in an area of the colliery which was not free from firedamp; the men were expressly ordered to use safety lamps. One man, John Moody, ignored this instruction and was seen using a candle. The overman ordered Moody to extinguish the candle, which he did. Shortly afterwards Moody was again found using a candle and reprimanded. He extinguished the candle and lit his lamp. The overman had just left him when the explosion occurred. 38 of the 41 men underground were killed, including a grandfather, his two sons and seven grandsons.

Two days later eight workmen descended Nova Scotia Pit, part of the same colliery. When they did not return another party went down to investigate but were forced back by chokedamp. Late on the following day six bodies were recovered and there was "little hope of recovery for the other two". All eight were recorded as being buried on 5th July.

Durham is a community in the Canadian province of Nova Scotia, located in Pictou County on Nova Scotia Route 376 alongside the West River of Pictou. It was named after Lord Durham who was Governor General of Canada in the 1830s.

NUTTY HAGG

Near St. Andrew Auckland. Nuttinghagge in 1647 – the place where you can find nuts. Middle English *nutting* + *hagg*.

OXHILL

The name quite simply means the hill where the oxen graze. West of Stanley, this small village is famous for being the birthplace of Hillary Clinton's grandfather, Hugh Rodham; he was born at Oxhill in 1879, the son of Jonathan Rodham, a coal miner. The family emigrated from here to the United States in the 1880s.

PELAW

The name means hill spur with a palisade from Middle English *pel* + Old English *hoh*.

Pelaw is a district in Gateshead between Heworth to the west and Bill Quay to the east. Pelaw owes its existence to the extensive Victorian factory complexes of the Co-Operative Wholesale Society (CWS), the manufacturing division of the Co-op company, which grew up along the mile long length of the Shields Road. This stretch of red-brick industry was home to factories making clothing and textiles, furniture, pharmaceuticals, household cleaning products, quilts, books and magazines and the world-famous 'Pelaw' shoe polish.

PELTON

Pelton is two miles to the north west of Chester-le-Street. The village of West Pelton is located to its west and closer to Stanley. The name means village with a palisade or situated by the shovel shaped hill. Alternatively it could mean the farmstead of a man called Peopla.

PERKINSVILLE

Perkinsville to the north west of Chester-le-Street was named in the 1840s by Charles Perkins (d. 1920), who ran the coal mines in High Urpeth near Chester-le-Street. He died in 1920. Perkinsville was originally laid out in a simple colliery housing style with streets named "A street" through to "E Street" and a North Street for good measure. The local pub, the Ship, has been demolished.

PETERLEE

Peterlee lies between Sunderland in the north and Hartlepool to the south. It was founded in 1948 under the New Towns Act 1946.

Peter Lee was a famous Durham miners' leader; the town is one of the few places in the UK to be named after an individual. The case for Peterlee was put forth in *Farewell Squalor* by Easington Rural District Council Surveyor C W Clarke; Peterlee is unique among the post-Second World War new towns in being requested by local people through their MP. A deputation, mostly if not all working miners, met the then Minister of Town and Country Planning to put the case for a new town in the district. The Minister, Lewis Silkin, responded by offering a half-size new town of 30,000 residents. The subsequent new residents migrated largely from surrounding villages in and around Easington.

The original plan was for tower blocks but this was rejected as unsuitable for the geology of the area, which had been weakened by mining works; the 'little boxes' that were built were rushed and of poor quality. Not quite that goodbye to squalor that was hoped for.

The Grade II listed Apollo Pavilion (1970) was designed by Victor Pasmore. It provided a social centre for the Sunny Blunts estate and was named after the Apollo moon missions.

Actress Gina McKee (born 1964), coal miner's daughter, was born here.

Peter Lee (1864–1935) was born at Duff Heap Row, Fivehouses, Trimdon Grange, into a poor family. When he was just ten, he was working ten-hour days at Littletown Colliery, Pittington, for a few pence a week, and by 21 he was a veteran of fifteen pits. He was a miner's leader, county councillor and Methodist local preacher. He rose to become the chairman of England's first Labour county council at Durham in 1919, served as general secretary and then president of the The Miners' Federation of Great Britain (MFGB).

All work and no play was not for Peter Lee; his curious mind and love of books was nurtured by his mother's regular reading sessions to the family. As he could not read himself, he took the courageous step at the age of 20 to return to the classroom, to learn the basics. He then sailed for America in 1886 to improve himself still further, working in the mines of Ohio, Pennsylvania and Kentucky for two years. On his return to England in 1888, Lee worked at Wingate Pit. His name lives on both in the town and in Peter Lee Methodist Church.

PHILADELPHIA

Near Houghton le Spring. Philadelphia (meaning brotherly love in ancient Greek) was a common enough name for a field and the mining village will have taken its name from that. It was so named in the American War of Independence 1776-83.

PIERCEBRIDGE

Piercebridge is a few miles west Darlington. Piercebridge is named after its Roman bridge or brigg: in 1104 it was Persebrig; in 1577 it was Priestbrigg. It is thought that pierce comes from *pershe*, meaning osiers (willows), perhaps because the bridge was at least partly made of osier twigs in 1050 when the name is first recorded. Alternative suggestions of "priest" and the name "Piers", have been rejeucted as being too modern.

Piercebridge is the southernmost of the Dere Street forts; its Roman name is Magis, Morbium or Vinovium. Excavations reveal that there were Romans on the site around the river from 70 CE because of its strategic value in guarding a bridging point of the Tees. The first bridge across the Tees here was wooden, built around 90 CE to carry Dere Street, but sometime in the late 2nd century the wooden structure was washed away as the river changed course from 130-80 CE. Remains of bridge timbers have been discovered under the water. It seems that a second bridge was built 180m downstream from the first, again of timber, but this time the timber was supported by stone abutments and a series of five thick masonry piers. The builders also laid down a series of paving blocks in the river bed to prevent the river from damaging the piers. It would not have suffered such intense flooding as the first bridge.

There was a *vicus* in Toft Field by 125 CE, and a military installation alongside Dere Street south of the Tees appeared later in the 2nd century. The fortifications which we see today on the north side of the river were not built until 260 to 270. The fort was maintained from around 290 to 350 CE and inhabited until the 6th century.

A 1973 excavation found a 3rd century rectangular bathhouse with hypocaust. A bronze figure of a ploughman with oxen, which is now in the British Museum, was found here along with Roman coins dated early 4th century. Other finds have included kilns and Roman pottery, a metalworking site, a carved stone altar and burials including gravestones and a lead coffin.

PITY ME

This Pity Me is a suburb of Durham; there are others: one north of Barrasford, near Hexham, and another outside Hartburn, west of Morpeth. Historians have floundered around trying to establish a viable etymology but perhaps we should just go with the *Oxford Dictionary of British Place Names* which says it is "a whimsical name bestowed in the 19th century on a place considered desolate, exposed or difficult to cultivate". Other less credible derivations include a shortened form of an earlier place name referring to a shallow lake or mere, such as Petit Mere (from Norman French), Petty Mere or Peaty Mere; that it comes from Pithead Mere, referring to an extended area of boggy waste ground onto which the outwash from minehead pumping engines was discharged, or that petite mer (French: small sea) is an ironic name for the settlement given the arid nature of the land.

Romantic folk etymologies include the legend that the coffin of St. Cuthbert was dropped near Pity Me on the way to Durham, at which point the saint sat up and begged the monks carrying him to take pity on him and be more careful; or that reaching here when fleeing from a Viking raid, a group of monks chanted the 51st Psalm, which includes the words "Miserere mei, Deus", English: "Pity me, O God".

POCKERLEY

Near Beamish. Early forms are Pokerleia (1183) and Pokerleye in 1389. It is associated with Middle English *pokere* meaning hobgoblin and thus Old Poker = the devil. It may also have a connection with poker, one who works with a poker or sack and appears in 1700 as a Newcastle word for someone who carries coal in sacks on horseback. It thus may mean a haunted clearing or a clearing where pokers pass. It may also have a link with the modern Norwegian word *pauk*, a dwarf.

Beamish Museum adopted the Pockerley name for a number of its superb exhibits, including Pockerley Gin Pit, the Waggonway, the Old Hall, New House, Old House, Pockerley Gardens and Pockerley Farmstead.

PODGE HOLE

Near Hamsterley, it means toad's hollow from Middle English *pode* + *hol*.

PORT CLARENCE

Port Clarence is on the north bank of the Tees at the northern end of the Middlesbrough Transporter Bridge. It was originally known as **Samphire Batts** and played an important part in the development of industrial Teesside during the prodigious growth around Middlesbrough fired by the burgeoning steel industry. The Clarence Railway was established to connect Stockton to the newly developed port at Samphire Batts and Haverton Hill upstream. Samphire Batts was then renamed after the port.

As for derivations, "batt" indicates "low-lying land by a river or by a shore subject to flooding". Samphire is an edible plant that grows in such places, like scurvy grass and is used in salads.

Samphire takes its name from St. Peter – saint Pierre – who is the patron saint of fishermen. It is known as "poor man's asparagus". The port on Samphire Batts was begun in 1828 by the Clarence Railway Company, which took its name from the Duke of Clarence, who became King William IV in 1830.

The *Whitby Repository or Album of Local Literature vol. 1* (1867) gives some detail:

> Up to the end of 1830 the Durham shore was one uninterrupted and waste blank, known by the name of the Samphire Batts. During that year, however, coal had been shipped from the Middlesbrough staithes, and incited by this the West Harbour and Railway Company extended their line to the Batts, and in so doing gave rise to Port Clarence. Simply at first a coal station, the rise of this district was extremely slow, and in 1836, with the exception of a single public-house, the trimmers' cabins in connection with the staithes formed the nucleus of the present busy village . . . Excepting as a coaling station, and a convenient ground ballast heaps, the railway company failed to see the benefit of the position, and it was left for Messrs. Bell Brothers, in 1852, to take the initiative. These gentlemen purchased of the railway company the waste ground, and in 1853 their ironworks were opened, and from the accessibility of the position to the coal field of South Durham flourished to an almost unprecedented degree. Furnace was added to furnace, and at the present time four are in full blast, two re-building, and around the works has arisen a village which has little to be ashamed of in comparison with similar works' communities. The population has been taken within the last fortnight, and the result is the discovery that "the one house" has, more than phoenix-like, arisen from its ruins, and become a village of 717 souls, 454 Catholics and 263 Protestants. In place of the one public-house there are now a public-house and beer-house. A policeman is stationed there, but it speaks well for the quiet character of the inhabitants that he describes his post as almost a sinecural one.

Wherever you have a river, people will need or want to cross it for one reason or another. The River Tees is no different. Mediaeval monks started it all with their ford opposite Newport. When the coal trade came to town in the 1830s, a ferry service was established to cater for the coal and the people employed in the industry; this was a private enterprise up to 1856 when Middlesbrough Corporation established a public wharf and passage over the Tees. In 1862 the Ferry Committee launched a steam ferryboat: the *Progress*, a shallow-draught wooden steam ferry licensed to carry 139 passengers. In 1872 things really started to happen when a visionary Charles Smith, Manager of the Hartlepool Ironworks, proposed a bridge on the transporter or aerial ferry principle costing £31,162. In 1874 the corporation ignored him and commissioned the *Perseverance* ferry instead – the first boat to ferry horses and carts over the Tees with 400 passengers at a cost of £2,975. The ferry steamer *Hugh Bell* came next costing £6,050, licensed to carry a massive load of 857 passengers. In 1901 the vexed question of bridging the river with a transporter bridge was revived and then developed from 1906. The Transporter Bridge was finally opened on the 17th October 1911 at a final cost of £84,000. It still stands today in its iconic magnificence.

PORTOBELLO

As with the Portobello near Edinburgh this namesake near Washington is named after the Porto Bello – beautiful port – in Panama. The legend is that Christopher Columbus originally named the port "Puerto Bello", meaning "Beautiful Port", in 1502. After Francis Drake died of dysentery in 1596 at sea, he was said to be buried in a lead coffin near Portobelo Bay. As part of the campaigns of the War of Jenkins' Ear, the port was attacked on 21st November 1739, and captured by a British fleet of six ships, commanded by Admiral Edward Vernon.

QUAKING HOUSES

The village of Quaking Houses is near to Stanley. The name comes from the fact that it was originally settled by Quakers before it developed into a mining village. The Quaker link is supported by the 1873 name for a local mine called Quaker House Pit. However, an alternative derivation may emanate from a colliery railway line here called the Quaking House Branch Line. A colloquial name for the village was Nanny Goat Island indicating the livestock kept locally.

QUEBEC
Quebec was a coal mining village west of the city of Durham, and close to the villages of Esh, Cornsay Colliery, Esh Winning and Langley Park. The village has a public house, the Hamsteels Inn and takes its unusual name from Quebec in Canada: the fields around the village were enclosed in 1759, the year Quebec was captured from France. It was standard practice at the time for small farms and smallholdings to be bought up together and merged or 'enclosed' and to then name those far away enclosed spaces after foreign lands. Toronto is close by while Philadelphia is at Houghton le Spring. There is a New York in North Shields and a California in Eston on Teesside.

Quebec Terrace in Mickleton is so-called because it was built on the site of the General Wolfe public house.

RAINTON GATE
Situated between Durham and Houghton-le-Spring. Reinuinton in 1123; Reiningtun in 1105 – estate named after Raegna from Old English. Symeon of Durham tells us that Franco, one of the seven bearers of the body of St. Cuthbert from Lindisfarne to Chester le Street was 'the father of Reinguald'.

ROLANDS GILL
Rowlands Gill is on the A694, between Winlaton Mill and Hamsterley Mill, on the north bank of the River Derwent. The arrival of the Derwent Valley Railway in 1867 brought with it opportunities to exploit the coal around here and so Rowlands Gill became a viable coal mining village. Pubs are The Railway Tavern and The Towneley Arms Public House; this latter pre-dated the village, being built in 1835 to serve travellers and their horses on the turnpike road through the valley. Col. Cowen's 5th Durhams camped in Gibside grounds nearby (Cowan was a local landowner and owner of the colliery). When Irish workmen came to build the railway a Special Constable was appointed to help the local priest to whip up his flock on pay-Friday nights and get them back from the Towneley to their billets. The pub was rebuilt in 1961 and demolished in 2002. The 1728 wagonway here was initially called the "Bucksnook Way".

Who was this Rowland? In December 1867 they constructed a railway from Scotswood in Newcastle to Leadgate and Consett passing up the Derwent Valley in front of the Gibside Estate in what was to become Rowlands Gill. This was on land owned by Robert Rowland; a railway station was built and named "Rowlands Gill". A road (Rowlands Gill Turnpike of 1835) also ran up the valley; the toll was a halfpenny for a donkey, a penny per horse and threepence for a horse with vehicle.

Profits allowed the colliery management to buy a strip of marshland near the river; "Ladysmith" was built to house miners working at South Garesfield Colliery near Low Friarside which opened in August 1887, but always known locally as "The Bottoms". A group of 44 businessmen drew up an "Indenture of Mutual Covenants" apportioning the land into building sites, and the general layout of the estate. These were the rules: no ale house nor Inn to be built. No part or the estate to be used for any offensive business such as chemical works or slaughter house. And not more than two pigs be kept in any garden.

ROMALDKIRK
Romaldkirk is supposedly named after Saint Rumwald of Brackley, sometimes called Rumwold or Rumbald of Buckingham, born 650 CE; he was the grandson of King Penda of Mercia, and the son of a pagan prince of Northumbria. Various legends surround him including one which has it that at three days old the prince at his baptism said the 'Creed' out loud, preached a sermon on the Holy Trinity and the need for virtuous living... and then promptly died.

The present church, often popularly elevated to Cathedral status as the 'Cathedral of the Dale', largely replaces a white plaster walled Saxon predecessor sacked by the Vikings. Pre-Norman elements can be seen at the base of the chancel arch. Rebuilding began about 1155 and continued into the 16th century. A 12th century cruciform church, St. Romald's, was the church for England's largest parish, extending from Barnard Castle into Lunedale.

The Domesday Book tells us, 'There is in Romoldscherce one carucate of land of the geld and there may have been two ploughs. Torfin held it, now Bodin holds it and it is waste'. The devastation was a result of the Harrying of the North.

Romaldkirk Fair was held twice a year in April and October until 1930 when 'inappropriate behaviour' brought it to an end.

In 1644 the plague claimed a third of the parishioners; they were buried down by the river. Grace Scott survived the plague by self-imposed quarantine, building a mud hut a mile from the village, and lived there until the risk of infection was over. A farm was built on the site, which is still called Gracie's Cottage.

In 1870 there was much (decidedly un-Christian) controversy surrounding restoration of churches in the neighbourhood as reported in the *Teesdale Mercury*: 'conceited mischievous, meddlesome country parsons who in the sublime audacity of a dense ignorance, sanction... the destruction of objects they are legally bound to protect'.

The Rose & Crown survives along with the Kirk Inn; however, in around 1910 there were no fewer than five drinking establishments; the King's Arms opposite the Kirk, the Bluebell and the Mason's Arms have since gone. The stocks are still there though and the pump is one of two that served the village – one dating from 1886. The pound is also still visible.

ROOKHOPE

Rochop in 1242 it comes from Old English *hroc hop* meaning the valley frequented by rooks.

Rookhope is a former lead and fluorspar mining community; the last mine closed in 1999. It started life as a group of cattle farms in the 13th century and is situated in the Pennines to the north of Weardale, 25 miles to the west of Durham. W. H. Auden once called Rookhope 'the most wonderfully desolate of all the dales', in *Vogue*, May 1954. The village has two pubs, the Rookhope Inn and the Swallow's Rest on the fell surrounding Rookhope.

Rookhope Arch is at Lintzgarth, and is one of the few remaining parts of the two miles long Rookhope Chimney. This "horizontal" chimney carried poisonous flue gases from the Rookhope lead smelting works up onto the high moor.

W. H. Auden knew the North Pennines and its derelict lead mines, having visited Rookhope at the age of 12 in 1919. In his poem *New Year Letter* (1941) he wrote that it was in Rookhope that he first became aware of himself as an individual person: *In Rookhope I was first aware/Of self and not-self, Death and Dread...*

ROWLEY

Near Consett and famous for having its railway station moved lock stock and barrel to Beamish Museum. The name means rough wood or clearing, from Old English *ruh + leah*.

The original Rowley railway station was opened in 1845 (as Cold Rowley, renamed Rowley in 1868) by the Stockton and Darlington Railway, consisting of just a platform. Under NER ownership, as a result of increasing use, in 1873 the station building was added. Beamish Museum acquired the building, dismantling it in 1972, and unveiled in its new location by Sir John Betjeman.

The station building we see is an Edwardian station, lit by oil lamp, having never been connected to gas or electricity. It features both an open waiting area and a visitor accessible waiting room and a booking and ticket office with the latter only visible from a small viewing entrance. One of those fabulous iconic tiled NER route maps adorns the waiting room.

SACRISTON

Sacriston is three miles north of the city of Durham; the first recorded settlement dates back to the 13th century to Sacristan's Heugh, known as Segrysteynhough in 1312. The farm and manor house here was once the residence of the sacristan, a monk who held the Office of the sacristan or sexton of the monastery at Durham Cathedral. The sacristan was responsible for providing the everyday services of the cathedral such as bread and wine, relics and the vestments. He was also responsible for repairs.

Sacriston Colliery shaft was sunk in 1838 by Charlaw and Sacriston Coal Co. Ltd and by the 1890s the pit employed 600 men, producing 1,000 tons of coal a day. Sadly, there were two notable disasters at the colliery. In November 1903 water flooded into the 3rd West district of the 'Busty' Seam. The inrush killed two miners: John Whittaker (25) and Thomas McCormick (52). When the workings were pumped out another man, Robert Richardson, was found on his coal tub having been stranded in the dark, surrounded by dirty flood water for 92 hours.

"The inquest found that the two men were accidentally drowned, and that, owing to the peculiar circumstances, no blame attached to the management." The Royal Humane Society awarded their silver medal to six mine officials. The inquiry lasted just five hours.

On 4th December 1941, a fall of stone on one of the work areas killed five miners: Joseph Welsh, 46; George W. Scott, 39; William Richardson, 50; William Smith, 40; John William Britton, 47.

The village website tells us that

> Sanitation presented a real problem as there was no piped water supply and the residents had to rely on a spring in a field on Plawsworth Road just below the Salvation Army Hall and one in Fulforth Dene known as the Springwell. There were also wells in the gardens of Lingey House Farm and the Vicarage. At Edmondsley there was a spring at the bottom of the field between east Edmondsley Farm and Daisy Hill, while at Nettleseworth there was a spring by the side of the road at the west side of the village. Earth closets and open ash pits very often shared by two or more houses were the only means of sanitation and in Sacriston rubbish was dumped at a spot known as the Gap, John Street was later built on this site.
>
> Many houses had no cooking facilities other than an open coal fire and in Sacriston one of the bakehouses undertook to bake the bread made by the housewives. At Edmondsley a communal oven was situated at the brickworks behind Hunter's Terrace and was probably heated from the waste heat of the brick kilns.

One pub, the Crossroads Inn, remains open. The others, The Village Inn, The Three Horseshoes (later the New Inn), The Daisy Hill, The Queen's Head (formerly the Boot and Shoe), The George and Dragon, The Colliery Inn and 'The Robin Hood', are now closed. Around 1920, the Robin Hood was noted for its "Five Court" (Handball Alley) and several notable matches were played there for stakes of £50 a side. Five Court is similar to Fives – a game played at posh schools. It was usual in those days for the colliery owner to build an inn which acted as an office where the miners could draw their pay, buy tools such as picks and drills – and of course, have a drink on the way home on "pay day". Wendy Craig (born 1934), English actress, and Sir Bobby Robson (1933–2009), football player and manager were both born in Sacriston.

SAMPHIRE BATTS
See Port Clarence.

SEAHAM
Quite simply ' sea town' Old English *sae ham* – the history is rather more exciting than the place name etymology. Seaham is six miles south of Sunderland; The parish church, St. Mary the Virgin, has a late 7th century Anglo-Saxon nave and is one of the twenty oldest surviving churches in the UK. Until the early 19th century, Seaham was a small rural agricultural farming community with nothing much going on – that is until the local landowner's daughter, Anne Isabella Milbanke, was married to Lord Byron at Seaham Hall on 2nd January 1815. Byron must have been bored very quickly with married life because he began writing his *Hebrew Melodies* while at Seaham; they were published in April 1815. He wrote to a friend:

> Upon this dreary coast we have nothing but county meetings and shipwrecks; and I have this day dined upon fish, which probably dined upon the crews of several colliers lost in the late gales. But I saw the sea once more in all the glories of surf and foam.

Seaham Hall was acquired by Charles William Vane, 3rd Marquess of Londonderry through his second marriage to Lady Frances Anne Vane-Tempest in 1819 – one of the greatest heiresses of the time.

The Byron marriage was short-lived, producing an only child, the mathematician Ada Lovelace. Things took a turn for the better when the Milbankes sold out in 1821 to the Marquess who built a harbour, in 1828, to facilitate transport of goods from local industries such as the first coal mine which opened in 1845. A deeper dock opened in 1905 under the auspices of the 6th Marquess. His harbour was unusual because it comprised a series of interconnecting locks, rather than the more typical two wall construction.

Seaham Colliery suffered a terrible underground explosion on Wednesday 8th September, 1880 at 2.20 am which resulted in the loss of over 160 lives, including surface workers and rescuers. durhamrecordsonline.com/library/seaham-colliery-disaster-of-1880/ sets the scene:

> The sound of the explosion was heard on ships in Seaham Harbour and as far away as Murton Colliery and the outskirts of Sunderland. Some men saw a great cloud of dust blown skywards out of the shafts. The Marquess [of Londonderry] heard the noise at Seaham Hall and was among the first on the scene.

The report goes on to describe the explosion in somewhat gruesome detail:

> Both shafts were blocked with debris and it was twelve hours before a descent could be made. Even then the rescuers had to use the emergency kibble (an iron bucket) for the cages were of course out of action. The cage remained out of action at the Low Pit for nine days. In the pit the engine house and stables had caught fire and many of the ponies were found to have suffocated. The hooves of some of them (complete with shoes) were preserved as souvenirs, polished, inscribed and adapted to various uses, such as stands for ink-wells, snuff-boxes and pin-cushions. Fifty four ponies and a cat survived. Further on the rescuers found debris and mutilated human corpses. Body after body was then located in the dark tunnels. Nineteen survivors from the Main Coal seam were brought up the Low Pit shaft which was not blocked at the level of that seam. The main rescue work was done from the High Pit shaft where it was also possible to use a kibble. Forty eight more survivors were brought out this way. Of the 231 workers only 67 had thus been rescued by midnight of the first day, leaving 164 unaccounted for. None of these survived. Some 169 men and boys had been working in the affected seam – only 5 of these survived and were rescued.

The disgusting voyeurism and gawping was just as nauseating:

> The roads into Seaham were completely blocked by people in the next few days. Most of these were simply morbid sight-seers who obstructed the way for the rescue teams despatched from other collieries near and far. Special trains from Sunderland to Seaham for the Flower Show (now cancelled) were instead packed with these 'spectators'. The families of those dead or missing were unable to get anywhere near the colliery. The crowd round the pit reached an estimated 14,000 on the Wednesday night (the day of the explosion). By Sunday there were an estimated 40,000 people in the vicinity to see the first mass funerals.

164 men and boys were dead. The flower of the village had been wiped out. There were thirteen dead from Seaham Street alone. California Street lost twelve, Cornish Street eleven, Australia and Hall Streets ten each. Every single street in the village lost at least two men or boys. Some of the bodies were recovered fairly quickly… the last of the bodies was not recovered until almost exactly a year after the explosion.

It was 82 years later when tragedy struck again. Seaham's first RNLI lifeboat, the Sisters Carter of Harrogate, arrived in Seaham in 1870. William Grainge in his *Annals of Harrogate & Pannal Vol. 2* tells us that it was

> A beautiful lifeboat, built at the cost of the Misses Carter…33 feet in length by 8½ feet wide, and rowed ten oars double banked. It possessed the usual valuable properties of self-righting, and self-ejecting water…The boat was afterwards sent to Seaham in the county of Durham, where a commodious house was erected for it by Earl Vane. This boat has since been the means of saving numbers of mariners from a watery grave.

Tragically, such a 'watery grave' awaited the crew of the RNLB George Elmy (and the men and boy they nearly saved) which washed up on Chemical Beach, just off Dawdon Colliery, on the morning of Sunday 18th November 1962 after capsizing the night before with the loss of nine lives. Over the

previous twelve years George Elmy and her crew had responded to 26 calls rescuing 20 people before she went to the aid of the fishing coble on that fateful night. She rescued all five on board; however, within a boat length of the South Pier a freak wave capsized the lifeboat and all but one of those on board was lost. The station was closed in 1979.
Here is the text inscribed on the memorial stone:

> **Remember the Heroes**
> This memorial is to commemorate the bravery of the five lifeboat men
> who lost their lives when, in the stormy seas on November 17th 1962,
> the Seaham lifeboat *George Elmy* capsized with the loss of it's crew.
> John T Miller (Coxswain), Frederick Gippert (Second Coxswain),
> Arthur Brown, Leonard Brown, James Farrington
> and all but one of the crew of the fishing cobble *Economy*,
> to whose aid the courageous men had gone:
> Gordon Burrwell, George Firth, Joseph Kennedy, David Burrell (aged 9)

California Row here was named after the still topical California Gold Rush while Butcher Row has nothing to do with butchers – it is named after a Mr Butcher who was a mining official. See also Dawdon.

SEATON CAREW

Since the reign of Henry I (r. 1100–35) the resort is named after the Norman French family de Carrowes or Carous, notably Robert de Carew – local landowners in the manor of Owton; Seaton means farmstead by the sea. Setone in 1189, Seton Carrou 1311 and Seton next Stranton 1502. Another coastal town with a remarkable history, Seaton Carew is just south of Hartlepool.

> Families of the first consequence – the peer, the prelate, the knight and the esquire, resort to Seaton. In fact, no place can be more conveniently situated for sea bathing; the salubrity of the air, the hospitable treatment, the cleanliness of the place...all greatly contribute to the gratification of the visitant.

So exaggerated William Tate in his *Description of Hartlepool, Seaton and Stranton* 2nd Ed 1816.
Tate again, condescendingly:

> It is very pleasant to behold numerous parties on the sands some in carriages, others on horseback...the Billiard Table has not found its way to Seaton yet, but the jack-bowls and quoits are frequently practised. Ladies sometimes amuse themselves with collecting sea-shells.

In 1667 a gun emplacement was built on the promontory of Seaton Snook to defend the mouth of the Tees, particularly against the Dutch—remnants of these fortifications can be seen today. In 1866 a riot took place here when the townspeople mistook Irish labourers for Fenian agitators. The Irishmen had come to salvage timber from the beached *Betsy Williams* but the timber failed to reach the shore and so they repaired to the Seaton Hotel. Here they joked with the barmaid that they were armed Fenians. The police were duly summoned and it all ended peacefully but not before the national press reported forces fifty strong marching on West Hartlepool armed to the teeth and causing a riot. As with the Hartlepool 'monkey' a poem celebrates the event:

> Bloodthirsty men with pikes and spears Were sackin' public 'ouses, And plungin' Seaton into tears... At midnight we arrove in haste The Fenians to secure, For Fenians is a kind of thing No Briton will endure.

Shades of misidentified French spies?

In the 18th and 19th centuries Seaton Carew evolved into a seaside resort for wealthy Quaker families from Darlington. From 1916–19 there was an RFC / RAF airstrip on open land to the south of Seaton Carew and seaplanes were stationed at Seaton Channel. This was a detachment of No. 36 Home Defence Squadron of the Royal Flying Corps stationed at RFC Station Cramlington, in Northumberland responsible for defending the north east of England and the Yorkshire coast.

Two German Zeppelin pilots are buried in the graveyard, shot down on 27th November 1916 but not before they had dropped 29 bombs on Hartlepool. A squadron of four Zeppelins attacked targets on the north east coast: *L34* was caught in a searchlight to the west of Hartlepool and Lieutenant Ian Vernon Pyott, the pilot of a Royal Aircraft Factory BE 2C biplane from A flight No. 36 Squadron based at Seaton Carew, on seeing the Zeppelin at about 10,000 feet gave chase for five miles, occasionally firing on the craft. The *L34* caught fire and, engulfed in flames, fell into the sea in Tees Bay with the loss of all crew while the other Zeppelins made their escape—apparently flames were seen as far away as Melton Mowbray.

Golf has been played at Seaton Carew since 1874, making it the tenth-oldest golf club in England. This is acknowledged as one of the most challenging links golf courses anywhere in the British Isles and regularly hosts top amateur championships such as the Brabazon Trophy – the English Amateur Championship.

'Welcome to Seaton Canoe – Twinned with Panama'. So said the sign which appeared on Seaton Lane during the 2007-08 Panama fraud investigation into the faked death of the British former teacher and prison officer John Darwin, who turned up alive in December 2007, five years after he was believed to have died in a canoeing accident.

SEDGEFIELD

Ceddesfeld in 1040 – the open land of a man called Secci; Seggesfeld 1174 and Sedgefielde in 1548. Sedgefield was home to Winterton Hospital, an isolation hospital and an asylum. The site was very much self-contained with its own fire station, bank and cricket team. Each Shrove Tuesday the Shrove Tuesday Ball Game still takes place – an example of Mob Football – or Medieval football, folk football, or Shrovetide football. Essentially, the games were played between neighbouring towns and villages, with an unlimited number of players, who would clash in the struggle to drag an inflated pig's bladder to markers at each end of a town.

SHADFORTH

Just to the east of Durham, this is the only village in England with this name; Shaldeford in 1183, it is from Old English *sceald* and means 'Shallow Ford'. Unusually for the area there has never been a pit in Shadforth.

SHILDON

Eleven miles north of Darlington Shildon, like Darlington and York, is synonymous with the railways in Britain. The name Shildon comes either from the Old English word *sceld*, which means 'shelf shaped hill' or 'shield, refuge'; or from Old English *sycl/fe* meaning 'shelf' and the suffix duri or dun meaning 'hill' which indicates the town's position on a limestone escarpment. This is how it looked before the railways, the Stockton and Darlington Railway no less, came:

> I have known Shildon for fifty years when there was not a house of any sort at New Shildon, much less a Mechanics Institute. When I surveyed the lines of the projected railway in 1821, the site of this New Shildon Works was a wet, swampy field – a likely place to find a snipe, or a flock of peewits. Dan Adamson's was the nearest house. A part of Old Shildon existed, but 'Chapel Row', a row of miner's houses, was unbuilt or unthought of.
>
> —John Dixon, *Bishop Auckland Herald* – 03/09/1863

A passenger service began from Shildon on 27th September 1825. The first train, *Locomotion No.1* started outside the Mason's Arms, the world's first railway station: tickets were sold at the bar and between 1833 and 1841 the company hired a room in the pub for use as a booking office. The railway ran from its northern terminus at Shildon along 27 miles of track to its southern terminus at Stockton. The Soho Engine Works opened in 1833, later to become the Soho Locomotive Building Company. Things started to really move with the opening of Shildon Colliery to the south of the Soho Works in 1873.

But this was no paradise, as the *Northern Echo* bluntly pointed out in its 8th November edition 1875:

> Shildon is one of the ugliest places on the earth's fair surface. It was once a swamp, the malaria from which laid many of its early inhabitants low with fever. It is now a hideous congerie of houses, growing like fungus on either side of a network of rails. A huge colliery rears its ungainly head close to the rails, and the noise of its working ceases not for ever. Engines are plying about with restless activity, like spiders running along the threads of their nets seeking for hapless flies.

The 1911 strike here was particularly shocking and saw violent scenes in the town with troops deployed to maintain order. A driver of a mineral train was stoned and dragged from his engine. He was pursued by an angry mob and had to be rescued by soldiers. Mineral wagons had their bottom doors undone, allowing the contents to spill out. Wagons in the sidings had their brakes undone and freewheeled for miles, railway signal cables were damaged and the cavalry had to be called. At one point soldiers mounted a bayonet charge in order to clear a bridge. Later, things progressed to the point where the Shildon Works became the largest wagon works in the world by 1976, employing 2,600 people. They built 1,000 wagons a year and repaired many more besides. The 27 miles of sidings made Shildon the largest sidings in the world. The works closed in June 1984, with the loss of 1,750 jobs. One glimmer of hope came with the 'Locomotion' railway museum, incorporating the existing Timothy Hackworth Museum as part of the National Railway Museum in York in October 2004.

SHINCLIFFE

'Shincliffe' is first attested in the *Liber Vitae Ecclesiae Dunelmensis* of 1085, where it appears as Scinneclif. It appears in the Charter Rolls of 1195 as Sineclive. The name means 'the cliff of the spectre or demon, haunted cliff' from Old English *scinna* = phantom + *clif*. Durham's first railway station was at Shincliffe in 1839 as the passenger terminus between the Durham area and Sunderland but closed in 1893.

SHINEY ROW

Shiney Row is in Houghton-le-Spring. The name probably means beautiful row (of trees): from Old English *scien raew* – the beautiful row.

SHOTLEY BRIDGE

Shotleybrigg in 1613 – clearing of the Scots from Old English *Scot* + *leah*. This village is adjacent to Consett and is famous for being at the heart of Britain's swordmaking industry. The bed of the river Derwent here was the source of stone for millstones, and licences for this are recorded at "Shotley Brig" in 1356. A water-powered corn mill was established in the 14th century, later replaced by a steam-powered version which was sold to the Derwent Co-operative Flour Mill Society Ltd in 1872, and continued until its closure in 1920. A paper mill opened in 1788 and was the first in the north of England and was by 1894 employing 300 workers half of whom were girls, and closing in 1905. Shotley Bridge had a reputation as a spa: a well produced unpleasant tasting water rumoured to be effective in curing disease and thus known as the "Hally Well" (hally = healthy, as in hale).

In the 17th century a band of swordmakers, Oley, Vooz, Molle and Bertram from Solingen in Germany (the steelmaking equivalent to our Sheffield) arrived and settled in Shotley Bridge as exiles from religious persecution. They chose Shotley Bridge because of the quality of the ironstone and the softness and swiftness of the River Derwent. The Oley family had a reputation as makers of the highest quality swords, using Damascus steel and rivalling those of Toledo. The Napoleonic Wars provided a ready market; they went on to be involved in the formation of the Consett Iron Company. However, they could not compete with Sheffield, so the sword works closed in 1840. Nevertheless members of the family moved to Birmingham, their business eventually became part of Wilkinson Sword.

Evidence of the industry can be seen in Cutlers Hall, 1767 and in the name of the public house The Crown and Crossed Swords. Before the last remaining cottages occupied by the swordmakers were flattened, there was an inscription over the door of the Oley house on Wood Street reading "Das Herren segen machet reich ohn alle Sorg wenn Du zugleich in deinem Stand treu und fleissig bist und tuest alle vas die befolen ist". This translates as "The blessing of the Lord makes rich without care, so long as you are industrious in your vocation and do what is ordered you".

Whinney House opened in 1913 for the care of people with mental issues; it was called "Shotley Bridge Mental Defectives Colony" from 1927 to 1940 when it was converted to an emergency hospital to treat patients in the Second World War; it was particularly noted for its plastic surgery.

SHOTTON AND SHOTTON COLLIERY

In 900 CE old Shotton was known as Sceotton, Old English for, ominously, 'of the Scots', Our first record of the village name came in 1165 as 'Sottun'; by the 16th century, when Easington was under the control of Prince Bishops, the village had become known as Shotton.

In 1833 the Haswell Coal Company sank pits to the west of Old Shotton, near Shotton Grange Farm. The pit was initially prosperous, but closed on 3rd November 1877. In 1900 the pit reopened and grew rapidly, leading to an increased population and overshadowing the coke works and the brick works. In 1972 the colliery closed with the loss of 800 jobs.

RIVER SKERNE

From end of 12th century *schyrna* from Old Scandinavian *skirn* or Old English *scir* = the clear or bright stream.

SNOTTERTON

Near Staindrop where the first record in 1411 names the place as Snotterton – just like today. It means farmstead of a man named Snotter.

SOCKBURN

Soccabyrig in 780, Socceburg in 1050 – the fort of a man called Socca.

Higbald, Bishop of Lindisfarne was crowned at Sockburn in 780 and Eanbald, Archbishop of York, in 796. In the middle ages Sir John Conyers reputedly slayed a dragon or "worm" that was terrorising the district. The stone under which the Sockburn Worm was supposedly buried was until recently still visible;the falchion (the weapon which killed it) is in Durham Cathedral Treasury.

The estate eventually went to the Blackett family, industrialists from Newcastle, who built a new farmhouse in the late 18th century. In 1799 this was occupied by Tom Hutchinson, who once bred a seventeen and a half stone sheep, and his sisters Mary and Sara. The Blacketts were distant relatives of William Wordsworth, who lodged with them for six months in 1799, and eventually married Mary. Coleridge who also stayed there. He fell in love with Sara, but he was already married; his feeling for Sara emerge in his poem *Love*, which references the church and the dragon legend.

Lewis Carroll, whose father was rector at Croft-on-Tees, was inspired by the legend of the Sockburn Worm which re-emerged in his *Jabberwocky*.

SOUTH CHURCH

South Church is a village just south of Bishop Auckland. Despite its small size it forms an important part of County Durham history. William de St. Calais had a major impact on Durham, establishing the Prince Bishops on what has been described 'as the first great northern powerhouse and starting the construction of the magnificent cathedral'. He was instrumental in changing the way the cathedral worked. Previously it had been looked after by clerks of St. Cuthbert, who were old-school monks – secular canons, encumbered with wives and children. William wished it to become a monastic cathedral, populated by celibate Benedictine monks.

In 1083, the secular canons were let go and sent to to live in Darlington, Norton-on-Tees and South Church. At South Church, the canons attached themselves to St. Andrew's Church, and became a college overseen by a dean.

In 1292 Bishop Antony Bek built them a deanery on the south bank of the Gaunless opposite the church – this is the oldest inhabited building in the county – a stronghold designed to withstand even the Scots – unusually and cleverly, it includes an anti-clockwise spiral staircase said to make it harder for right-handed attackers to wield their swords.

In the 1540s, Henry VIII gifted the Deanery to Sir Hugh Ascne who used it as a farmhouse which gradually fell down. It was abandoned in the 1960s; in the 1990s the Deanery became a restaurant and is now a private house.

SOUTH SHIELDS

Historically part of County Durham. Shelis 1296; le Shels 1365. The name South Shields developed from the Middle English *Schele* or *Shield*, which was a small fishermen's or shepherd's dwelling.

The Roman fort of Arbeia has been partially reconstructed based on archaeological excavation: the Roman gatehouse, barracks and commanding officer's house have been reconstructed on their original foundations. Overlooking the Tyne, the fort was founded in 120 CE to guard the main sea route to Hadrian's Wall; later, it was to become a huge maritime supply base providing logistical support for the wall, and, to that end, contains the only permanent stone-built granaries found in Britain. Over 600 troops were stationed there.

Arbeia is as good a place as any to illustrate the thoroughly cosmopolitan and mobile nature of the Roman world. One epigraph commemorates Regina, a British woman of the Catuvellauni tribe, who was first the slave, then the freedwoman and wife of Barates, a merchant from Palmyra (now part of Syria) who, obviously missing her, set up a gravestone after she died at the age of 30. Barates himself is buried at the nearby fort of Coria (Corbridge). Another commemorates Victor, another former slave, freed by Numerianus of the Ala I Asturum, who also arranged his own funeral ('piantissime', with all devotion) when Victor died at the age of 20. The stone records that Victor was 'of the Moorish nation'.

The excellent museum has an altarpiece to a previously unknown god and a tablet with the name of the Emperor Alexander Severus (d. 235 CE) chiselled off. Two more altarstones are of interest: Brigantia was the patron deity of the local British tribe in the area, who was worshipped throughout the iron-age world as Brigit. She was the tripartite goddess of wisdom, also known as the Mother of Memory, a daughter of Dana the iron-age mother goddess.

Soon after the Romans left, as a British settlement the place became a royal residence of King Osric of Deira. Bede tells how Oswin gave land to St. Hilda for the foundation of a monastery here in *c.*647; the present-day church of St. Hilda, by the Market Place, is thought to stand on the monastic site.

The South Shields of today was founded in 1245 and developed as a fishing port. Salt-panning was important too, particularly in the 15th century. In the 19th century, coal mining, alkaline production and glass making led to prosperity in the town. The population mushroomed from 12,000 in 1801 to 75,000 by the 1860s. Shipbuilding was another major industry, with John Readhead & Sons Shipyard being the largest yard.

In the Second World War, the Luftwaffe made South Shields and its people suffer: a bomb shelter in the Market Place of South Shields was the location of many casualties. On the night of 4th October 1941 a German plane dropped its bombs on to the Market Place and nearby rows of terraced houses and strafed the streets with machine gun fire. St. Bede's Junior School received a direct hit, Laygate School was wrecked, Croftons, Woolworths, the Grapes and Black's Regal were hit and Binns was badly damaged. One bomb killed several people and injured many more who were huddled in the air raid shelter. In the end 68 men, women and children lay dead or dying and 117 were seriously injured. More than 2,000 people were made homeless. South Shields lost more seafarers than any other port in Britain during the Second World War.

Since the 1890s South Shields has been home to a Yemeni British community who came to the town as seamen in crews of British merchant vessels. In 1909, the first Arab Seamen's Boarding House opened in the Holborn district of the town. At the end of the First World War, the Yemeni population of South Shields was over 3,000. South Shields had lost one of the largest proportions of Merchant Navy sailors in the war: one in four casualties was of Yemeni background. Disputes over jobs led to race riots – the Arab Riots – in 1919 and 1930. The Bangladeshi community here is the third largest in the north east of England.

Notable South Shields people include Catherine Cookson and Eric Idle. In 1977 Muhammad Ali visited the Al-Ahzar Mosque in Laygate and had his marriage blessed. Ali visited the town after receiving an invitation from a local boys' boxing club. L S Lowry painted a number of artworks in South Shields while staying at the Seaburn Hotel in Sunderland.

People from South Shields are sometimes called Sandancers. This originates from the town's beach and history with the Arabic peoples dating from a 19th century music hall act of the same name.

SPENNYMOOR

Spennymoor is seven miles south of Durham city. Spennymoor is built on what was moorland covered with thorn and whin bushes, hence Spenny Moor. Some believe the name to be derived from the Latin *spina* which means a thorn and *mor*, Anglo-Saxon for a moor. Others suggest the Scandinavian *spaan* meaning shingle-hut and Anglo-Saxon combination involving *mar* – Spennymoor thus being the moor called after the shingle-hut erected thereon. Others still go for *spenning mor* – the moor with a fence, hence Spendingmore in 1336.

Up to 1800 some of the biggest horse-race meetings in the north of England took place on the moor, with miners and their families attending in their holiday best.

When the Wittered Pit was sunk in 1839 shabby houses were built for the workers –with two rooms and a loft, more like "piggeries than human habitation" according to one historian. The coal mining at Whitworth and a small foundry at Merrington Lane were the earliest industries, but in 1853 the Weardale Iron and Coal Company opened its great ironworks at Tudhoe attracting hundreds of immigrant workers from the Midlands, Wales and Lancashire.

Spennymoor was encircled by collieries, belching furnaces and coke ovens and the new prosperity showed itself in the building of better houses and in the opening of Co-operative stores. A National School opened in 1841. A branch railway from the main line at Ferryhill opened in 1876. The horrendous explosion at Tudhoe Colliery in 1882 claimed 37 lives; a thirteen week strike in 1892 brought the area to its knees in 1892, although it did result in the introduction of new machinery at the Tudhoe Iron works and a new mill. The works then could claim to have the largest mill in Europe, capable of rolling plates up to 13 feet in width.

In an area generally noted for its poverty and squalor Spennymoor was notoriously bad. In 1874 the then Local Government Board reported:

> Nothing could well exceed the nuisance attendant on the disposal of excrement and refuse in Spennymoor. There are entire streets without any closet accommodation whatever and in its stead open wooden boxes are placed opposite nearly every doorway for the reception of the excrement, ashes and other refuse; an arrangement which, besides being revolting to every sense of decency, is stated to be offensive in the extreme, especially in hot weather. It is impossible to walk between the rows of cottages without being convinced that the surface of the ground is to a large extent composed of the overflowing contents of these midden boxes. The back streets stand deep in filth and mud.

Not much had changed by 1920 when less than 10% of the town houses had water closets. In 1923 only four houses were built and there was still massive overcrowding in back to back properties. In the next few years only between one and four houses were built in any year and in 1929 the housing situation was still reported as acute. The dawning of the 20th century witnessed depression beginning with the closure in 1901 of the ironworks which was now obsolete. Even before the strike of 1926 the collieries had begun to close. Three closed in 1924 and the strike took another two. In 1930 the coke ovens were only working intermittently. Coulson's engineering works, Kenmir's furniture factory and the newly-opened brickworks at Todhills were now the main sources of employment. Unemployment was over 33%.

The Second World War brought with it the opening in 1941 of a Royal Ordnance Factory at Merrington Lane. On Christmas Eve 1944, Tudhoe's cricket ground took a hit from a rogue V-1 flying bomb, which had been air-launched by a German Heinkel He 111 aimed at Manchester. This was the furthest north any V-1 had landed during the war.

Later, with the coal industry gone manufacturers of consumer goods moved in. Electrolux, Thorn Lighting and Black and Decker opened factories as did Rothmans International employing more than 400 people in Spennymoor from 1980 up until 2000.

The Durham Mining Museum is in Spennymoor Town Hall "dedicated to the memory of more than 24,000 men, women and children who have lost their lives in mining related accidents in the North of England since 1293".

STAINDROP

Derives from Old English Standropa around 1040 from *staener hop* = the valley with stony ground.

Jeremiah Dixon is buried in Staindrop. His unmarked grave is in the Quaker burial ground next to the old Friends' Meeting House. Thomas Pynchon's novel *Mason & Dixon* mentions Staindrop as the location of Jeremiah Dixon's favourite pub.

King Canute gave the manors of Raby and Staindrop to Durham Priory in about 1018. In 1131 Prior Algar granted the manor to an Anglo-Saxon named Dolfin "son of Uhtred", the earliest recorded direct male ancestor of the great Neville family who built Raby Castle as their seat in the north part of the manor.

STAINTON

Old English *stan tun* as in Stanton in the mid 12th century – stone settlement.

Stainton is north east of Barnard Castle, famous for its army camp, one of a group of camps built near Barnard Castle out of range of German bombers at the beginning of the war; the fall of Norway changed all that bringing the area back in range. The local camps held around 20,000 members of the Royal Armoured Corps as well as being a GHQ Battle School.

STANLEY

Stanley is south of Gateshead; the name is derived from the Old English, *stan leah*, for 'stoney field'. John Speed's map of County Durham gives Standley while a 1130 document gives Stanlega.

In 1882 an underground explosion killed thirteen men. However, the West Stanley Pit Disaster, one of the worst coal mining disasters in British history took place in Stanley at West Stanley Colliery on 16th February 1909 when 168 people died in the Burns Pit Disaster.

In 2000 Stanley became famous when local curry house owner Harresh Ramadan turned his Indian takeaway restaurant on Front Street into a fish-and-chip shop and renamed it Harry Ramadan's, a nod to Harry Ramsden's chain, with signage in an identical font and colours. The Harry Ramsden's chain sued…

STARTFORTH

We first hear of Startforth – a village near Barnard Castle – in 1050, when it is Stretford. It is mentioned in *The Domesday Book* of 1086 where it appears as Stradford. The name means 'street-ford', and refers to the paved ford by which the Roman road which passes through the village crosses the River Tees to link the Roman forts of Bowes and Binchester. The paved ford is still visible when the water is low.

STILLINGTON

Stillington means the estate named after Styfel – Stillingtune, 1190 and Stillyngton, 1400. Stillington lies north west of Stockton-on-Tees. In 1866 Samuel Boston founded the Carlton Iron Works and built 111 houses to add to the existing three. In 1932 the original blast furnace was demolished. The company still exists which operates in Stillington under the name of Metabrasive, including North Eastern Iron Refining company, manufactures chilled iron particles and refined iron ingots (pig iron).

STOCKTON-ON-TEES

Stoc tun in 1006, Stoktona 1193 – farmstead of the outlying place. Stockton has its origins with the Anglo-Saxons; it was described in the *Boldon Book* of 1183 as having 'eighteen farms, three families with a cottage but little land, a smith and a ferry across the River Tees'.

Later, Bishop Pudsey of Durham, (Hugh de Puiset c.1125–95), made his residence in Stockton Castle, a glorified, fortified manor house. Our first recorded reference to the castle was in 1376.

> The only reputed relic of the old Castle is a wrought stone, about three feet in length, on which are the figures of two couchant lions. This was formerly built up in the wall of a cow-byer in Hartburn, but was afterwards placed in the grounds of the late Colonel Sleigh at Elton
>
> *An Historical, Topographical, and Descriptive View of the County ..., Volume 2*
> By Eneas Mackenzie, Marvin Ross 1834

King John stayed here in 1200, 1210 and 1212.

During the Civil War Stockton Castle was a Royalist stronghold and in 1640 when a treaty was signed making the Tees a boundary between the forces of Scotland and the English King, the castle stayed in Royalist hands. Scottish forces under the Earl of Callendar finally captured Stockton Castle in 1644 and it was garrisoned by them until 1646. In 1647 the House of Commons gave the order that the castle be 'made untenable and the garrison disgarrisoned'. Only the castle barn – a 'castellated cowhouse' – remained until its demolition in 1865.

Stockton's famous market on the High Street goes back to 1310 when Bishop Bek of Durham granted a market charter in perpetuity – *to our town of Stockton a market upon every Wednesday for ever.*

Hiring fairs were also called mop fairs. They date from the reign of Edward III (r. 1327–77), and his attempt to regulate the labour market by the Statute of Labourers in 1351 in response to the national labour shortage caused by the depredations after the Black Death. Subsequent legislation, in particular the Statute of Apprentices of 1563, legislated for a particular day when the high constables of the shire would proclaim the stipulated rates of pay and conditions of employment for the following year. The fairs acted like a magnet and quickly turned into the place for matching workers and employers. Hiring fairs continued well into the 20th century, up to the Second World War in some places.

Farm workers, labourers, servants and some craftsmen worked for their employer from October to October the following year. At the end of their employment they would go to the mop fair smartly turned out in their Sunday best, carrying an item signifying their trade. A servant with no specific skills would carry a mop head: The 'tassle' everyone wore on their lapel was another emblem of the employee's trade and was known as a 'mop'. Hiring fairs were also known as statute fairs (or statutes) because that was where an Act of Parliament of 1677 endorsed the yearly bonds made between masters and servants. Once agreement was reached the employer would give the employee a small token of money, known as the "fasten-penny," usually a shilling, which "fastened" the contract for a year. The employee would then remove the item signifying their trade and replace it with bright ribbons to indicate they had been hired.

Shipbuilding began in the mid 17th century with 60 ships built between 1780 and 1800; the yards were at Smithfield and near to Stockton Bridge.

In 1718 75 corn ships entered the Port of London from Stockton, more than the combined total from Sunderland and Hartlepool. By the end of the 18th century Stockton had taken over from Yarm as the principal port on the Tees; bigger boats and tides saw to that. In 1767 9,600 tons of grain, 1,400 tons of butter, cheese, pork and ham, 70 tons of ale, 900 tons of alum, and 900 tons of other products left the port. Grain was in decline, though, with 124 ships in and out in 1760, falling to 23 in 1769.

The famous Town House (now known as the Town Hall) was built in 1735; The first factual reference is in *Hatfield's Survey* from 1382, when a plot of land available for the Manor (the site of the Town House) existed on payment of four pennies per year to the Bishops of Durham. The Town House, described as a 'mean building' was in effect the Mayor's house which received rents, tolls, fines and admittances to the market.

History was made here in 1810 for it was at a dinner to celebrate the opening of a new "cut" in the River Tees that Leonard Raisbeck, Recorder of Stockton, first suggested a railway or canal to link Stockton with the "interior country". Fifteen years later, the famous Stockton and Darlington Railway opened and, on 27th September that year, a celebratory dinner took place at the Town Hall after George Stephenson had driven the first train into the town.

In 1771 the Bishop's Ferry was replaced by a five arch stone bridge – the lowest bridging point of the Tees until the Middlesbrough Transporter Bridge opened in 1911.

The Industrial Revolution had a dramatic and pronounced effect on Stockton. The Portrack Iron Works opened in 1806 under Brown and Goundry; Stockton Iron Works had been opened in 1770 by John Jackson in West Row; Fossick and Hackworth started Blair's Engine Works in 1839 producing locomotives and stationary engines. Tees Glass Works opened their bottle factory in 1839.

Nevertheless, it was all about to change, beyond recognition, due to the emergence of Ironopolis nearby: growth in what was to become Middlesbrough was biblical and swift; from the middle of the 19th century Stockton began to decline in the face of Middlesbrough's explosive growth: generally, the area went very quickly from farm to furnace, from cattle to crane.

In 1887, John Bartholomew's *Gazetteer of the British Isles* described Stockton-on-Tees as follows:

> Stockton: manufacturing town, river port, parish and township,, on river Tees, 4 miles from its mouth, 4 miles SW. of Middlesbrough and 236 from London by rail; population 42,242; 4 Banks, 2 newspapers. Market-days Wednesday and Saturday. Stockton was long under the bishops of Durham, one of whom built its castle, which was dismantled after the Civil War, and has now totally disappeared, its last remains having been removed in 1865. Its commerce rose to importance through the decline of Hartlepool about 1683, and was checked by the recent rise of Middlesbrough, but is still large and flourishing. The mfrs. formerly consisted almost exclusively of linen and sailcloth, but the development of the iron mines of Cleveland has led to a rapidly increasing trade in iron smelting and rolling, iron shipbuilding, and the mfr. of iron rails, iron bridges, marine engines, boilers, gasholders, &c. There are also potteries and bottle works. It returns 1 member to Parliament.

The local shipbuilding acted as a magnet for smaller industries such as brick, sailcloth and rope making which is remembered today in local names such as Ropery Street. Just how important rope making was to the town is underlined by the fact that in 1825 1,178 tons of hemp were landed at Stockton. Cotton was important too: a cotton mill was established in 1839 to work this while the Stockton Sugar Refinery had set up at 'Sugar House Open' – the only sugar refinery between Hull and Newcastle.

There was thriving brick-making in Stockton too – bricks were much in demand as towns continued to spring up in the region and with them the urgent need for houses and other community buildings.

Stockton then was the principal port for County Durham, Yorkshire's North Riding and even Westmorland, mainly exporting rope, agricultural produce and lead from the Yorkshire Dales, trading extensively with the Baltic states.

By 1867 there were three blast furnaces, 144 puddling furnaces and six finishing mills in action in Stockton. The companies were Stockton Rail Mill Co; The Malleable Iron Co; Holdsworth & Co; and the West Stockton Iron Co. They were later joined by Pickerings who manufactured lifting gear, Bowesfield Iron & Steel Co; and Lustrum Iron Works amongst others. There were more in Eaglescliffe and Thornaby.

John Walker Strikes a Light – The Man of the Match

A light came on in Stockton in 1827 when local chemist John Walker invented the friction match in his shop at 59 High Street. Walker was born in Stockton in 1781 and was apprenticed to Watson Alcock, the town's principal surgeon. Walker, however, could not stomach the surgery and changed to chemistry. After studying at Durham and York, he returned to Stockton and set up as a chemist and druggist at 59 High Street around 1818.

The discovery of the match was serendipitous: Walker had been routinely selling concoctions of combustible materials in powder form to smokers and to a gunsmith; in 1826 he was experimenting with these combustibles when, by chance, he scraped the mixing stick against his hearth: the stick caught fire. In 1830 enter an intrigued Michael Faraday who came to visit urging Walker to apply for a patent. The reasonably well off Walker did nothing and inevitably a man called Samuel Johnson took out a patent for 'Friction Matches', branding the matches as 'Lucifers'. The devil, as ever, is in the detail.... Walker died in 1859 aged 78 *sans brevet* and is buried in St. Mary's Church in Norton.

Thomas Sheraton – furniture maker with no furniture

Thomas Sheraton, famous furniture designer, was born in the town in 1751 where he served his time before moving to London. Sheraton achieved no fame during his lifetime and died in poverty. A pub on Bridge Road bears his name. He authored a number of what came to be regarded as bibles for furniture designers: in 1791 the influential four volume *The Cabinet Maker's and Upholsterer's Drawing Book* was published. In 1803 he released the cutting edge *Cabinet Dictionary* a definitive rule book on the techniques of cabinet and chair making; in 1805 he released the first volume of *Cabinet Maker, Upholsterer and General Artist's Encyclopaedia*. Sheraton himself never made any of the pieces described and depicted in his books and no surviving pieces of furniture can be credited to him directly. So, a 'Sheraton' always denotes the design and not the maker. He died in Broad Street in 1806 of 'phrenitis', an inflammation of the brain accompanied by fever and delirium, leaving his wife Margaret and their two children in poverty.

Sheraton was forever the bridesmaid to the likes of Otley's Chippendale, just as his hometown was to become bridesmaid to Middlesbrough.

SUNDERLAND

Historically a County Durham place, Sunderland is one of three contiguous settlements at the mouth of the River Wear. On the north bank, Monkwearmouth was settled in 674 when King Ecgfrith of Northumbria gifted land to Benedict Biscop to found Monkwearmouth Monastery. In 685, Ecgfrith further granted Biscop the land adjacent to the monastery on the south side of the river. With the river in between it was henceforth referred to as the "sunder-land", a separate land; from Old English *sundor land*. It would grow as a fishing settlement before being granted a charter in 1179. The medieval village of Bishopwearmouth was founded in 930 to the west of Sunderland. Sunderland flourished as a port shipping coal and salt. Shipbuilding sprang up on the river in the 14th century. By the 19th century, the port of Sunderland had swallowed up Bishopwearmouth and Monkwearmouth, thanks to the shipbuilding.

Sunderland can claim to have, at one time, been the "Largest Shipbuilding Town in the World", with ships under construction from at least 1346 onwards and the mid-18th century. By 1815 it was 'the leading shipbuilding port for wooden trading vessels' with 600 ships constructed that year across 31 different yards. By 1840 the town had 76 shipyards and between 1820 and 1850 the number of ships being built on the Wear increased fivefold. From 1846 to 1854 almost a third of the UK's ships were built in Sunderland. One particularly famous vessel was the *Torrens*, the clipper in which Joseph Conrad sailed, and on which he began his first novel *Almayer's Folly* in 1895.

During the Second World War the Wear yards launched 245 merchant ships totalling 1.5 million tons, a quarter of the merchant tonnage produced in the UK during the war. The last shipyard in Sunderland closed on 7th December 1988.

And then there was coal. Sunderland was part of the Durham coalfield; at its peak in 1923, 170,000 miners were employed in County Durham but as demand for coal declined following the Second World War, mines began to close across the region, causing mass unemployment. The last coal mine closed in 1994. The site of the last coal mine, Wearmouth Colliery, is now occupied by the Sunderland AFC Stadium of Light, and a miner's Davy lamp monument stands outside of the ground to honour the site's mining heritage. Archives relating to the region's coal mining heritage are stored at the North East England Mining Archive and Resource Centre (NEEMARC).

James Hartley & Co., established in Sunderland in 1836, grew to be the largest glassworks in the country and produced much of the glass used in the construction of the Crystal Palace in 1851. A third of all UK plate glass was coming out of Hartley's by this time. Other manufacturers included the Cornhill Flint Glassworks established at Southwick in 1865, which went on to specialise in pressed glass, as did the Wear Flint Glassworks which had originally been established in 1697. In addition to the plate glass and pressed glass manufacturers there were sixteen bottle works on the Wear in the 1850s, with the capacity to produce between 60,000 and 70,000 bottles a day. In 1855 John Candlish opened a bottleworks, producing glass bottles, with six sites at nearby Seaham and at Diamond Hall, Sunderland.

Overseas competition accelerated the closure of of Sunderland's glass-making factories. Corning Glass Works, in Sunderland for 120 years, closed in 2007; that same year the Pyrex manufacturing site also shut its doors. There has been some rejuvenation with the opening of the National Glass Centre which provides international glass makers with working facilities and a shop to showcase their work, predominantly in the artistic rather than functional field.

Vaux Breweries was established in the town in the 1880s and for 110 years was a major employer; the brewery was finally closed in July 1999.

Victoria Hall was the scene of a tragedy on 16th June 1883 when 183 children died. During a variety show, children rushed towards a staircase to get their treats. At the bottom of the staircase, the door had been opened inward and bolted in such a way as to leave only a gap wide enough for one child to pass at a time. The children surged down the stairs and those at the front were trapped and crushed by the weight of the seething crowd behind them. The suffocation of 183 children aged between three and 14 is the worst disaster of its kind in British history. The memorial, a grieving mother holding a dead child, is in Mowbray Park. Newspaper coverage triggered a mood of national outrage and an inquiry recommended that public venues be fitted with a minimum number of outward opening emergency exits, which led to the invention of 'push bar' emergency doors. Victoria Hall remained in use until 1941 when it was destroyed by a German bomb.

During the Second World War German bombing claimed the lives of 267 people, caused damage or destruction to 4,000 homes, and devastated local industry.

TANTOBIE
Tantobie is a former colliery village two miles north west of Stanley; the etymology is uncertain although the ending may be Old Norse *by* "village", "farm", as in Lockerbie and Formby. To the east is a housing estate named 'Sleepy Valley'.

THORNLEY
Known as Thornhlawa in 1071 – the name derives from Old English thorn hlaw, the place that is the thorn tree hill or mound. There was a castle here in the early Middle Ages. Thornley is five miles west of Peterlee and is a former mining town. The first shaft was sunk here in 1835 and the first coal was delivered by a new mineral railway line to Hartlepool soon after. Thornley, therefore, played a major role in the development of Hartlepool as a port. Thornley miners also played a key role in the formation of the Durham Miners' Association, the first meeting of which was held in the grounds of the village's Half-Way House public house in 1869. The colliery closed in 1970 with the loss of over 900 jobs.

There is another Thornley, in Weardale, about one mile south of Tow Law.

THORPE THEWLES
Thorpe Thewles lies between Stockton-on-Tees and Sedgefield; Thorpe Thewles was originally settled in 1692 with only two farmhouses but has grown to have more than 182 households today. *Thorpe* is a Danish word which means farm, while Thewles was the name of a family that owned land hereabouts in the Middle Ages. The earliest record is 'Thorpp' Thewles' in 1265. The surname Thewles probably comes from the Old English *theawleas* 'immoral', though the meaning of the placename is the farm of the Thewles Family rather than, as sometimes recorded, the Immoral Farm.

TORONTO
Toronto is just to the north west of Bishop Auckland. The village is named after Toronto, Canada, derived from the Mohawk word *tkaronto*, meaning "place where trees stand in the water". A coal baron, WC Stobart, was visiting the Canadian city when he was told that coal had been discovered under his estate back home. He called the mine Toronto, and the village took its name.

TOWDY POTTS
Near Wolsingham, Thottypotts in 1545 from *totty* – quaking grass + *pot*, a hole or pitt.

TOW LAW

This interestingly named place is to the south of Consett and gets its name from the Old English *tot hlaw* meaning "lookout mound"; we get Tollawe in 1424. Tow Law House was the name of the solitary house which stood there predating the iron works and the village. By 1851 the population of the town was almost 2,000. By the early 1870s the population was 4,968 reaching a peak in 1881 of 5,005 inhabitants.

Charles Attwood lived in the house; in 1845 he established an iron works near to this solitary house to exploit the iron ore in upper Weardale and the coal reserves in and around Tow Law. Six blast furnaces were the result, built for for the "Weardale Iron and Coal Company". A large colliery was sunk to the north of the area named 'Black Prince'. The merchant-banking house of Baring Brothers bankrolled the expansion of the Tow Law Iron Works.

One of the specialities at Tow Law was the manufacture of rails and chairs for the railways, not just in the UK but, unsuccessfully, in the US too. The end of the Tow Law Iron Works came in 1882 when all production of the iron and steel moved to the Tudhoe works at nearby Spennymoor. The mining continued and at its peak Black Prince employed over 600 men working four coal seams; over 1,000 men had been employed at the iron works. The last deep mine in the town, 'Inkerman', closed in 1969.

During the Crimean War of 1853 cannon balls fired were made from Tow Law iron; the hamlet to the east of the town called Inkerman takes its name from the Battle of Inkerman.

Joseph Bond carried on the iron making in the town. He had the enterprise to establish his Castle Foundry and Patent Steel Works in 1868. They are still going as are the steel works of George Blair and Company, founded in 1941 just to the north of Tow Law.

The town is mentioned in the Mark Knopfler song *Hill Farmer's Blues* on his album *The Ragpicker's Dream*.

TRIMDON, TRIMDON COLLIERY and TRIMDON GRANGE

Tremeldona in 1196; Tremedun in 1183 meaning hill with a wooden cross – Old English *treo-mael* + *dun*. Reference is to a wooden preaching cross which predated the church.

At 14.40 on 16th February 1882 Trimdon Grange Colliery was afflicted by a major explosion resulting in the deaths of 69 men and boys. It is interesting to paraphrase the coroner's (TW Snagge) report to both Houses of Parliament; it tells us a lot about mining in the Durham coalfield and its ever-present dangers:

> The mine was a dusty mine and watering should have been daily but it was done "not in all places, but where it was absolutely necessary." The mine was not "more than ordinarily gassy", but there is some evidence that the identified points of leakage might have been points of accumulation from leaks elsewhere.
>
> The lamps in use were Davy pattern and naked lights called "midgies" in some areas. The coroner found no evidence that the midgies were connected with the explosion. [Miners in the north eastern pits have traditionally preferred the Geordie lamp which incorporates a glass inner tube through which the flame cannot be blown].
>
> Good order and discipline prevailed in Trimdon Grange Colliery.
>
> The air pressure had been exceptionally low, the lowest it had been that month, falling to 29.10 inches of mercury (985 mbar) on the morning of the explosion.[Low air pressure will encourage gas to leak out of the seams]. The roof above the workings in the narrow pit district had been observed to be dangerous.
>
> There is no room for doubt that the explosion had its origin in the Pit Narrow Board District, and that it was caused by the diffusion of a sudden "squeeze" or outburst of gas forced, with accompanying dust, towards the working face by a heavy fall of roof over the northern edge of the Pit Narrow Board goaf, and driven out with a velocity which sent the flame through a miner's lamp.
>
> The result of this inquiry is a further proof, if further proof were needed, that the Davy lamp affords no security whatever against the occurrence of grave disasters of a similar kind, and that its employment in dusty mines during long-wall working operations, carried on under conditions of ventilation and roof formation similar to those prevailing in Trimdon Grange Colliery, ought to be absolutely prohibited.
>
> Not all the men were killed by the explosion and fire. After the explosion the burnt methane (firedamp) forms carbon dioxide (then called carbonic acid gas) and carbon monoxide. The resulting mixture is called afterdamp and will suffocate and kill. Indeed, the gas forced its way through a passage into the adjoining Kelloe Pit where six men died from the afterdamp.

UNTHANK

It seems that Unthank has always been Unthank, even in 1254. It comes from Old English *unthanc* which means the land held without consent – ancient squatters. Alternatively it could mean land that was not very giving, as ungrateful or stubborn.

There is a tradition of place names demeaning unproductive land; for example Carry Nothing, Dear Bought, Little Grace, Mount Poverty, Never No, Small Gains. The opposite is found in Thanky Furlong. In *Buddenbrookes* Thomas Mann's character lives on an estate called *Ungnade* – thankless. Why? 'Because it did not bring in a penny's income.

URLAY NOOK

Lurlehou in 1220; Lurelau in 1250, Urley 1614; Early Nooke 1739. All mean Lurla's hill spur from Old English *Lurla + hoh* and then law from Old English *hlaw*, a hill.

URPETH

Urpath in 1183 and Urpeth meaning bison's path from Old English *ur*, bison + *paeth*. Or, more likely, the wild ox Urus or Aurochs (*bos primigenius*) as described by Julius Caesar (100–44 BCE), in *The Gallic War*, when spotted in southern Germany; Caesar tells us about Germans living in the semi-mythological Hercynian Forest full of oxen with horns in the middle of their foreheads, elks without joints or ligatures, and uri who kill every man they encounter.

Urpeth is near Beamish. Urpeth Colliery was owned by the Birtley Iron Company and during its heyday employed 300 men and boys. The on-site coke ovens churned out up to 470 tons of coke every day. More recently Urpeth had the dubious privilege of hosting a controversial landfill site used for the disposal of low level radioactive waste along with three other sites at Kibblesworth, Ryton and Cowpen Bewley. However, in the late 1990s the site was closed and a methane burner now stands sentinel there.

USHAW MOOR

Ushaw Moor is a former pit village on the north bank of the River Deerness to the west of Durham. The name 'Ushaw' is Scandinavian from *wulf scaga* and means 'wolves' wood', so, with the addition of moor we find ourselves at 'the moor near the wood of wolves'. It was Ulveskake in the 12th century. There are variant eytmologies: the first tells us Ushaw comes from *Yew-shaw*, Old English for a yew tree wood. Yew trees were brought by the French to England to plant around the graves of their dead. This wood was eventually cut down for firewood and to make bows and arrows: only one tree survived; which stood in the grounds of Ushaw College, eventually rotting away with age. Other spellings are Ushshaw, Usshaw, Ushoa. In 1183, according to the *Boldon Buke*, Ulf held 60 acres in the manor of Lanchester for which he paid fifteen shillings, ran the bishop's errands, and with one hound attended the great hunt in Weardale. This gives us Ulvskahe then Ulfshaw. It was Ulveskake in the 12th century.

In 1804 Bishop William Gibson ordered the building of St. Cuthbert's College, now Ushaw College, which opened in 1808. A chapel was added in 1847, as well as a library and exhibition hall. In 1858 a drift mine was established at Ushaw Moor Colliery selling coal on the landsale system. This was purchased in 1879 by Henry Chaytor of Witton Castle.

Ushaw College closed in 2011; it was a Roman Catholic seminary and one of the constituent colleges of the University of Durham.

Father Fortin introduced education to the mining population of the Deerness Valley, in 1874 erecting a corrugated shack near Ushaw Moor Colliery naming it St. Joseph's School. Both Catholic and Protestant children paid one penny each Monday for their education – an early fee-paying school. The school officially held 100 but had an average attendance of 130. With the closing of the 'tent school'as it was called during the strike in 1882, the Catholic children then attended the school at Newhouse, Esh Winning, transported there each morning by horse-drawn brake. The fare was six pence per week although each evening the children walked back to Ushaw Moor. In 1898 the school was dismantled and shipped to Newhouse where it was re-erected and repurposed as the first Newhouse Working Men's Club.

VINOVIUM
See Piercebridge.

WACKERFIELD
Wackerfield is close to Staindrop and was Wacarfeld in 1040, Wakerfeld in 1283 – meaning open ground growing with osiers from Old English *wacor* + *feld*.

WALWORTH
Walworth and Walworth Gate are thought to be on the line of the Roman road, Dere Street north west of Darlington. The village is triangular, with Walworth Castle and Walworth Park as its focus. North Farm and the lost settlement of Walworth are at the north corner; Castle Farm and Tomtit Wood are at the south west corner, and Walworth Grange at the south east corner. Walworth Castle is a large, 16th century mansion built in the style of a medieval castle and is now a hotel.

The name "Walworth" means Welsh settlement from Old English *walh* + *worth*; it was known as Waleberge in Saxon days. Walworth may have been planned as a village with the previous castle around 1150 by the Hansard family as part of their 1,100 acres estate. Malcolm III of Scotland probably sacked the village on his way along the River Tees.

WASHINGTON
Historically in County Durham, Washington is equidistant from Newcastle, Durham and Sunderland. Washington DC in the USA is named after our Washington which was designated a new town in 1964, absorbing parts of Chester-le-Street.

An early Old English reference from around 1096 was Wasindone but the etymology is disputed and confused with some asserting that Wasindone means people of the hill by the stream, 1096, or Wassyngtona is the settlement of Wassa's people, 1183. However, the origin of most support is that Washington is derived from Anglo-Saxon *Hwæsingatūn*, which means "estate of the descendants (family) of Hwæsa". Hwæsa (Wassa or Wossa in modern English) is an Old English name meaning "wheat sheaf".

William de Wessyngton was a forebear of George Washington. Though George Washington's great-grandfather John Washington emigrated to Virginia from Hertfordshire, Washington Old Hall was the family home of George Washington's ancestors. American Independence Day is marked each year by a ceremony at Washington Old Hall.

The parents of Gertrude Bell, Sir Isaac Bell and his wife Margaret, lived in Washington New Hall on The Avenue. After Margaret's death in 1871, Sir Isaac established an orphanage in the house, named Dame Margaret Home in his late wife's honour. It later became a Barnardo's home until the Second World War.

Coal mining apart Washington supported a chemical industry – the Washington Chemical Works was a major employer in the 19th century. This later became the Cape – Newalls Works, which produced insulating materials.

The North East of England Japanese Saturday School (北東イングランド補習授業校 Hokutō Ingurando Hoshū Jugyō Kō), a Japanese weekend supplementary school, holds its classes in the Oxclose Community School in Oxclose. Car makers Nissan obviously has an influence here.

Gertrude Bell was born at Washington Hall. Bryan Ferry comes from Washington and attended Washington Grammar School, now Washington School; Heather Mills, one time wife of Paul McCartney, attended Usworth Grange Primary School and Usworth Comprehensive School.

WEST AUCKLAND
West of Bishop Auckland, West Auckland possesses one of the largest village greens in the country, lined with 17th and 18th century buildings.

West Auckland Town FC is the 'Home of the First World Cup': its football team was the winner of the Sir Thomas Lipton Trophy, one of the first international footballing competitions, in its two initial years 1909 and 1911 and were, therefore, by the rules of the competition, awarded the trophy to keep in perpetuity.

The Trophy was instigated by Sir Thomas Lipton, who wanted to establish a competition between the leading football clubs of Europe. The football associations of Italy, Germany and Switzerland duly complied. The Football Association of England refused to nominate a club and approached Woolwich Arsenal FC instead, addressing the invitation to WA AFC. The letter was sent to the wrong team, West Auckland AFC, and so a group of coal miners pawned their belongings and made the journey to Turin.

They beat Stuttgarter Sportfreunde in the semi-finals 2–0; in the final, on 12th April 1909, West Auckland faced Swiss side FC Winterthur and beat them 2–0 to win the trophy. Two years later, West Auckland beat FC Zürich 2–0, and won 6–1 in the final against Juventus. The story was made into a TV film in 1982 called *The World Cup: A Captain's Tale*.

The club was forced to pawn the trophy to the landlady of the local hotel on their return home because of financial difficulties. It remained with her family until 1960 when a village appeal raised money to return the cup to the club. It was stolen in 1994 and despite the efforts of the police and a £2,000 reward was never found. A replica now resides in the West Auckland Working Men's Club.

WHAGGS

Near Whickham and Gateshead, we get Whagge in 1674 from Old English *cwagga* and *cwabba* meaning bog.

WHAM

Near Hamsterley it is Quwam and Qwhom in 1315 and Whom, le Whamshele in 1382 from Old English *hwamm*, the name of a shieling. There is a Wham in Yorkshire near Giggleswick.

WHICKHAM

Whickham was Quicham in 1196 and Wicham in 1354 and probably derives from the Old English *cwic hege* or *ham* – the homestead with a quickset hedge.

WHITBURN

Whitburn is halfway between South Shields and Sunderland, in the ceremonial county of Tyne and Wear, but historically part of County Durham. A record gives Wituberne in 1182; Whitborn in 1385. The "Whit" is the Old English word *hwit* meaning "white"; the "burn" component may come from the Northern English term *burna* meaning a stream, or it may be a corruption of "barn" from *bern*. Whitburn is listed in the *Boldon Buke* of 1183 as "Whitbern".

Following the Spanish Armada attack on England in 1588, the defeated Spanish fleet dispersed up the east coasts of England and Scotland. Two Spanish galleons ran aground on Whitburn Rocks in rough seas and local inhabitants duly plundered the wreckage. The bell from one of the galleons was salvaged and installed in Whitburn Church. Spanish oak beams removed from the shipwrecks could still be viewed in the roof of the Whitburn lawnmower shop in the 1950s before it was demolished.

In 1874 Marsden Pit was sunk; Whitburn Colliery closed in 1968. Lewis Carroll wrote *The Walrus and the Carpenter* while on holiday at his cousins' house in Whitburn; there is statue of Carroll in the library. Gone are the days when Whitburn supported three pubs: The Grey Horse (now closed) on North Guards, the Jolly Sailor on Front Street and the Whitburn Lodge (closed) on the Coast Road, formerly part of the former Whitburn Colliery buildings.

WHITWORTH

Qwyteworth in 1293 meaning Hwita's enclosure.

Whitworth is close to Spennymoor, the most prominent building being Whitworth Hall (now a hotel). The house was the home of the Shafto family, whose most famous member, from the 18th century, was Bobby Shafto, of English nursery rhyme fame: "Bobby Shafto's Gone to Sea" (*Roud Folk Song Index* #1359).

Robert Shafto (1732–97) was a Tory politician between 1760 and 1790. He was educated at Westminster School and Balliol College, Oxford and became one of the two members for County

Durham in 1760, using his nickname "Bonny Bobby Shafto" and the now famous song in his electioneering. The song tells how he broke the heart of Bridget Belasyse of Brancepeth Castle, County Durham, where his brother Thomas was rector, when he married Anne Duncombe of Duncombe Park in Yorkshire. Bridget Belasyse is said to have died two weeks later of a broken heart after hearing the news, although the crueller reality is that she died a fortnight before the wedding, of pulmonary tuberculosis.

> Bobby Shafto's gone to sea, Silver buckles at his knee; He'll come back and marry me, Bonny Bobby Shafto! Bobby Shafto's bright and fair, Combing down his yellow hair; He's my love for evermore, Bonny Bobby Shafto!

His supporters added a verse for the 1761 elections with the lyrics:

> Bobby Shafto's looking out, All his ribbons flew about, All the ladies gave a shout, Hey for Bobby Shafto!

Bobby Shafto is top of the pops at Imperial College, London, School of Medicine Squash Club where all members of the club claim to be descended from Bobby.

WILLINGTON

Willington is a former mining village on the River Wear close to Crook, Bishop Auckland and Durham City. It was Wyvelintum around 1190 which means the estate of a man called Wifel, or the estate at Wifeling. Nothing to do with beetles (Old English *Wifel*, beetle) as has previously been suggested.

George Burdon McKean was born in the village in 1888, before moving to Canada in 1902. He was a very brave and highly decorated man, who came back to England in the First World War in the Canadian Expeditionary Force. His first gallantry award was as an NCO, in 1917, when he won the Military Medal. A year later, as a commissioned officer, he took part in a trench raid for which he was awarded the Victoria Cross. He was one of a small number of soldiers to be awarded both the Military Medal and the Military Cross – having served as a both a junior rank and an officer.

The Lion & Unicorn pub reminds us of the proximity of the border with Scotland – the lion is England, the unicorn Scotland.

WINGATE

Seven miles north west of Hartlepool this former pit village expanded rapidly with the advent of coal mining in the region. The name Wingate derives from the Anglo-Saxon words *windig* (windy) and *geat* (road) meaning windy road.

In 1906, a mine explosion killed 26 pit workers in Wingate. Four other men – Maddison, Bloomfield, Elliott and Dixon received injuries that probably caused their deaths from the force of the explosion itself. The deaths of all the others were attributed to after-damp or chokedamp. Evidence showed, and expert witnesses agreed, that the explosion was of coal dust and air.

This report on the disaster is extracted from www.dmm.org.uk/pitwork/html/wingate.htm

> All the bodies of the victims were recovered, except that of Elliott, and rescue of the surviving miners were completed by 9 a.m. on Tuesday the 16th October. The body of Elliott was only found after a long search, but it was surmised that he might have been blown into the downcast shaft, and his body was eventually found in the sump of that shaft on October 23rd.
>
> In the stables in the Low Main seam 56 horses and ponies were killed, all appear to have sunk down quietly and died from inhaling afterdamp; except for two near the engine plane whose bodies indicated some struggling.

These are just a few of the fatalities with cause of death from the list at the same source:

> Ainsley, James. 20 years of age, occupation Pumper. Choke damp. Carbonic acid.
> Bloomfield, George. 41, occupation Shifter. Injuries: Fractured skull, singed and other injuries.

Maddison, John Thomas. 24 years of age, occupation Stoneman. Burns by flame. Broken neck, Pieces of coal in face.

WITTON GILBERT

Witton Gilbert is situated to the north west of Durham close to the River Browney. It is a medieval town with Saxon origins. Witton was originally spelled Witun (*wit* meaning white house and *tun* meaning fortified place). "Gilbert" was added later and refers to the Norman lord Gilbert de la Ley, a 12th century landowner, or maybe a later lord Gilbert de la Latone.

Around 1175 Gilbert de la Ley, Lord of the Manor and tenant of the Bishop of Durham, financed the building of a leper hospital which originally admitted five lepers, soon increasing to eight. The hospital had its own chapel and continued to operate until the dissolution of the monasteries when the inmates were evicted to fend for themselves. The hospital was converted to a farmhouse and is still in use.

Nearby collieries employed numerous workers, many of whom settled in Witton Gilbert, so that the population reportedly increased to about 4,400 persons in 1896. Some of England's first council houses were built here at the beginning of the 20th century.

WOLSINGHAM

Wolsingham is in Weardale, by the River Wear, between Crook and Stanhope. It is one of the earliest market towns in County Durham, getting its name from Waelsingas, or Sons of Wael, an ancient Saxon family that once lived there. Wulsyngham in 1183. Alternatively, homestead at Wulsing, a place named after Wulfsige. The earliest known record of the town comes in Reginald of Durham's *Life of Godric* which records that the saint lived there for almost two years *circa* 1120 CE with Elric the hermit.

The bishops' hunting forest here was the second largest in England after the New Forest. The former Pack Horse Inn was where Edward III rested on returning from his unfruitful encounter with the Scots in Weardale in 1327. Charles II is reputed to have ridden his horse up the internal staircase of the house.

Charles Attwood built an ironworks – a major employer from 1864, producing steel from Weardale iron ore. Steel castings were produced for use in shipbuilding and munitions. Attwood built his home Holywood Hall, which after his death became a hospital – the regional sanatorium for the treatment of tuberculosis with open verandah rooms. 1962 saw the transfer of elderly patients from Sedgefield Mental Hospital to Hollywood. The patients were mainly elderly, long-term residents of impaired mental faculty, who had no living relatives to care for them and were 'institutionalised' and would have been unable to cope with independent living.

Local residents have included botanist David Bellamy and Neil Tennant of the Pet Shop Boys.

WOLVISTON

Wolviston is to the north of Billingham. The village name is Saxon (Oluestona in 1091 and Wluestuna in the 12th century) although people like to think that it was named after the local wolf packs. More likely it derives from Wulfestun – or Wulf's (Uluf's) estate – an early landowner. Another possibility is that it is from a local Saxon dignitary named Wolvis.

WOOLEY HILL

Near Cockfield.

Situated to the south west of Evenwood the Randolph Colliery was opened in 1893. The colliery and its associated coke ovens attracted the attention of Zeppelin *L16* on the night of the 5/6th April 1916. *L16* had orders to bomb Leeds but had drifted off course in the dark and mistook the smoke and glow of the colliery and its coke works for the city.

The coke ovens at Trimdon Grange. Coke is made by heating coal in an oxygen free environment. This forces the oily components and impurities from the coal out leaving behind a carbon rich residue or coke. It is an excellent fuel for iron smelting because the lack of impurities prevents it from contaminating the metal.

The Rivers of County Durham

RIVER BALDER
The Balder rises on the eastern slope of Stainmore Common in the Pennines and flows eastwards for about thirteen miles to join the River Tees at Cotherstone.

RIVER BROWNEY
Aqua de Brun in 1125 and Brune Flumen in 1170; both mean brown waters, *ea* being Old English water. The River Browney is the largest tributary of the River Wear. It rises from a spring in Head Plantation, on the eastern slope of Skaylock Hill, about a mile south east of Waskerley. It flows eastwards towards Lanchester and continues eastwards past Langley Park and Witton Gilbert before skirting the western edge of Durham. The Browney is joined by the River Deerness north of Langley Moor and finally joins the Wear south of Durham, close to Sunderland Bridge.

The Browney suffered badly from industrial contamination, particularly lead and coal mining, but has recovered in recent years. The river was stocked with around 3,000 grayling in 2006.

It has been argued that the river name forms the first element of 'Brunanburh', as in the Battle of Brunanburh; 'Brunanburh' is 'stronghold of the Browney', referring to the Roman fort of Longovicium.

[Breeze, Andrew (2014-12-04). "Brunanburh in 937: Bromborough or Lanchester?". *Society of Antiquaries of London: Ordinary Meeting of Fellows*].

RIVER DEERNESS
The River Deerness is a tributary of the River Browney, itself a tributary of the River Wear. It rises near Tow Law and descends through the Deerness Valley for 11½ miles passing Waterhouses, Ushaw Moor and Esh Winning. The Roman road Dere Street passes through Ragpath Woods to cross the river as it heads northwards to the site of the Roman fort at Lanchester.

Its confluence with the River Browney is near Langley Moor. In 1197 it is Diuerness then Dernesse in 1418 from Primitive Welsh *dubr* + pre-Celtic river name *ness*, as in Loch Ness and Inverness. Its name means 'rushing or roaring river'. It contends for the title of the oldest place name in County Durham.

As mine after mine opened the sparse population of the valley increased significantly, with labour converging from Durham, Cumberland, Northumberland and Westmorland, as well as from other areas of England and Wales. There were also a number of Irish emigrants, fleeing the famines of the 1840s and 1850s. There were no facilities for these workers, so the mine owners built housing, first of wood, but gradually replaced by brick and stone dwellings. Schools, chapels and shops followed. While villages such as Waterhouses were praised at the time with their garden plots, Miners' Institute, school and Co-operative Store, sanitation, as ever, was an issue, resulting in outbreaks of typhoid and scarlet fever in the 1890s. There was also a long-running strike at Ushaw Moor from 1881 to 1883, with workers evicted from their houses which were then promptly boarded up. Most of the mines closed in the 1950s and 1960s, with the last one being at Esh Winning, which closed in 1968.

RIVER DERWENT
The River Derwent flows between the borders of County Durham and Northumberland and into the Derwent Reservoir, west of Consett. The 35 mile long Derwent is a tributary of the River Tyne, which it joins near Gateshead.

Derewenta in 1138; Dyrwente in 1758, the name Derwent comes from the Brythonic/Early Welsh word for oak *derw* and valley *–went*; alternatively water *dour / der/ dar* and white – *went*. So, oak tree river or white water.

RIVER GAUNLESS
The River Gaunless received its name from the no-nonsense Vikings. They found nothing to commend it or any use for it so they named it Gaunless, meaning 'useless'.

Its source is just south of the village of Copley, by the confluence of Arn Gill (to the south, coming west from south of Langleydale Common) and Hindon Beck (to the north and coming east from Langleydale Common). The Gaunless goes east, passing the settlements of Butterknowle, Cockfield and through West Auckland before skirting Bishop Auckland on its way to join the River Wear.

The Gaunless Viaduct, built in 1825, however, was much more useful and productive than the river it spans. At the time it was the highest viaduct on the South Durham & Lancashire Union Railway. Also known as the 'Lands Viaduct', it carried the South Durham and Lancashire Union Railway between Bishop Auckland and Barnard Castle over the River Gaunless at Lands. It opened on 1st August 1863, at a cost of £15,422. It was 161 feet high with a total span of 640 feet.

The viaduct played a crucial role in the transportation of ore and coal to the foundries and ports at Hartlepool and Teesside.

RIVER GRETA

A tributary of the River Tees it rises in the Pennines and drains Spittal Ings, Roper Castle (or Round Table) and Beldoo Moss to the east of Moudy Mea, before flowing east through Stainmore Forest. The river eventually reaches Bowes, where, at the site of the Roman fort of Lavatrae, the Pennine Way traverses it. The Greta has been made world famous through the work of John Sell Cotman and Turner.

RIVER SKERNE

From end of 12th century *schyrna* from Old Scandinavian *skirn* or Old English *scir* = the clear or bright stream.

The Skerne is 25 miles long and rises between Trimdon and Trimdon Grange and ends at Hurworth Place where it joins the River Tees. Three miles from the source the Skerne enters Hurworth Burn Reservoir near Stockton-on-Tees; it then heads south west towards Sedgefield, flows between Fishburn and Sedgefield as "the fish-stream" that gives Fishburn its name.

RIVER TEAM

Tame in 1127 and Tayme in 1485. The River Team is a tributary of the River Tyne in Gateshead. Team may have an origin from the Brittonic root tā-, meaning "melting, thawing, dissolving". The river was once one of the most polluted rivers in the area due to the discharges from sewage works near Lamesley and heavy industry in the Team Valley. It is called "The Gut" by the residents of Dunston.

RIVER TEES

The River Tees rises on the eastern slope of Cross Fell in the North Pennines at 2,401 feet, and flows eastwards for 85 miles reaching the North Sea between Hartlepool and Redcar. The name Tees is possibly of Brittonic origin. The element *tēs* meaning "warmth", even "boiling, excitement" *Teihx-s*, a root possibly derived from Brittonic *ti* (Welsh tail, "dung, manure" may also explain the name Tees. Thesa in 1026, Tese in 1100. Before the 1974 reorganisation the river formed the boundary between County Durham and Yorkshire.

Before the heavy industrialisation of the lower reaches of the Tees, the flats at Seal Sands in the estuary were home to common seals. For around 100 years this species was absent from the estuary but have now returned.

In a bid to keep Stockton viable as a port a number of projects were completed. In 1810 The Mandale Cut was opened, constructed by the Tees Navigation Company: it cut off one of the Tees meanders, reducing the distance from the Tees Estuary to Stockton by more than two miles. Soon after, a second cut, the Portrack Cut, further reduced the River Tees distance between Stockton and Newport by three quarters of a mile. Portrack was a response to the ominous growth of Middlesbrough as a port. In the event, the increasing size of ships and the 1827 decision to extend the railway direct to Middlesbrough and by-passing Stockton sounded the death knell for the town. The Tees Barrage is close to the site of the Mandale Cut.

English folklore gives us Peg Powler – a hag and water spirit who lurks around the River Tees. She drags children into the water if they get too close to the edge and is an archetypal bogeywoman figure who is or was invoked by parents to terrify children into good behaviour. The 19th century folklorist William Henderson describes Peg Powler as having green hair and "an insatiable desire for human life", and she is said to lure people into the river to drown or be devoured. The foam or froth which is often seen floating on parts of the Tees is called "Peg Powler's suds" or "Peg Powler's cream".

A similar creature named Nanny Powler is said to haunt the **River Skerne**, a tributary of the Tees. Michael Denham asserts that she is either the sister or daughter of Peg Powler. Elliott O'Donnell sees Peg Powler very differently in his 1924 book *Ghosts, Helpful and Harmful*. He describes her as a spirit who lures men and boys to their doom in the River Tees by appearing as a beautiful young woman with green hair and pretending to drown so that her victim will enter the water to save her. Sometimes she may even appear on land on foggy nights and lead men astray until they stumble into the river.

RIVER WEAR

The River Wear rises in the Pennines and flows eastwards, mostly through County Durham to the North Sea in Sunderland. It extends for 60 miles and is one of the region's longest rivers, wending its way through the city of Durham and finally reaching the sea at Sunderland. It lends its name to Weardale in its upper reaches and to Wearside at its mouth.

The origin of Wear is not altogether clear but is generally believed to be Celtic. The Roman River Vedra may be the River Wear. The name may be derived from Brittonic *wejr* which meant "a bend" Also possible is a derivation from the Brittonic root *wei-*, which meant "to flow". Wear has also been posited as being an ancient Celtic name meaning "river of blood".

The windmill at Grangetown, Sunderland had several names. It was known as Stoup Mill, Hendon Grange Mill, and Burton's Stob Mill. A post mill, it had wheels that allowed the upper body to be turned on the base. The mill was demolished in 1926 after consultation with the Admiralty because it had become a seamark used by mariners for navigation.

The family of Mr Barrow, a builder from Jarrow, posing in a cornfield behind Croft Terrace, 1908.

The coaling staithes in Dunstan allowed coal to easily be transferred to ship for transportation around Britain and the world. The staithes are the largest wooden structure to have been built in Europe, and were constructed by the North Eastern Railway in 1893. With the decline of the coal industry they fell into disrepair. In 1990 they were restored as part of the site of Gateshead Garden Festival. However, in 2003 a section was destroyed by fire and fundraising continues to repair the damage.

The Highest Hills and Mountains in Durham

In the United Kingdom and the Republic of Ireland, a hill qualifies as a mountain when its summit is at least 2,000 feet (610 m) high.

BURNHOPE SEAT
Burnhope means broom valley from Old English *brom* + *hop*. Burnhope Seat is between the heads of the Rivers Tees, South Tyne and Wear. The summit is crossed by the boundary between County Durham and Cumbria. At 2451 feet it is the highest point in County Durham. The highest point of the hill lies in Cumbria, some 200 metres west of a trig point on the border.

HARTER FELL, LUNEDALE
Harter Fell, 1447 feet, in Lunedale is an area of upland heath to the west of the county which lies on the watershed between the River Tees to the north east and the River Lune to the south and reaches its maximum height just north of the hamlet of Thringarth.

KIRKCARRION
Two miles to the south west of Middleton-in-Teesdale is the Lunedale Ridge close to Harter Fell. On top of the ridge there is a tree-covered burial mound or round barrow, locally known as Kirkcarrion or Caryn's Castle. It stands some 380 feet high. This was once thought to be a Roman site but the name derives from Prince Caryn of the Brigantes, the local tribe. In 1804 local men came to the ridge to gather stones for building walls. As they were digging around they came upon what was a stone-lined burial chamber in which was an urn that contained a cremation and tiny bone fragments.

The old Celtic name for Kirkcarrion was Carreg Caryn. Modern Welsh for rocks is *cerrig*. So, this was a burial chamber for a Bronze Age chieftain.

MICKLE FELL
Mickle Fell forms part of the Pennine range; it is 2,585 feet high and part of southern Teesdale, and thus is also the highest point in ceremonial County Durham.

The name Mickle Fell derives from the Old Norse word *mikill* meaning great, and *fell* or *fjäll* meaning mountain or hill. The fell is a Marilyn – rare in the area but separated from its neighbours by over 200m of relative height. A Marilyn is a hill over 150m (492 feet).

Mickle Fell and the surrounding moorland form part of the Warcop Training Area, a Ministry of Defence firing range. As a result, public access to the fell is limited.

Queen Alexandra Bridge, Sunderland shortly before it was opened in 1909.

Newcastle-based Brough's ran a chain of grocery shops in the north east. This is their shop in Ryton. Established in 1894 they became a common sight on streets of the region. Brough's were pioneers, in Britain, of collecting your own shopping instead of going to a counter to ask for goods. Their first purpose-built self-service store was opened in Sunderland in 1952, a year after Premier Supermarkets built the first in Streatham, London. The Brough's name lasted until 1972, when their parent company, Allied Suppliers, was taken over. The new owners rebranded the shops as Liptons, another former Allied Suppliers' grocery chain.

Turkeys for Christmas hanging from Thomas Brown's shop at 24 Silver Street, Durham.

Some Interesting Durham Pubs

I would give all of my fame for a pot of ale and safety.

William Shakespeare 1564-1616

there is nothing which has yet been contrived by man, by which so much happiness is produced, as by a good tavern or inn.

Samuel Johnson 1709–1784

This is a selective list of some of the more interestingly named pubs in County Durham, including those which have a particularly significant or fascinating history or, indeed which have been preserved in more or less their original state – dodging what T.P. Cooper so accurately called 'The destroying hand of progress.' in his 1897 *The Old Inns and Inn Signs of York*. More recently, CAMRA cautions that

> there are more than 3,500 pubs in the North East but less than 2 per cent have escaped drastic alteration in recent times; the number whose interiors can be considered to be of significant heritage interest has dwindled to less than 50.

People come to the county from all over the world for many reasons, for the breathtaking scenery, the peaceful solitude, the buzzing towns and villages, the rivers and hills and waterfalls, the fascinating industrial heritage, and for…the pubs..

In the days before Sat Nav, if you stopped and asked a stranger the way to somewhere, anywhere, you would most likely be directed by way of the local church (if there was one) or via the local pub or pubs. Generally speaking, pubs are still, despite all the closures, the second most ubiquitous feature of most high streets, be they urban or rural or suburban. That tells you just how important pubs are to any local community; like churches, they can be the focal point of a street, estate, village, town or city centre. Like churches they can, for some, satisfy a very real need for refuge, companionship, comfort and joy.

Time is being called for the last time all the time. The message I offered in my book on the pubs of the Yorkshire Dales is just as valid here: 'So, if there is a message to take away from this book it is simply put the book down, get up, go out and call in at your local for a pint or two and help preserve and extend this most British of social institutions. Once the pub, your favourite pub, has gone, it's often gone for good'.

But don't take it from me – in the words of no less an authority than the ever-cautious Hilaire Belloc (1870–1953):

> When you have lost your inns drown your empty selves for you will have lost the last of England.

He's right. Ask any villager whose local has been cruelly erased from the face of his main street.

To give some historical perspective – and to highlight the seemingly inexorable decline of pub culture – back in 2003 the average pub price per pint of draught bitter was £1.95. Times have indeed changed since then: then, the average adult drank 218 pints per person; by 2011, that same adult downed just 152 pints, a 30 per cent drop. In 2002 there were 60,100 pubs in the UK. There were 50,300 pubs at the end of 2016, down from 54,194 in December 2014, according to CAMRA.

How did our pubs come about? In the beginning, pubs, particularly pubs out in the country, brewed their own ale in brewhouses next to the pub; women often did most of the work. 'Brewsters', or 'alewives' brewed ale in the home for domestic consumption and commercial sale, albeit on a small scale. These brewsters made a substantial and vital contribution to the family income. It was good ale that attracted neighbours into their houses and eventually led to the birth of the public house.

Yorkshire's Stingo, Knockerdown and Rumtum were famous strong Yorkshire brews with well-earned reputations as far south as London's Marylebone. Stingo even had pubs named after it. Hopped ale was imported from Flanders around 1400, after which hops were home-grown in England for beer production: ale usually has a lower hop content than beer. At the same time, hostelries were set up by the roadside catering for travellers. This had started with the Persians and Hellenistic Greeks in the 2nd century CE and perfected by the Romans locating *tabernae* on their extensive road network to proffer wine to marching legions and various other travellers. Essentially, this *cursus publicus*, public way, was made up of thousands of posting stations along the major road systems of the empire where riders and travellers took food and refreshment and horses were watered, shoed, cared for by vets, stabled, and passed over to fresh dispatch riders. Durham would have benefitted enormously from this with its communications with Hadrian's and Antonine's Walls and the garrisoning and resupply thereof. Later on vehicles were garaged here and the taverns provided for merchants, refugees, magistrates or court officials in transit between cities.

Catering on the hoof continued apace with merchants from the Middle Ages plying between markets, as well as long-distance drovers, commercial travellers, monks commuting from monastery to monastery, pilgrims (as exemplified by Chaucer's *Canterbury Tales*) and all manner of other people moving from village to village or from town to town. Lords of the manor sometimes provided refreshing and sustaining beer-house facilities for the thirsty workers toiling in their fields.

Ale was an important part of the Durham diet, being affordable, and unpolluted unlike water. It is estimated that the average adult then drank up to eight pints a day. Taverns, though, got off to a bad start when Ecgbert, Archbishop of York, around 735 CE declared ale houses to be off limits and decreed that 'no priest go to eat or drink in taverns'. Nevertheless, during King Alfred's reign (871–899) alehouses proliferated, identifiable by the ale stake – a long pole stuck outside along with a bush if wine was also on offer. In 997 CE alehouses, and their tendency to foster anti-social behaviour, entered the statute book when King Ethelred (979–1013) tried to put a price on drink-fuelled disorder with an edict that stated 'in the case of a breach of the peace in an alehouse 6 half marks shall be paid if a man is slain'. He introduced prohibition when he closed down many a tavern and restricted them to one per village. He was also the inadvertent inventor of the drinking game tradition when he introduced pegs in drinking horns – the drinker was not to go beyond the next peg with each draught. The 1215 *Magna Carta* had a go at establishing 'standard measures of wine and corn'. In 1267 the Assize of Ale and Bread was the first attempt, by Edward III, to establish the price of ale and minimise extortionate overpricing. It laid down conditions on brewers and ale wives, taverners and hostelers (innkeepers). From this we start to see a distinction between inns, taverns and alehouses: innkeepers provided accommodation for travellers, taverners bought wine from vintners (wine wholesalers) and resold it to their customers for consumption off their premises, ale brewers sold ale to alehouse keepers for resale in the alehouse. Licensees of ale houses were later described as tipplers and ale drapers.

In 1393 Richard II introduced more regulation when he saw the tax potential to be had in ale and decreed that 'whosoever shall brew in the town with the intention of selling it must hang out a sign'. In so doing he not only gave birth to the fine tradition of pub signage, he also made life easy for his revenue men and for law enforcers to spot potential tax and trouble. Hitherto, most early ale houses were located in private houses, so there was no need for regulation or the signage that went with it. Richard II's action also explains why many pub names have associations with the Wars of the Roses (1455–87) – Rose & Crown, White Hart, Blue Boar, and so on; the decree came relatively soon before the start of the war, which will have provided a source of fresh, new names.

Thanks to their general unsavoury reputation, alehouses later got sucked into 1496 legislation relating to 'vagabonds, idle and suspected persons' when justices of the peace gained powers to 'rejecte And put away common ale selling in townes and places where they shall think convenyent'. In 1552 keepers of alehouses and tippling houses were required to be licensed; tippling houses were places where beer specifically could be sold but not brewed.

By the mid-16th century there were 19,759 taverns or inns in England and Wales, or 1:187 people compared with 1:650 today.

The Alehouses Act of 1551 was a central government attempt to deal with the 'abuses and disorders as are had and used in common ale houses'. Justices of the Peace could apply sanctions to rowdy establishments enabled as they were 'to remove, discharge and put away common selling of ale and beer'. The apparent problem with taverns was that there was deemed to be too many of them and that the wine served was usually of dubious quality. So, in 1553 the number of taverns was restricted by law: London was allowed forty, York a mere eight and Hull and other comparable sized cities a miserable four. However, legislation so universally, yet gleefully, ignored and unenforced would be hard to find: in 1623 there were still 13,000 licensed premises in England.

In 1572 Elizabeth I's Council of the North, established in York, demanded yet more robust regulation; in 1604 legislation – An Act to Restrain the Inordinate Haunting and Tippling of Inns, Alehouses, and Other Drinking Places – was passed to redefine the very role of drinking establishments: they were definitely not for 'Entertainment and Harbouring lewd and idle People to spend and consume their Time in lewd and drunken Manner'. What they were for was the 'Receipt, Relief and Lodging of Wayfaring people from place to place'. Having fun, social cohesion and inculcating a community spirit then, were officially subsidiary to the provision of board and lodge.

In 1577 the Elizabethan authorities carried out a survey which found there to be about 24,000 alehouse keepers in England. In 1585 it was stipulated that the maximum number of alehouses in Westminster was to be 100; by 1631 there were 551. Population increase generally did little to help: in 1577 the population of England was about 3.4 million; by 1636 it was nearer 4.9 million with 5.5 million in 1688, half of whom were on poor relief. In 1577 the ratio of ale retailers to population was 1:142; by 1636 it was nearer 1:95. A stroll from Charing Cross to the Tower would take you past a tavern every 80 yards. In 1629 Durham city magistrates threw their hands in the air in despair because it was quite impossible to count the number of alehouses due to the huge numbers.

Ironically, and awkwardly, things then became very confusing when tipplers were required by law to 'serve all the Queen's people, without refusal for their ready money'; trouble makers or not, they had to be served. In this blizzard of well-meaning but ineffective legislation, evasion was rife, especially illegal brewing and keeping an alehouse without a licence; the production of illicit ale was far too profitable for it not to be; the corollary to this was the effect of strong beer on the average temper and temperament, effects that were all too predictable. And so the bar room brawling continued. But it was by no means wall-to-wall violence: in the ongoing battle against illicit production and rowdiness some progress appears to have been made by 1743; new laws restricted the issuing of licences to keepers of public houses: only one licence could be held, licences could only be issued at Brewster Sessions and transfers at Transfer Sessions, licensees had to be of a higher social standing and were required to produce sureties of good behaviour. A black market in licences soon emerged and in Durham it is reported that blank licences were filled out in advance and completed at the discretion of the Clerk of the Peace.

Things had started to change nationally in the 17th century when in 1657 turnpikes led to a huge increase in the number of horses and coaches full of passengers crisscrossing the country. Two inns in Sunderland High Street, The Gardener's Tavern and The Grey Horse were the termini for the stage coaches to Durham and Seaham. The railways 200 years later brought the next seismic change with the establishment of railway inns at stations; a third development was the now ubiquitous motor car and the transportation of goods by road, all of which necessitated catering for day trippers, business people, long-distance lorry drivers and other travellers – often in the very pubs that once served coach and railway travellers.

The first common brewers were the Nesfield family of Scarborough established in 1691; the end of the 18th century saw the emergence of the common brewery; this was boosted by Wellington's Beerhouse Act of 1830 with names from the 19th century like Cameron's of Hartlepool, Castle Eden and Vaux, still very much alive in the 20th century and, in the case of Cameron's, into this century. Beer brewing had moved out of the home and was an industry in its own right, supplying a growing number of public houses and hotels. The aim of the Beerhouse Act was to encourage people to drink beer rather than spirits, gin mainly. Any householder who paid the poor rate could sell beer, ale or porter by buying an excise licence; they did not now need a justices' licence but spirit selling retailers did. Sellers of ale had to promise to give correct measures, maintain good order, to allow no drunkenness or gambling, and not to dilute the beer! The Beerhouse Act abolished the beer tax, and extended the opening hours of licensed public houses, taverns and alehouses to from fifteen to eighteen hours a day.

The Act also gave rise to the beerhouse and beershops that were permitted to sell only beer. Opening hours could be from 4 am. to 10 pm. – good for a breakfast pint. For two guineas payable to the local excise officer, anyone could now brew and sell beer. The excise licence would stipulate whether the beer could be consumed on the premises (beerhouse) or as off-sales only (beershop). Supervision by local justices was severely curtailed leading to complaints by magistrates and local gentry keen to control the working classes in their area.

Unsurprisingly not everyone warmed to the Act, driving the making of beer underground and doing nothing for the fight against intoxication: many beerhouses emerged from the back streets of large cities and became working class drinking dens. The Beerhouse Act of 1830 also saw licensed premises double in ten years with 24,000 new licences issued within three months of the legislation. It also galvanised the rise and rise of the common brewery, brewing beer and selling it to other outlets rather than brewing for oneself.

Beerhouses provided not just beer, but food, games and some even lodging. They were also known by the name 'small beer' or 'Tom and Jerry' shops. In villages and towns many shopkeepers opened their own beershop and sold beer alongside their usual wares. Beer would be brewed on the premises or purchased from brewers. Many beerhouses inevitably became the haunt of criminals and prostitutes, with some eliding into thinly disguised brothels. The official reaction was to raise the excise fee to three guineas and to introduce property qualifications. But only the Wine and Beer House Act of 1869 brought the licensing of the beerhouses back under the control of the local justices. Many then closed, or were purchased by breweries and changed to fully licensed public houses.

Pubs were never always just pubs. Many doubled up as coroners' and magistrates' courts, as markets, morgues and as smugglers' dens: others were also blacksmith's (as in West Hartlepool), cobblers or carpenters – often the landlord's day job. The George Inn in Sunderland's High Street was the location for Sunderland magistrates court in the late 18th and early 19th centuries. Inquests were held in The Mountain Daisy which is still in Hylton Road.

Pub signs and the names and the images depicted on them make an intriguing subject on their own. The Romans started it all with a welcoming sign showing a bunch of vine leaves representing the wine god Bacchus to denote a *taberna* – the place for a legionary, government official, itinerant or a merchant to slake his thirst. As with any other commercial enterprise, pubs use signs or symbols to signify the nature of the business going on within. The barber's pole and the pawnbroker's balls still survive; until the end of the 19th century most people could not read, so word signage would have been quite useless: a symbolic, graphic sign, however, clearly spoke volumes. For pubs, a garland on a pole, the alestake, denoted a place where drink could be had. Red lattices on glassless windows also gave the game away for what was on offer within. From 1393 it was a legal requirement for innkeepers to display a sign: pub owners accordingly invented names and signs to differentiate their pub from the one up the road: your sign set you apart from other inns and taverns in the locality; it might also advertise what might be found inside (for example, cold meats or board games as well as lodgings and ale), or indeed the political leanings of the landlord and his clientele. Coats of arms reflect the custom adopted by noblemen in which they displayed their banners outside the inn to show that they might be found within.

The name Royal Oak (as at Cornsey Colliery) indicated a supporter of Charles II (he hid in an oak at Boscobel after the battle of Worcester in 1651 before restoring the monarchy in 1660); Punch Bowl (as at Edmunbyers, Consett and at Stanley) denoted a Whig establishment and their patrons' predilection for punch. The Tories still preferred port and red wines. The Marquis of Granby (as at Framwellgate Moor) reflected the philanthropy of said Marquis to his veterans. Chequers (as at Darlington) denoted board games available while The Board (as in Sunderland, Esh and Durham city) proclaimed that cold meats were on offer inside.

WHAT'S SO SPECIAL ABOUT COUNTY DURHAM'S PUBS?

To the casual, or uninterested, observer, a pub in Durham is very much like one in London, York or Belfast. Not so. Here are some distinguishing features which set pubs here apart from those elsewhere. Ceramic frontages on their ground floors were a particularly popular feature, as in the Wheatsheaf in Felling built in 1907 and in Hebburn's Wardle's, once the Albert Hotel, with its attractive brown and orange ceramic frontage from 1908; also the Black Swan in Darlington and the Half Moon in Durham (1908–09), the Central Borough in Darlington (1906), and the Three Horseshoes in Leamside (1907).

In addition, the foundation dates of these and many other pubs in Durham extend into the 1900s when the pub-building boom in London and elsewhere came to a jarring and ruinous end by 1902. This is because north eastern brewers were able to benefit from a still buoyant local economy in which workers retained a comparatively high level of disposable income, much of which was spent on beer.

Some of the room names were different too. The 'select bar' was a popular place and, for a few pennies more on your pint, allowed you to sit in a room just a cut above the public bar. We see this at the Victoria in Durham, the Delaval and the White Swan in Greenside. The 'sitting room' was a place where you sat and imbibed drinks brought to your table by the staff (hence the survival of bell-pushes still seen in some pubs) or purchased at a small hatch to the servery. The Smith's Arms in Greatham was a good example of this in the 60s and 70s, as is the Fleece in Pelton. Another name largely unfamiliar further south, was 'family department' which described the once-common feature of a small compartment or room for the sale of drink for consumption off the premises; this was more commonly known as 'the off-sales department', 'bottle & jug', 'jug & bottle', or 'outdoor sales' etc. An example is at the Victoria in Durham.

'Banking the Beer' is a uniquely north east method of pulling a pint, specifically in the south of the region. To get that much-desired good head on your pint the server slowly pulled the beer through a tight sparkler, allowing it to settle before topping up. This, of course, entailed a bit of a wait for the customer who, more often than not, was thirsty after a hard worked shift and maybe had to get home soon for his tea.

CAMRA tells how this conflict was resolved:

> 'Some beer was pulled quickly and fiercely (which produced a foamy head) into a series of pint glasses; these were put aside (or 'banked') for a couple of minutes or more while the liquid settled to a third or so of the glass (still with a deep head in place). As customers came in they would get a glass topped up to a pint but the head rose and rose, appearing above the brim rather like an ice cream in a cone'.

To see this in action CAMRA recommends you go to the Sun Inn, Knowles Street, just off the High Street in Stockton-on-Tees where there are always trays with glasses of 'banked' Bass. Banking also goes on at the Masham, Hartburn, near Stockton-onTees but only on request.

An asterisk * after a pub's name indicates that it is closed or has been demolished at the time of writing

ADAM & EVES 1851, SEAHAM *

Before it was a pub this building was called Garden House; also called The Pear Tree. Closed in the 30s. Of the first 133 buildings completed in Seaham Harbour by 1831, twelve were pubs.

THE ALUM ALE HOUSE, SOUTH SHIELDS

An unspoilt part-17th century traditional pub which stands on the site of a former brewery and close to an alum and alkali works. The alehouse stood on what was originally Alum Ham, the public landing place where scullermen once gathered to row passengers across the Tyne.

Not always a pub, it was used by the Home Guard during the Second World War, as offices of Tyne Dock Engineering and by a furnishing company.

Alum production was an appalling industry causing massive damage to the landscape and environment. Entire cliffsides were quarried away to extract the alum rich shales. The shale was then piled in stacks up to 100 feet high and burned. The charcoal needed to keep the shale burning for nine months required tree felling on an enormous scale. The sulphuric acid and ash produced by the burning shale poisoned the surrounding land. Once burned, what was left of the shale was sent to a leaching works to extract the aluminium sulphate. It was a disgusting process that required thousands of gallons of human urine. The resulting liquid evaporated and then crystalised requiring yet more charcoal. Eventually the crystals were milled for use as a dye fixative.

AMERICAN TAVERN, STOCKTON *

Apparently got its name because of the many Americans who drank there during the Second World War. Demolished in 1991.

THE ANCIENT UNICORN INN, BOWES

A 16th century coaching inn which can claim Charles Dickens and Turner as guests.

THE ARGO FRIGATE, SUNDERLAND *

Next to the *Sunderland Echo*'s old offices in Bridge Street. Named after the Royal Navy frigate (there were five in all at different times), in turn named after Jason and the Argonauts' *Argo*.

THE BALANCING EEL, SOUTH SHIELDS *

Assumed its intriguing name in 1969 through inspiration by *Alice in Wonderland*: 'Yet you balanced an eel on the end of your nose – what made you so awfull clever?' The sign depicted a mariner holding a rope while at the same time balancing an eel on the end of his nose. Later the name changed to the banal Bizz Bar.

THE BEACONSFIELD, BARNARD CASTLE*

Named after Benjamin Disraeli? Indeed, he became the Earl of Beaconsfield.

BEAMISH MARY INN, NO PLACE

Opened in 1897, the Beamish Mary Inn was originally known as the Red Robin until 1987 but was renamed after the nearby Beamish Mary Coal Pit. There is a Beamish Ann Colliery but no corresponding pub.

THE BELSAY CASTLE INN, ALLENSFORD

Allensford Mill farmhouse was originally called the Belsay Castle Inn, named after the estate of the Middleton family of Belsay Castle. Part of the inn was built in the late 17th century and may have been a bastle. Later additions continued throughout the 18th and 19th centuries. The inn was licensed until 1869. The upper room in the outbuilding served as a nonconformist chapel.

Bastel, bastle, or bastille houses are found along the Anglo-Scottish border, in areas formerly terrorised by border Reivers. They are fortified farmhouses, characterised by security measures against raids.

THE BIRDS NEST, HARTLEPOOL*

Called The Palace from 1904, before this Stein's Hotel. It was demolished in 1996.

THE BOTTLEMAKERS ARMS, SEAHAM *

Opened in 1873 but was an unnamed beer house in 1856. Popularly known as **The Red Light**. Wonder why. Closed *c*.1935.

THE BRITANNIA, DARLINGTON
Built 1830 and a pub from 1858. The bar was extended about 1960 and refitted. On the right is a well preserved snug with fireplace, fixed bench seating, bell pushes and baffles all dating from 1920.

Pubs called the Britannia usually take the name from the Roman appellation for Britain; the familiar idealised female figure was first minted on British coins after 1665 and show Frances Stewart (1647–1702), mistress of Charles II, lady-in-waiting to Charles II's bride, Catherine of Braganza, Duchess of Richmond and Lennox. After the war with the Netherlands, Charles commissioned a commemorative medal, in which her face was used as a model for Britannia; this subsequently became standard for medals, coins and statues. Wonder what Catherine thought? Ms Stewart continued to appear on some of the copper coinage of the United Kingdom until the decimalization of the currency in 1971 and on the fifty pence piece from its introduction in 1969 until 2008.

THE CASTLE EDEN INN, CASTLE EDEN
Birthplace of the famous Castle Eden Brewery. The beer came on tap here in 1826 when John Nimmo (*c*.1801-67) began to brew at the Castle Eden Inn which had its own brewhouse.

THE CATCOTE, HARTLEPOOL*
Opened in 1956 as the Catcote Hotel. A favourite haunt of Hartlepool Grammar School sixth formers spending their dinner money there on a Friday lunchtime. In 1998 it was renamed the Shakespeare, before being demolished in 2008.

CAUSEY ARCH INN, CAUSEY
Sunniside Local History Society tells a wonderful story about Causey Arch Inn and one of the customers on its website

> The characters who drank there were a mixed lot, the most well known was Jack Cutter. Jack had been barred from drinking in all pubs in Stanley. The only place he could get a drink was the Causey Arch Inn. Cutter must have been 18 or 19 stone, his head was as big as a coal scuttle. With hard wooden pads attached, and two short crutches he used to walk about on his knees, his legs were useless from the knee down over. Jack's means of transport was a grey pony called Dolly. About 12 hands high, and a tub trap. When I was about 13 years old I saw him come out of the Causey Inn, Cutter on getting into the back of his trap, chucked in the crutches, one knee went onto the step, and the shafts shot into the air. I waited for his other knee to come up and put his full weight onto the trap, wondering which would give first would it be the pony? Would the shafts break? Or would the belly band give?

THE CENTRAL BOROUGH, DARLINGTON
This is formed of two terraced houses knocked together and a pub since 1906. Happily, it retains its original layout of three rooms with off-sales window in the passage.

THE COLPITTS HOTEL, DURHAM
Unspoilt (very early) Victorian pub, phone free. Say no more… 'The real draw here is the unadorned interior, which is a real throwback…it's worth going here to see how pubs used to be' [*Beer in the Evening*]. Built around 1836, the bar sports a U-shaped 1890s carved wood counter and part-mirrored bar back. The cast-iron fireplace is a 1950s replacement; a small smoke room offers a fine tall bar back fitting and another ornate bar counter.

THE COMEDIAN, BISHOP AUCKLAND
Named after Arthur Stanley Jefferson, better known as Stan Laurel, who spent his early days in Bishop Auckland. He was born in Ulverston on 16th June 1890, but moved to Bishop Auckland where he lived in Princes Street with his parents. He was baptised in St. Peter's Church in the town in October 1891. He moved to North Shields in 1895 at the age of five and remained, when not away at school, until he was fifteen. His father managed a local theatre there. From 1903 he attended Gainford Academy (or Bowman's Academy) for a few months.

THE COMET, DARLINGTON
Nothing astronomical here; this old coaching inn is in fact named after a prize shorthorn bull which won a prize of 1,000 guineas.

THE COMPANY ROW, CONSETT
In 1841 the Derwent Iron Company built rows of houses, known as Company Rows, for its workers. The Rows – which were later renamed Queen Street, King Street, Prince's Street and Trafalgar Street – stood parallel to Front Street, between Middle Street and what is now Medomsley Road. The earliest was Staffordshire Row, built in 1841 and said to have been named after the home town and county of many of the first workers to arrive here. Consett Terrace and Puddlers' Row, and Front Street, were also constructed in the 1840s. The Rows stood near the main ironworks and were often covered in red dust. They were mostly pulled down in 1924. The cleared area later became the Market Place.

THE COOKSON, CHESTER LE STREET *
Named, of course, after Catherine Cookson. Now out of print, as it were.

THE CROWN & CROSSED SWORDS, SHOTLEY BRIDGE
Formed from two pubs which were combined in 1812 – the right-hand side was the Commercial, the left side the Swords Inn. The right-hand side remains unchanged since c.1955.

In the 17th century a band of swordmakers, Oley, Vooz, Molle and Bertram from Solingen in Germany (the steelmaking equivalent to our Sheffield) arrived in Shotley Bridge as exiles from religious persecution. They chose Shotley Bridge because of the quality of the ironstone and the softness and swiftness of the River Derwent. The Oley family had a reputation as makers of the highest quality swords, using Damascus steel and rivalling those made in Toledo. The Napoleonic Wars provided a ready market; they went on to be involved in the formation of the Consett Iron Company. However, the swordmakers could not compete with Sheffield, so the sword works closed in 1840. Nevertheless, members of the family moved to Birmingham where their business eventually became part of Wilkinson Sword. Evidence of the industry can be seen in Cutlers Hall, 1767 and in the name of the public house.

THE CUMBY ARMS, HEIGHINGTON
Remembers Captain William Price Cumby (1771–1837), an officer in the Royal Navy whose valour during the French Revolutionary and Napoleonic Wars reached its peak at the Battle of Trafalgar. When the French almost took his vessel, the ship of the line the *Bellerophon*, despite mounting casualties, heavy bombardment and the death of John Cooke, the ship's captain, Cumby took command, leading a charge and repelling all boarders.

THE DAVY LAMP, DURHAM*
The Davy lamp is a safety lamp for use in flammable atmospheres, invented in 1815 by Sir Humphry Davy comprising a wick lamp with the flame enclosed inside a mesh screen. It was created for use in coal mines, to reduce the danger of explosions due to the presence of methane and other flammable gases – firedamp or minedamp. The Davy lamp was first trialled at Hebburn Colliery in 1816. Davy was awarded £2,000 worth of silver while George Stephenson was accused of stealing the idea from Davy with his 'Geordie lamp'. Lamps are still made in Eccles, in Aberdare, and in Kolkata, India.

THE DEVON, HARTLEPOOL *
This pub was downstairs in this Church Street building. Popular haunt of foreign sailors, hence its reputation in the 60s.

THE DIAMOND, BUTTERKNOWLE
Named after Diamond Hill, the diamond shaped hill nearby.

THE DUKE OF WELLINGTON, HIGH CONISCLIFFE *
The Duke of Wellington pub was notable for perversely having had a portrait of Napoleon, Wellington's defeated enemy, on its sign from 1975 to 1988.

THE DUN COW, DURHAM
18th century pub with a splendid Tudor Revival four-sectioned bar back with mirrored panels, a panelled bar counter and a carved wood surround fireplace. A delight to drink in.

THE DUN COW, SUNDERLAND
A fine-looking corner site built in 1901–02, next door to the Empire Theatre and patronised by many of the stars who performed there. Designed by architect Benjamin F. Simpson of Newcastle to replace a pub that had been on the site since at least the 1830s. CAMRA says

> The Dun Cow retains much of its original layout but is most notable for its powerfully detailed bar counter and one of the country's most striking bar-back fittings. It has three sections, divided by semicircular projections, and is richly decorated with delicate Art Nouveau style woodcarving and curious reliefs in plaster in some of the recesses. Formidable bar counter with strong detail.

THE DURHAM LIGHT INFANTRYMAN, DURHAM*
Named after the distinguished regiment of the British Army that was the Durham Light Infantry, a light infantry regiment from 1881 to 1968, headquartered in Durham City. The regiment served with distinction in the Second Boer War, the First and Second World Wars, the Korean War and the Indonesia–Malaysia conflict. It now forms part of the much amalgamated The Rifles.

THE DURHAM OX, COUNDON
The Durham Ox was a steer who became famous in the early 19th century for his shape, size and weight. He was an early example of what became the Shorthorn breed of cattle and helped establish the standards by which the breed was to be defined. The beast was born in March 1796 and was bred by Charles Colling of Ketton Hall, Brafferton; Colling and his brother Charles were pioneers of the cattle-breeding movement of the late 18th and early 19th centuries. The animal eventually known as the Durham Ox was the grandson of Colling's original bull Hubbach or Hubback and became known as the Ketton Ox when he was shown in Darlington in 1799. In 1801 the ox was sold to John Day of Harmston, near Lincoln, for £250 (2010 = £14,900); Day renamed him the Durham Ox and had a carriage custom-built to transport him, drawn by four horses. For the next five years the ox was toured the length and breadth of England and Scotland, exhibited at agricultural fairs and shows.

A dedication on a painting of the ox by John Boultbee (1753–1812) in 1802 gave the animal's weight as 171 stone but later estimates go as high as 270 stone. On show in Oxford in February 1807, the ox injured his hip as he was getting out of his carriage. The injury failed to heal, and on 15th April 1807 he was slaughtered. His weight at death was reported to be 189 stone. There is an **Ox Inn** in Stanley named after the Durham Ox; and there was a **Durham Ox** in Stockton and a **Wild Ox** there too.

THE EARL OF STOCKTON, STOCKTON *
This pub was previously known as The Newlands but changed its name after Harold Macmillan became Earl Of Stockton.

THE FALCHION, DARLINGTON*
The Falchion was at 8 Blackwellgate, previously known as The Three Blue Bells. The original pub was named after the curved broadsword used to slay the legendary Sockburn Worm and traditionally presented to a new Bishop of Durham on crossing the Tees into the diocese.

THE FARRERS ARMS, CROOK
Reginal Farrer (1880–1920), the famous botanist, inspired this. The Farrer Medal takes its name from him. He grew up in the village of Clapham under Ingleborough in the Yorkshire Dales and authored a number of books, the most famous of which is *My Rock Garden* (1907) and *The Garden of Asia* (1904).

THE FIGHTING COCKS, DURHAM
Cockfighting presumably took place here in the earlier of its 300 years as a pub. The Romans introduced it but it is much older than that; Cromwell banned it in 1653 only to drive it underground until its elimination (or so we think) in the 19th century.

THE FIVE ALLS, BISHOPGARTH
The name derives from the four universal aphorisms: The King (or Queen) rules for all; The Priest prays for all; The Soldier fights for all; The Ordinary Man or Farmer pays for all; The Lawyer pleads for all – sometimes omitted in pubs named the Four Alls. There is another **Five Alls** in Stockton.

THE FIVE QUARTER, PETERLEE
Unusually named after one of the three seams in the coal mine nearby at Horden.

THE FLASS INN, DURHAM
Gets its name from Flass, once The Flash and Flashes – from Old French *flasque* – a pool or bog.

THE FREEMASONS ARMS, CONSETT
Gets its name from stone masons in mediaeval Europe who operated a closed shop system, using secret signs to exclude 'cowboy' builders. Once a popular ballroom and banqueting suite. The Freemasons was but one stop in the famous Consett pub crawl as immortalised in this anonymous 'poem' from the 1930s:

> Let's start at the "Stirling Castle" And admire the "Royal Oak" Let's watch the "White Swan" swimming From "The Turf" I'm a happy bloke Let's climb the "Mount Pleasant" And look around "The Park" Have a good drink at "The Burton" Before it gets dark Let's stop next at "The Railway" The beer is a real treat We can look through the stained glass windows At "The Shakespeare" across the street Next let's visit "The Queens" Mine host Albert Pigg Then pop into "The Mason's Arms" And do an Irish jig We can shake hands with the "Duke of Wellington" Meet "Alexandra" with all her charm Who took "Britannia" to the "Fountain" In front of the "Freemasons Arms" Then through "The Edinburgh House" To "The Wheatsheaf" we can stray Then take the "Coach and Horses" The "Black Horse" and "The Gray" We'll take "The Imperial" route to "The Commercial" Skirt "The Beehive" what a test Let's stop at "The Railway Tavern" As we will need "A Traveller's Rest" Now I think I'll finish I am full of beer and gin But if you can manage a walk up John Street You can sleep at "The Old Board Inn".

THE GEORGE HOTEL, PIERCEBRIDGE
The George in Piercebridge is famous for the clock that inspired American composer Henry Clay Work to write his famous *My Grandfather's Clock* when he visited in 1878. Today the tune is a standard of British brass bands and colliery bands, and is also popular in bluegrass music repertoires. All long case clocks were henceforth called 'grandfather' clocks. The clock stopped at the precise moment of its owner's death and never ticked again.

THE GOLDEN FLEECE, CROOK*
Such pubs are named after the golden fleece in Greek mythology, the fleece of the golden-woolled, winged ram, Chrysomallos, in Colchis. The fleece is a symbol of authority and kingship. It features in the myth of Jason and his crew of Argonauts. In some places there is an obvious association with a local wood trade.

THE GRETNA GREEN WEDDING INN, AYCLIFFE
Now the Gretna Green Hotel. The Gretna Green Wedding Inn opened in the 1930s on the A167. The origin of the delightful name is revealed in the sign which shows a former landlord of the pub in his real life wedding ceremony at the celebrated smithy in Gretna.

THE GREYHOUND, DARLINGTON
This pub was rebuilt 1903 when it doubled up as a hotel. CAMRA invites us to

> 'Note the floor mosiac at the entrance, the large etched windows and the pretty Art Nouveau-style leading above them. The public bar on the right remains largely in its original state with fixed wall seating, red tile floor, panelled counter and triple-arched bar back. The latter is interesting because, although it has thin shafts with disproportionately large foliage capitals, there is a restraint that contrasts with the ornateness of Victorian work that might be expected a decade or so earlier'.

THE HALF MOON INN, NEW ELVET, DURHAM
Stand-out feature is the buffet bar at the back, dating from 1908-09. It has a semi-circular, segmental-shaped mahogany counter, heavily detailed, and a fine Queen Anne-style bar back with a pair of high-level glazed cupboards and bevelled mirror panels.

THE HAPPY WANDERER, FRAMWELLGATE MOOR
The Happy Wanderer pub recalls a group of miners who migrated to Durham from Yorkshire when their pits closed in the 1930s. The pub can boast a peerless collection of mining lamps.

THE HARBOUR OF REFUGE, HARTLEPOOL
Always useful in a place like Hartlepool where the sea has claimed many a life over the years. Built in 1895 it was preceded by a beer-house-cum-grocers. It was also known as The Pot House on account of the glazed pottery tiles on the outside walls.

THE HAVELOCK ARMS, DARLINGTON
Honours General Sir Henry Havelock (1795–1857), hero of the Indian Mutiny, Cawnpore. and the Siege of Lucknow. There is a statue of Havelock at the top of Building Hill in Mowbray Park, Sunderland.

THE HONEST LAWYER, CROXDALE
The joke here is that the only honest lawyer is a dead one, hence the frequent inn sign depicting a headless lawyer; the joke persists with the upstairs restaurant being named The Gallows.

THE INN BETWEEN, SEAHAM *
Another joke; compare the various Nobody Inns. The Inn Between opened in 1868 and was on South Railway Street; previously known as The Northumberland Arms and The Masons Arms.

THE IRON HORSE, NEWTON AYCLIFFE
Apparently echoes the words of native Americans when they first saw a railway locomotive.

THE KICKING CUDDY INN, COXHOE
Kicking Cuddy is Scottish dialect and speaks of a donkey. Once home to the shove ha'penny world championship no less, and once the Clarence Villa, the pub takes its name from the 19th century donkey – or "cuddy" – races which were held nearby. Now dual purpose with the Italian Farmhouse pizzeria and Clarence Villa pub.

THE KINGS ARMS, SUNDERLAND
Notable for its stunning Victorian exterior, and an an L-shaped main bar with a notable High Victorian bar-back with decoratively carved brackets and mirrored panels. Of 1860s/1870s vintage which would make it very early in terms of surviving pub fittings.

THE LITTLE BLACK BOOK, WEST HARTLEPOOL*
In Whitby Street. Formerly The Victoria.

THE LIVE AND LET LIVE, SUNDERLAND *
Pubs with this name (there are at least 23 of them in the UK) are telling the world that their business has been encroached upon and compromised by a rival setting up to give competition close by.

THE LORD BYRON, SEAHAM *
Locally also known as The Cuddy and, before that, the Kicking Cuddy. Byron would have been impressed.

THE MALT AND HOPS, WEST HARTLEPOOL *
Alfred Ernest (Fred) Priest was the the landlord here and first manager and captain of Hartlepools Utd from 1908 to 1912. Previously, he played for England (in 1900) and Sheffield United (as a left winger or inside left); he was also assistant coach at Middlesbrough for a time. At Sheffield he won League Championship and Cup Winners medals; in 1897/98 when 'The Cutlers' won the league title, Fred was leading goalscorer. Fred's three year contract at Hartlepool showed him to have been paid £3 a week. Fred's son, Eric Priest, carried on the footballing tradition when he became manager of Richardsons Westgarth; Eric was also landlord of The Malt and Hops in Albert Street in the 1950s – it closed in 1959. Eric's brother, Jackie, was landlord of The Dun Cow Inn on the corner of Northgate and Francis Street in 1950. Fred's grandson, also Eric Priest (1936–2018), was chief fire officer of Cleveland Fire Brigade.

THE MASON'S ARMS, SHILDON
A passenger service began from Shildon on 27th September 1825. The first train, *Locomotion No.1* started outside the Mason's Arms, the world's first railway station: tickets were sold at the bar and between 1833 and 1841 the company hired a room in the pub for use as a booking office.

THE MCORVILLE, ELWICK
Elwick boasts two pubs: the **Spotted Cow** (opened 1780 and was the village hall before that) and the McOrville, named after two famous local horses – Old and Young McOrville.

THE MILLBANK ARMS, BARNINGHAM
One of only twelve pubs in the UK which have no counter, so drinks are brought up a flight of stairs from a cellar.

THE MOUNTAIN DAISY, SUNDERLAND
According to CAMRA: https://pubheritage.camra.org.uk/pubs/151

> A large, imposing pub rebuilt in 1900-2 as a hotel by the local architects, William & T.R. Milburn for W B Reid & Co. Limited, brewers and wine & spirit merchants of Newcastle upon Tyne. It is a three-storey red brick building with stone dressings and a black marble facing on the ground floor…It has a slightly Queen Anne revival style emphasised by a metal plaque on the west facade with an impression of a mountain daisy; also '1901' in stone…
>
> …the Sitting Room on the rear left, which was converted into a Buffet Bar, remains intact and is one of the most spectacular pub rooms anywhere in the country. It is visual feast of ceramic work made by Craven Dunnill & Co. of Jackfield, Shropshire, one of the leading manufacturers of the day. The walls are tiled from floor to ceiling with a dado of floral tiles with bands of green tiling and one of brown, then yellow tiles in relief up to a frieze of large floral tiles in pink, cream and green with a deep cornice with brackets picked out in a pale brown colour. It has wonderful display of mosaic covering the floor.
>
> There is a stunning quarter circle ceramic bar counter faced with green and yellow faience in an animal head pattern with a marble top and is one of only fourteen remaining in the whole of the UK… Craven Dunnill also specialised in tile pictures and here there are seven of them depicting north eastern scenes – one of the most impressive displays of tiled paintings in any pub in the UK…
>
> Other original fittings in the Buffet Bar include a floral tiled, cast iron and wood surround fireplace with a mirror in surround above, and three stained glass window screens showing scenes of eating and drinking, but any fixed seating was removed in late 1980s. If the snug is closed ask staff and they will open it up for you. The entrance

on Cromwell Street leads into a fine vestibule with stained and leaded panels up to the ceiling. On the servery side of the screen is a blocked up hatch with a figure '1' above, which was the family department (off sales).

The main bar was refitted in the 1970s but you can still see the remains of the two vestibule entrances on the Hylton Road side with stained and leaded panels – the left hand side one is blocked up with the right hand side one is in use; also good stained and leaded top lights above plain front windows.

Some detail from *The Northumbrian Pub* by Lynn F. Pearson.

THE MORRITT ARMS HOTEL, GRETA BRIDGE

J. B. S. Morritt of Rokeby Hall was the benefactor who provided this sixty-foot-high road crossing that is Abbey Bridge. It opened in 1773 with a Masonic ceremony and became such a busy route into Barnard Castle that the post office was persuaded to move from Bridgegate to Newgate, en route from the bridge. Coleridge came in 1779 and Sir Walter Scott in 1791 remarking on its 'walls with battlements' and that the Tees was 'condemned to mine a channel'd way/o'er solid sheets of marble grey', referring to the Tees marble (limestone slabs) that was mined here. Can boast an intact bar from 1946 with the walls covered in murals of Pickwickian characters painted by J. V. Gilroy of Guinness advertising fame.

THE NORTH BRITON, AYCLIFFE*

Named after one of the mail coaches that ran between Newcastle and Leeds. There is a pub of the same name at 26 High Street, Darlington – also closed.

THE PAINTED WAGON, SUNDERLAND *

The Painted Wagon was a western-themed bar on the corner of Holmeside and Park Lane. It opened in 1974, and closed when the ABC cinema which housed it closed in 1999.

THE PENNYWEIGHT, DARLINGTON

Noted for its distinctive sign featuring a set of scales and, therefore, reminiscent of the local dealers in weights and measures: apothecaries and jewellers, for example. A pennyweight was exactly that: the weight of the old penny, ie 1/240th of the weight of a Troy pound, with 240 old pennies = £1. The Troy pound and the pennyweight (dwt) lost their official status in the United Kingdom in the Weights and Measures Act of 1878; only the Troy ounce and its decimal subdivisions remained official. The pennyweight is the common weight used in the valuation and measurement of precious metals. Jewellers use the pennyweight in calculating the amount and cost of precious metals used in fabricating or casting jewellery. Similarly, dentists and dental labs still use the pennyweight as the measure of precious metals in dental crowns and inlays.

Pennyweight and grains are still used to weigh gooseberries in competitions in Cheshire; in Yorkshire the alternative drams and grains measurement has been used since a new set of scales was purchased by the Egton Bridge Old Gooseberry Society in 1937.

THE PINK DOMINO, HARTLEPOOL *

The Pink opened in 1958 and closed in 2013. One Hartlepool's first 'themed' pubs it was built by local builder Cecil Yuill. The interior was elm panelled with pit props facing the counters.

THE PIT LADDIE, SPENNYMOOR*

Originally the Shamrock. Children, laddies, performed a number of vital tasks underground in the pits – door keepers who operated the ventilation doors to let coal carts through, drammers, who pulled coal carts to and from the coal face, colliers' helpers who assisted the actual coal cutting, usually alongside their fathers or older brothers, and drivers who led the horses which pulled wagons along the main roadways. And it wasn't just 'laddies', 'lassies' too worked underground in shocking conditions and in considerable danger. The Coal Mines Regulation Act was finally passed on 4th August 1842: from 1st March 1843 it became illegal for women or any child under the age of ten (yes ten) to work underground in Britain. But evasion of the Act could not have been easier – there was only one inspector to cover the whole of Britain and he had to give prior notice before visiting collieries.

There are similarly named pubs: **The Boldon Lad** at Boldon; **The Bonnie Pit Lad** at Hetton le Hole; **The Collier Lad** at Hazelrigg and **The Pit Laddie** at Shirecliff.

THE PLAINSMAN, STANLEY
A rare case of a pub named after a Hollwood movie, although there is another pub with the same name in Nottingham. *The Plainsman* is a 1936 Western directed by Cecil B. DeMille and starring Gary Cooper and Jean Arthur. The film is a highly fictionalized and anachronistic account of the adventures and relationships between Wild Bill Hickok, Calamity Jane, Buffalo Bill Cody, and General George Custer, with a gun-runner named Lattimer (Charles Bickford) as the main villain.

THE PRINCESS HELENA, HARTLEPOOL
Opened in 1866. Princess Helena of the United Kingdom (1846–1923) was the third daughter and fifth child of Queen Victoria and Prince Albert. She was one of the founding members of the British Red Cross, founding president of the Royal School of Needlework, and president of the Workhouse Infirmary Nursing Association and the Royal British Nurses' Association.

THE QUAKERHOUSE, DARLINGTON
Reflects Darlington's close association with Quakerism, the Society of Friends. The Quakerhouse opened in 1998 having undergone major alterations from the old Quaker Coffee House. The building was originally three cottages built in the late 1700s when the yard was used by tradesmen such as coopers and blacksmiths. Mechanics Yard as it is now used to be known as Betty Hobson's Yard.

THE RATTLER, SOUTH SHIELDS *
The Rattler pub on the seafront was named after the passenger service run for miners by the Harton Coal Company between Westoe Lane Station and Whitburn Colliery, using a motley collection of second-hand rolling stock, which gave a very rough ride and resulted in its rather unflattering name.

THE ROYAL TELEGRAPH, AYCLIFFE
Another pub named after a mail coach.

THE SEATON COLLIERY INN, SEAHAM *
Opened 1856 as the Colliery Inn. Bombed during the Second World War on 25th November 1941 when two people were killed. Rebuilt as the fittingly named *The Phoenix* in the late 1950s.

THE SHADES, HARTLEPOOL *
Long closed and in a state of advanced dilapidation in Church Street. It is shameful that such a beautiful building with its breathtaking exterior tiling has been allowed to fall into such a state. Get a grip Hartlepool!

THE SHEPHERD AND SHEPHERDESS, BEAMISH
The pub was built in the 18th century, and altered in the late 19th century. It boasts two life-sized painted lead figures of a shepherd and a shepherdess said to date from the Napoleonic wars (1796–1815) when England's armaments and munitions capability was restricted by a French blockade on lead. As part of clandestine measures to import the metal without detection, lead works of art were commissioned abroad. One of ten pairs of figures brought from the continent to be melted down for weaponry, the shepherd and shepherdess eluded their fiery fate when the squire of Beamish Hall purchased them.

Originally installed above the entrance to the Hall, they were later moved to the lawn where a storm destroyed the accompanying figure of a dog. Sometime in 1870, according to local legend, the squire was returning home after a night's drinking and stumbled on the figures in the dark. The experience was such a shock that he gave the pair away to the inn at Beamish. Thereafter the pub was known as the Shepherd & Shepherdess Inn.

THE SHUTTLE AND LOOM, DARLINGTON
Named in memory of the early flax weaving industry here.

THE SLATERS ARMS, DARLINGTON
Remembers roofers and builders generally. Early-mid 18th centuary two storey listed building.

THE SMELTERS ARMS, CASTLESIDE, CONSETT*
An industrial echo of the ore smelting in the area.

THE SMITH'S ARMS, GREATHAM
In 1902 it was run by Rachel Whitfield who died that year. Her widower, Robertson Whitfield sold it to Mr J. W. Baird who then, astutely, sold it to local brewers Cameron's. His profit was a considerable £1,230, which he used to pay for a new forge.

THE SPECULATION, WASHINGTON
The right-hand 1920s bar is a sight to behold, probably from the 1920s, with its semicircular bar counter, mock rustic timbering and stained glass in the rear and entrance lobby windows.

THE SQUARE & COMPASS, CORNFORTH
Indicative of the tools used by various tradesmen – carpenters, joiners, masons and the like.

THE STAGS HEAD, SOUTH SHIELDS
Very unusual in that this 1897 Victorian pub has a two-storey arrangement of two bars one above the other – a unique and inspired space-saving answer to its narrow site.

THE STUMBLE INN, SUNDERLAND
…and out no doubt.

THE SUN INN, BEAMISH MUSEUM
A marvellous and atmospheric reconstruction which uses genuine historic fittings taken mostly from other pubs in the region. The pub opened in the museum in 1985. It had been in Bondgate in Bishop Auckland, and was donated to the museum by Scottish & Newcastle Breweries. Originally a "one-up one down" cottage, the earliest owner we know of was James Thompson, on 21st January 1806. Known as The Tiger Inn until the 1850s, from 1857 to 1899 under the Leng family, it flourished under the patronage of miners from Newton Cap and other collieries. The pub features fully operational front and back bars. Interior decoration includes the stuffed racing greyhound 'Jake's Bonny Mary', which won nine trophies before being put on display in The Gerry in White le Head near Tantobie.

THE THOMAS SHERATON, STOCKTON-ON-TEES
Thomas Sheraton, famous furniture maker, was born in the town in 1751 where he served his time before moving to London. Sheraton achieved no fame during his lifetime. He authored a number of what came to be regarded as bibles for furniture designers. Late in life, he was ordained a minister – a devout Baptist, and returned to Stockton in the early 1800s to lead its Baptist congregation. He died in Broad Street in 1806 of 'phrenitis', an inflammation of the brain accompanied by fever and delirium, leaving his wife Margaret and their two children in poverty.

THE TIMOTHY HACKWORTH, SHILDON
Timothy Hackworth (1786–1850)) was a prominent steam locomotive engineer who lived in Shildon and was the first locomotive superintendent of the Stockton and Darlington Railway. Hackworth was heavily involved in the development of the first Stephenson locomotive intended for the Stockton and Darlington Railway during his time at the Forth Street factory. That locomotive, then named *Active*, now known as

Locomotion No 1, was delivered just before the opening ceremony on 27th September 1825. In 1836, he constructed the first locomotive to run in Russia for the Tsarskoye Selo Railway. In 1838, the *Samson* was built for the Albion Mines Railway in Nova Scotia, and was one of the first engines to run in Canada.

THE TROTTERS INN, BISHOP AUCKLAND*
Horses', not pigs'.

THE VICTORIA INN, DURHAM
According to CAMRA
> The best historic multi-room pub interior in the North East. The pub was built in 1899 to the designs of successful Newcastle architect, Joseph Oswald. Perhaps its most interesting feature is the Family Department. This tiny space is accessed from the side entrance and has cut-glass panels and a small hatch to the servery… the Victoria still keeps its original separate rooms and fittings almost exactly as they were when the pub was built in 1899.

THE VOLTIGUER INN, SPENNYMOOR
Winner of the Epsom Derby in 1850.

THE WHEATSHEAF, CARLISLE STREET, FELLING
Rebuilt in Edwardian style in 1907 with a particularly striking green and yellow ceramic facing on the ground floor.

THE WHITE HART, HART NEAR HARTLEPOOL
Many ships have been wrecked off Hartlepool: perhaps the worst night for this was the Great Storm of 9th February 1861, when 60 vessels were wrecked or beached between the Old Town Pier and Seaton. One of the casualties that night was the *Rising Sun*, whose figurehead now graces the White Hart at Hart.

YE OLDE WHEEL TAPPER INN, DARLINGTON
Part of Darlington's railway heritage. The wheeltapper checked for cracks in railway engine and carriage wheels. He would go down the side of a train when it pulled into and paused at a station and, using a special hammer, would tap each carriage wheel, listening for any defects. Defective carriages were then removed from the train before it proceeded. The 'Ye Olde' bit is daft: it first appeared from the USA as recently as the late 19th century so is not 'olde'; what's more 'Ye' means 'you', not 'the'.

Three places in particular have a particularly rich pub heritage and so merit separate treatment: they happen to be three of the bigger urban districts in the old ceremonial county of Durham and are Gateshead, South Shields and Sunderland.

GATESHEAD
Much of what follows owes a debt to Jon and Rob Bratton who compiled the excellent and informative www.gateshead-history.com/gateshead-pubs website.

Today, Gateshead supports about 150 pubs, much reduced from the earlier years of the 20th century. Here are some of the pubs that have closed their doors for the last time over the years:

Beacon, Crown, British Lion, British Queen, Beeswing, Bugle, Deckham, Five Wand Mill Inn, Half Moon, Half Moon, Honeysuckle, Magpie, Mulberry, New Collingwood, Nine Pins, Perseverance, Ship, Swan, Trafalgar, Vigo, William IV Hotel, Willows, Wrekendyk, Bourgognes, Gamekeeper, Board Inn, Stella.

The preponderance of names associated with patriotism and sea-faring is unmissable. Likewise these:

The Brandling Arms, before a pub it was a rectory and stood where the **Sage** now is. The **Brandlings** of Newcastle were a wealthy family of merchants and land and coal owners in Newcastle upon Tyne and Northumberland. **The Barge Inn** in Hillgate; **The Anchor** opened to slake the thirsts of the keelmen and others working around the Dunston Staithes. It is now called the **Tudor Rose**; **The Wherry Inn** in Swalwell – a wherry being a large light barge.

In the 19th century, Durham and Northumberland were top of the inebriation leagues. Temperance halls were set up but in 1846 there were reported to be a mere 73 adult teetotallers in Gateshead along with 49 juveniles, and only four ministers. In 1851 one in every 168 people of Gateshead had had a conviction for drunkenness. According to George Lucas, a temperance activist, there were 170 public houses in the 1860s. The population of Gateshead was only 35,000 at this time making 205 people per pub. Nowadays in the extended borough of Gateshead, comprising some 200,000 people, there are less than 200 pubs or 1,000 people per pub.

The High Street

At its peak there were 25 pubs on the High Street, 32 including ones on Bottle Bank and Brunswick Street. They are **Brunswick Hotel**, Brunswick Street; **Argyle**, Brunswick Street; **Blue Bell**; **British Lion**; **Peareth Arms**; **Golden Fleece**; **Rector House**; **William IV**); **Ye Olde Fleece**; **Butcher's Arms**; **Phoenix** (Curley's); **Park House Hotel**; **Metropole Hotel**; **Atlas Hotel**; **Waggon Inn**; **Grey Nag's Head**; **British Queen**; **Ellison Arms**; **Albion**; **Ship Inn**; **Crown**; **Lord Raglan**; **Grey Horse**; **Coach and Horses**; **Dun Cow**; **Turk's Head**; **Old Nag's Head**; **Half Moon Hotel**; **Queen's Head**; **Wheatsheaf**; **Black Bull Hotel** and **William IV**.

Pubs in Central Gateshead not in the High Street

Albert, Albert Street; **Prince Alfred**, Prince Consort Road; **Alma Inn**, Hopper Street; **Barley Mow**, **Crawshay Inn**, both on East Street; **Beaconsfield Hotel**, Askew Road; **Black Swan Inn**, Park Lane; **Castle**, Bensham Road; **Crystal Palace**, Oakwellgate; **Elephant Inn**, Swalwell/Whickham; **Flying Horse**, Oakwellgate; **Gardeners Arms**, Bensham Road; **Northumberland Arms**, Coatsworth Road; **Princess of Wales**, Ellison Street West; **Richard Cobden Inn**, Chandless Street; **Shipcote Hotel**, Sunderland Road; **Wylam Hotel**, Hector Street.

Today there remain only ten or so pubs on the High Street three of which are closed. Pubs in what was Brunswick Street are: **The Bluebell**, **The Grove**, **O'Keefe's** and **The Moon and Sixpence**.

Of particular interest is **The Goat Inn** on, aptly enough, Bottle Bank, christened in 1672 after some local confusion regarding the etymology of the town's name being a corruption of Goat's Hill. The pub, fittingly enough, sported a rather grand wooden carving of a goat over the door which now adorns Shipley Art Gallery in Gateshead. The pub was demolished in 1928 – not unreasonably in this case – to make way for the Tyne Bridge. In 1616, it was called "The Bell of the Hoop"; in 1627, "The Spread Eagle" and by 1672, the "Goat Inn".

The 1854 **Central Bar** was the setting for a scene in the film *Women in Love*, starring Glenda Jackson and Oliver Reed.

SOUTH SHIELDS

The following list of old South Shields pubs was posted anonymously on the internet:

1. Ship Inn Harton 1803
2. Marine 1871/72 (there was an inquest there in August 1872
3. Adam and Eve Rebuilt *c.*1873 (earlier pub there in 1827
4. Criterion 1875
5. Westoe Hotel 1875/6 on site of old Crown Inn
6. Brunswick 1879/80 (earlier pub there in 1848)
7. Pier 1879/80
8. Ship and Royal (then known as the Royal 1879/80)
9. Lambton Arms 1885
10. County Hotel 1893 on site of Westoe Tavern 1829
11. Stags rebuilt 1895 (earlier pub on site, dates back to 1859/60

A number of local pubs were either built or rebuilt in the 1890s e.g a pub called the **Neptune** was on the present site in 1859/60, but the present building was built in 1901. The **Britannia** in Charlotte Terrace was built in 1898. The **Cyprus** was rebuilt in 1900, the original building was there in 1882. There was a beer house on the **Lord Clyde** site from 1870/71, but at present we do not know when it became a full public house or whether this is the same building. The first directory entry for a pub called the **Railway Inn** in Coronation Street was in 1848, but again this could have been rebuilt.

SUNDERLAND

I am indebted to Sunderland Antiquarian Society's website and their 'A few notes on Sunderland pubs' page for some of the content here.

Sunderland has never been short of a pub or two and vies with numerous other places with the claim to have the most per head of population, not least Newcastle over the old ceremonial county border. It is reported that in 1880 there were 262 fully licensed houses and 377 beer houses in South Shields; that there was a place selling drink for every 90 adults and that every twentieth house sold drink of some kind. However, this was down on 1820 when Low Street, for example, boasted 41 pubs. By 1888 in the same street there were only twelve and by 1916 only three.

Coronation Street could boast twelve pubs in 1914, including **Engineers Arms**, **Grace Darling**, **Holy Island Castle**, **Robert Burns Arms**, **Meux Arms** and **Nutwith Hotel**. By 1924 only seven remained open. This reduction continued during the first half of the 20th century and by the 1950s Sunderland was reduced to 150 pubs and 50 beer houses

The Holy Island was one of a number of pubs named after local castles; others included **Alnwick Castle**, **Bamburgh Castle** and **Tynemouth Castle**.

The Nutwith was bought by Robert Ord (then it was The Borough) in the 1840s, a vet and farrier; his practice was next door. Nutwith won the 1843 St. Leger at Doncaster. It was served a Compulsory Purchase Order in 1962 and sold for £2,900. The Grace Darling was the scene of a drinking competition in 1897, after which one of the drinkers, Robert Archibold, 30, downed a ½ pint of Irish whiskey in one, on top of copious amounts of beer. He later died from 'an overdraught of neat whisky, which caused paralysis of the nerve centre of the brain'. Landlady Rebecca Potts was fined £5 plus costs for selling alcohol to a drunken person.

Exotic names include **The Smyrna Hotel**, the ancient name for Izmir; **The Alma** after the Crimean Battle. Then we have the **Vulcan**, the **Grapes**, the **Olive Branch**, the **Pear Tree** and the **Pineapple Hotel**.

In Sunderland it wasn't all work and industry. Some of the names of old Sunderland pubs had a rural flavour to them, for example **The Dog and Pheasant** in Coronation Street, **Green Shutters** in High Street and **Strawberry Cottage** in Tunstall Lane. **Maple Bar**, **The Rosedene**, **The Ashbrooke**, **Hollymere**, **Laburnum Cottage**, **Ivy House**, **Linden Arms**, **Bee Hive** add a countryside feel to this industrial place. **The Saltgrass** gets its name from the tidal wetland where it stood. And, of course, the **Mountain Daisy** which in 1904 was proud to have 'the most handsome and select [two table]billiard saloon in town'.

The Clipper Ship in Monkwearmouth reminds us of when vessels like *The Torrens* were built at Sunderland, while shipyard and waterfront trades are echoed by **The Boilermakers Arms**, **Smiths Arms**, **Waterman's Tavern**, **Trimmers Arms**, **The Masons Arms**. **Engineers' Arms**, **Engineers' Tavern**, the **New Clipper**, the **Sheet Anchor** and **Shipwrights Arms**. **The Ship Isis** was originally the **Ship Tavern** but changed its name in 1857 because the crews from the *Isis* always got paid off there. The **Skiff Inn** recalls skiffs, light sculling boats used for rowing on the Wear. It closed in the 1930s having opened in the 1850s. The **Trimmers Arms** won its fame when in May 1905 it was raided by the police for illegal betting. The **Colliery Tavern**, the **Colliery House** and the **Waggon Tavern** recall local mining history. Transport inspired names are the **Bus** and the **Tram Car Inn** while the **Pedestrian Arms** begs to differ. The **Saddle Inn** is named after the saddler, Martin Stephenson, who bought the tavern in the 1770s. Perambulating the parish boundaries was an old Sunderland custom – in 1853 this terminated at the inn which then hosted a dinner for dignitaries. Closed in 1919.

Famous people crop up quite a lot in Sunderland pubs. The ubiquitous **Robin Hood** is in High Street, the Scottish bard is in **The Burns Arms** in Coronation Street, **General Wolfe** and **Lord Byron** are in Malings Rigg, **William Pile** is in Dame Dorothy Street and **Jack Crawford** is in Whitburn Street.

William Pile (1823–73) was the first to introduce the Clipper class of ship onto the River Wear. Aged 18 his right hand was almost severed in an accident. On his recovery, he started with a shipbuilder in Monkwearmouth to complete his apprenticeship where his talent was recognised; he was promoted to foreman and was soon in charge of a busy yard. His brother, John Pile, was born at Sunderland in 1820, and served his apprenticeship in Yarm-on-Tees. In 1852 he moved to Hartlepool to develop a shipyard in the newly opened Jackson's Dock. In 1889 the people of West Hartlepool presented him with a marble bust of himself, now in the Gray Art Gallery, Hartlepool, in recognition of the role he played in the industrial development of the town.

Jack Crawford (1775–1831) was a sailor of the Royal Navy known as the "Hero of Camperdown." Born in Thornhill's Bank (now Pottery Bank) in the east end of Sunderland he was a keelman until 1786 when, aged 12, he joined the crew of the *Peggy* at South Shields as an apprentice. In 1796, he was press-ganged into the Royal Navy and served on HMS *Venerable* under Admiral Duncan, the Royal Navy Commander-in-Chief of the North Seas.

At the Battle of Camperdown off the Dutch coast (11th October 1797), *Venerable* was Admiral Duncan's flagship. During the action, part of the *Venerable's* mast was felled, including the admiral's flag. Lowering the Admiral's personal flag was an unmistakable sign of surrender. Despite intense gunfire, Crawford sought to avoid such a defeatist signal and shinned up the mast and nailed the colours to the top.

Vividly named pubs include **The Hat and Feather, Coach and Horses, Argo Frigate**, **Shoulder of Mutton**, the **Aquatic Arms** and **New Shades**. Havelock, the hero of the Relief of Lucknow was commemorated by two **General Havelocks** and the **Havelock Hotel** whilst multiple pubs shared other names – there were three **Bee Hives**, three **Oddfellows Arm**s and three **Wheatsheafs** in various parts of the town. **Blue House** is next to Blue House Field, Sunderland AFC's first ground in 1879. Then there is the **Antelope**, the **Phoenix**, the **Round Robin**, the **Eagle** and the **Dolphin**.

Nicknames abounded, including: **The Scotch House** (Tea Shop), **Neptune** (No.9), **Laings** (Vestry), **Commercial Vaults** (Long Bar), and the **Theatre Tavern** (Polly's). Who knows why? The name Tea Shop was given because tea was once served from canisters behind the bar. The tables and chairs were made from barrels; it was previously known as Laing & Company. Closed in 1983. Long Bar came about because the **Commercial Vaults** had the longest bar in town. In 1940 a discarded cigarette did the Luftwaffe out of a target when the pub burnt ot the ground and the long bar was no more. Finally closed in 1984. The **Neptune** is less exciting – it was nicknamed after the number of the place in Dunning Street, although the landlord was fined £25 for illegal betting on the premises. **The Gannet** was called the Dive Bar because it was below street level; the real name came about because gannets are noted for their supreme diving skills.

The River Derwent near Rowlands Gill.

Seaham Harbour was established by the 3rd Marquess of Londonderry, Charles William Vane, as an outlet for coal from his collieries. The harbour is comprised of a series of docks. The oldest, the North Dock, was opened for shipping in July 1831, and was followed shortly after by the South Dock in 1835. The harbour was extended again at the turn of the 20th century and again in the late 1920s. It is still a working port handling about 600,000 tonnes of goods a year.

The Olympia Rink (roller skating) in South Shields. The rink, designed by the architect Joseph H. Morton opened on 17th June 1909. In addition to skating it was used as a dance hall and a regular venue for boxing matches, which probably helped it to survive once the popularity of 'rinking' declined. Many of its contemoraries closed when the short lived Edwardian craze for roller skating faded (1908 to 1912). It was renamed the Spa Rink in 1931, but disaster struck on 26th January 1932, when the rink burned down. Within a few minutes of the discovery of the blaze the roof had collapsed. Within the hour, all that was left of the wooden building was a few of the pillars at the front and the boilerhouse.

Further Reading

Anderson, M. (2008) *Durham mining disasters c.1700-1950s.* Barnsley
Appleton, A. *A Colony of Workmen: The Socio-Economic Development of Port Clarence 1851-1881*
Blair, P. H. (1977) [1956]. *An Introduction to Anglo-Saxon England* (Second ed.). Cambridge
Brandon, D. (2010) *Discovering Pub Names and Signs*, Oxford
Brandwood, G.(2011) *Licensed to Sell – The History and Heritage of the Public House*, 2nd edition, Swindon
Brett, A. (2003) *Sunderland Public Houses*, Sunderland
Bruning, T. *Historic Pubs of England*, London, 2000
CAMRA https://camra-phg.s3.eu-west-1.amazonaws.com/RealHeritagePubsOfNorthEast.pdf
Chrystal. P. (2016) *Harrogate Pubs including Knaresborough*, Stroud
Chrystal, P. (2017) *The Place Names of Yorkshire, including Pub Names*, Catrine
Chrystal, P. (2017) *Hull Pubs*, Stroud
Chrystal, P. (2018) *Pubs in & Around York*, Darlington
Chrystal, P. (2019) *Pubs in & Around the Yorkshire Dales*, Darlington
Chrystal, P. *Lifeboat Stations of the North East Coast*, Stroud
Chrystal. P. (2019) *Old Hartlepool & West Hartlepool*, Catrine
Chrystal. P. *Hartlepool Through the Ages with Stan Laundon*, Stroud
Chrystal. P. *Hartlepool Through Time*, Stroud
Chrystal. P. *Hartlepool, The Postcard Collection with Stan Laundon*, Stroud
Chrystal. P. *Hartlepool History Tour with Stan Laundon and Simon Crossley*, Stroud
Chrystal. P. *Darlington Through Time*, Stroud
Chrystal. P. *Barnard Castle & Teesdale Through Time*, Stroud
Chrystal. P. *Barnard Castle Shops, Pubs & Trades Through Time with Carol Dougherty*
Chrystal. P.(2019) *The Romans in the North of England*, Darlington
Chrystal. P. (2020) *Old Stockton*, Catrine
Chrystal. P.(2020) *Old Yarm*, Catrine
Chrystal, P. *Darlington Through Time*, Stroud
Clark, P. (1983) *The English Alehouse: A Social History 1200–1830*, London
Davis, B. (1981) *The Traditional English Pub: A Way of Drinking*, London
Dobson, S. (1986) *Larn Yersel Geordie*
Dufferwiel, M. (2004). *Durham: Over 1,000 Years of History and Legend.* Edinburgh
Durham Bishops (1960). British History Online. University of London & History of Parliament Trust.
Durham mining Museum. *Mining History*. The Durham Mining Museum and its contributors.
The Durham landscape (PDF). Physical influences. durham.gov.uk.
Eilert E., *The Concise Oxford Dictionary of English Place-names*
Flagg, A.C. (1979), *The History of Shipbuilding in South Shields 1746-1946*
Fordyce, W. (1857), *The History and Antiquities of the County Palatine of Durham*, A. Fullarton and Co.
Forster, E. (1969) *The death pit: the untold story of mass death in a mine.* Newcastle upon Tyne
Fox, B. (2007) *The P-Celtic Place-Names of North-East England and South-East Scotland,* The Heroic Age (2007)
Gilbert, C. (2000) *Billingham, Haverton Hill and Port Clarence*
Girouard, M (1984). *Victorian Pubs*, London
Gorham, M. (2007) *Back to the Local*, London
Gorham, M. (1950) *Inside the Pub*, London
Graham, F. (1979). *Roman Durham*. Newcastle upon Tyne
Graham, F. *Roman Inscriptions of Britain – the Northern Borders* (Lanchester)
Graham, F ed (1987)., *The New Geordie Dictionary* (1987)
Green, A. (2010), *Northern Landscapes: Representations and Realities of North-East England*, 136-137, 2010
Greenwell, William (1857). *Bishop Hatfield's survey, a record of the possessions of the see of Durham, made by order of Thomas de Hatfield, bishop of Durham. Durham:* Surtees Society.

Griffiths, B. (2004) *Dictionary of North-East Dialect*, Northumbria University Press
Griffiths, B. (2007) *Pitmatic: The Talk of the North East Coalfields*, Northumbria University Press.
Guy & Atkinson, *West Durham: the archaeology of industry*, Phillimore 2008
Halpin, Joe (2004). *Mining in the Deerness Valley Area* (PDF). Durham in Time.
Hatcher, Jane. *Annfield Plain—a short history*. Durham Miner Project
Hatton, C. (2005) *Haverton Hill: Port Clarence to Billingham*
Haydon, P.(1994) *The English Pub: A History*, London
Heslop, R.O (1892) *Northumberland words: a glossary of words used in the county of Northumberland and on the Tyneside*
Hutchinson, T. (2005), *The History of Bishop Auckland*, Seaham: The People's History
James, A. G. *A Guide to the Place-Name Evidence – Guide to the Elements* (PDF). Scottish Place Name Society – The Brittonic Language in the Old North.
Johnson, M. (1992) *"Finchale Priory" in Durham: Historic and University City and surrounding area*. Sixth Edition. Turnstone Ventures
Lewis, S. (1848). *A Topographical Dictionary of England*
Mackay, M.L (2008) *The Lion Roars and the Monkey Bites – The Pubs of Hartlepool*, Hartlepool
Mawer, Allen (1920), *The Place-Names of Northumberland and Durham*, Cambridge
Mills, A.D. (2011) *A Dictionary of British Place Names*, Oxford
Monckton, H.A.(1969) *A History of the English Public House*, London
Monson-Fitzjohn, G.J. (1926) *Quaint Signs of Olde Inns*, London
Oliver, B. (1947) *The Renaissance of the English Public House*, London
Page, W. (1907). *A History of the County of Durham: Volume 2*
Pearce, M, (2009) 'A perceptual dialect map of North East England', *Journal of English Linguistics*, 37 162-92
Pearson, L.F. (1989) *The Northumbrian Pub*, Morpeth
Pevsner, N. (1985). *The Buildings of England: Durham*, London
Proud, K. (1990) *The Prince Bishops of Durham*
Purdon, G. (1992). *Chester-le-Street and district – The people and the place*.
Redman, N. (1993) *The History of the Castle Eden Brewery, County Durham* (Whitbread plc, London)
Selkirk, R. (2000). *Chester-le-Street and Its Place in History*. Birtley
Simpson, D. A (1991), *Prince Bishop country: the people history and folklore of County Durham and the River Wear*, North Pennine Publishing
Wales, K. (2006) *Northern English: A Social and Cultural History*
Watts, V. (2002). *A dictionary of County Durham place-names*. Nottingham
Whellan, W. (1856), *History, Topography, and Directory of the County Palatine of Durham*, William Whellan and Co.

The ferry in Cox Green which carried passengers across the River Wear to Washington.